To my beloved wife Mehroo,
whose support for me has been exceeded only by her
caring, devotion, and love

Special discounts on bulk quantities of AMACOM books are available to corporations, professional associations, and other organizations. For details, contact Special Sales Department, AMACOM, a division of American Management Association, 1601 Broadway, New York, NY 10019.
Tel.: 212-903-8316   Fax: 212-903-8083
Web site: www.amacombooks.org

This publication is designed to provide accurate and authoritative information in regard to the subject matter covered. It is sold with the understanding that the publisher is not engaged in rendering legal, accounting, or other professional service. If legal advice or other expert assistance is required, the services of a competent professional person should be sought.

Library of Congress Cataloging-in-Publication Data

Bhote, Keki R.
    The power of ultimate Six Sigma : Keki Bhote's proven system for moving beyond quality excellence to total business excellence / Keki R. Bhote.
        p.   cm.
    Includes bibliographical references and index.
    ISBN 0-8144-0759-5
    1. Process control.   I. Title.
TS156.8 B485   2003
658.5'62—dc21   2002011379

Printing number
10 9 8 7 6 5 4 3 2 1

The Power of
Ultimate Six Sigma™

Keki Bhote's Proven System for Moving Beyond
Quality Excellence to Total Business Excellence

KEKI R. BHOTE

AMACOM
American Management Association

New York • Atlanta • Brussels • Buenos Aires • Chicago • London • Mexico City
San Francisco • Shanghai • Tokyo • Toronto • Washington, D. C.

Contents

Contents

Foreword

C. Jackson Grayson, Ph. D.,
Chairman, American Productivity and Quality Center

It is a pleasure to write this foreword to Keki Bhote's book *The Power of Ultimate Six Sigma*. I have had a most productive association with Keki for more than fifteen years. He helped me in enlarging the horizons for APQC's pioneering work on the Malcolm Baldrige National Quality Award for the United States. Keki also introduced his simple but highly effective and statistically powerful Design of Experiments to the American Productivity and Quality Center staff and to many companies around the world.

Keki was among those who helped develop Motorola's renowned Six Sigma process. As the Chief Corporate Consultant for Quality and Productivity Improvement at Motorola, he was responsible for many of the leading innovations in the company. In 1995, Keki was selected as one of the new quality gurus of America by *Quality Digest* magazine.

His first book on Six Sigma, *The Ultimate Six Sigma*, expanded the concept of Six Sigma from mere quality excellence to total business excellence. Its great popularity has created a demand for this latest book—*The Power of Ultimate Six Sigma*. It focuses on several themes vital for America:

- It challenges the business community to initiate a business Marshall Plan to solve the world's social and economic problems, with profit at the end of the rainbow.

- It develops 200 disciplines by which a company, mired in anemic profits, can capture the El Dorado of maximum customer loyalty, together with maximum profits.

Three chapters are devoted to the powerful tools of quality, cost, and cycle time improvement. Further, each chapter is illustrated with a case study of a benchmark company that excels in one of the twelve areas of a company's business. Finally, there is a self-assessment/audit guide by which a company can measure its overall corporate health.

The Power of Ultimate Six Sigma adds another of Keki Bhote's impressive contributions to stimulating and helping improve companies around the world.

Preface

Larger Horizons for
"The Power of Ultimate Six Sigma"

My first book on the Ultimate Six Sigma has been immensely popular for breaking new ground on the subject of Six Sigma, first developed by my associates and myself at Motorola. It enlarged the scope of Six Sigma—as slavishly practiced by hundreds of companies—from the narrow confines of quality excellence to total business excellence. By turning the searchlight on to the issues of customers, leadership, organization, employees, and suppliers, the Ultimate Six Sigma represented a quantum leap over the standard treatment of Six Sigma. By highlighting the ten powerful tools of the twenty-first century, it left far behind the obsolete problem-solving/improvement tools employed by Six Sigma black belts. Why, then, the necessity for another perspective on the Ultimate Six Sigma? As the title *The Power of the Ultimate Six Sigma* indicates, there is an urgent need to give a high-octane boost to the top management of business enterprises.

Two cataclysmic events—one global, the other within the world of business—have converged to expand the horizon of the Ultimate Six Sigma even further and with greater urgency. The first represents a golden opportunity for pursuing the Power of the Ultimate Six Sigma to unprecedented heights for business. The second represents a Power of Ultimate Six Sigma message for business to reform itself or else witness the precipitous slide in the stock market, the disillusionment of the stockholder, and the gradual atrophy of the glorious engine of capitalism.

The Aftermath of September 11:
A Rousing Challenge for Business

The catastrophe of September 11 impacted the American psyche as no other single event in its history. The response of the U.S. government to fight the cancer of terrorism has been splendid in conception and brilliant in its execution.

However, the underlying, deep-rooted cause of terrorism—the utter hopelessness that festers among the masses of the Third World and that provides fodder for the terrorists—cannot be effectively tackled by governments. It can only be addressed by business. But it will require a veritable *business Marshall Plan*—specifically, the solving of the world's social ills by business—that can be executed at a profit for business. One of the messages of Chapter 1 is lifting the vision of the business community from its current focus on a narrow, private customer base to the larger social responsibility of solving the ills of one-half of mankind, with the profit motive remaining a viable output.

Enron—Greater Impact Than September 11?

While September 11 has the potential to elevate business to a new and enlightened mission, the Enron, Andersen, and WorldCom scandals have dragged it to a new low. Businessmen are being cast as villains with their collusion and corruption in high places, while their working stiffs are being bilked of their hard-won pensions. Paul Krugman, an economist turned columnist, contends that the Enron debacle will prove to be a greater turning point for America than even September 11. Enronitis is pervading the stock market. How many other Enrons are likely to surface? How many more Arthur Andersens can cook the books? The public is being treated to a scandal a day! Business must change public perceptions from "what is good for business is good enough for the country" to "what is good for the country is good for business!" Chapter 1 outlines ways by which business must burnish its tarnished image in the public mind. Business, after all, derives its legitimacy from the public. If it forfeits that legitimacy, it forfeits its right to exist.

From Concepts and Principles to Lighting a Fire Under Management

My Ultimate Six Sigma book was a *tour de force* of the concepts, philosophies, and principles needed to overcome the mediocrity of traditional Six Sigma practices. With this groundwork laid, there is a sense of urgency among my clients, readers, and the public for a new book focused on:

- The need for an order-of-magnitude improvement in the anemic profits of most companies, which have lost their skills—though not the appetite for profit improvement

- A clarion call to the top management of companies to get personally involved in Six Sigma as a way of life, rather than delegating it to their professionals with limited power

- A hard-hitting, practical implementation of the original treatise—in short, a more hands-on approach and "how to" recipe

Leadership—A Call to Greatness

Besides calling for a business Marshall Plan and for the captains of industry to reform themselves, this book (in the five chapters that comprise Part 2) highlights the crucial role of leadership to better serve all of its stakeholders—customers, employees, suppliers, as well as the public itself.

Essential Disciplines for Practical Implementation

In Parts 2, 3, 4, and 5, there is an unfolding of 200 *disciplines and techniques* that must be embraced for practical implementation if a company is to reach for the Ultimate Six Sigma. The reader can still refer to the original Ultimate Six Sigma book for in-depth background and rationale, but the emphasis here is on unleashing the Power of Ultimate Six Sigma by pursuing each discipline to completion. It is about going from intelligence quotient to action quotient. To sum up, business needs all three Qs—the IQ of all its people, the EQ (emotional quotient) of its leaders, and the AQ (action quotient) of the organization!

Implementation Timetable by Three Different Company Types

Another distinctive feature of the book is a recommended timetable within which each of the 200 disciplines/techniques can be implemented. Recognizing that companies have different characteristics (e.g., size and corporate cultures) as well as different levels of urgency, receptivity to the required disciplines, and expertise to run with the disciplines, I have divided them into three company types:

Type A companies have the greatest urgency, either because of ambition or competitive pressures, to embrace as many of these vital disciplines as possible and propel themselves into world class. Type A companies can be big or small. Size is not a limiting factor.

Type B companies are typically smaller, and though they may possess the same ambition to excel as a Type A company, they are limited by resources, manpower, and expertise. The implementation timetable is, perforce, drawn out further.

Type C companies are the most unreconstructed. A Type C company is comfortable with the *status quo*. It is generally large in size and tends to be bureaucratic. It may even look upon itself as successful (at least in the short run) and may not have gone through the tempering fires of competition. It often lacks the vision and the drive to improve. It may be somewhat skeptical of the remedies proposed and is years behind in the knowledge and power of the required disciplines. As a result, there could be a long delay in implementation or even a rejection of a discipline.

Some of the characteristics of these three types of companies are discussed in Chapter 3.

A Regrouping of the Disciplines of the Ultimate Six Sigma

The original Ultimate Six Sigma book grouped the key characteristics and success factors of a Six Sigma drive together, by area. *The Power of Ultimate Six Sigma* retains the key characteristics in each area, but converts the success factors into essential disciplines that must be put into effect for achieving breakthroughs. In addition, the entire scope of the Power of the Ultimate Six Sigma is divided into four distinct areas: stakeholders, high-octane disciplines, major line functions, and results.

1. *Stakeholders.* As shareholder value gives way to stakeholder value, these important constituents—customers, leaders, corporate organization/culture, employees, and supply chain partners—are accorded special treatment, and in Part 2 of this book there's a chapter devoted to each constituent. (Traditional Six Sigma pays scant attention to any of them.)

2. *High-Octane Techniques.* The concentration here is on powerful tools for quality, cost reduction, and cycle time. Each of these topics is accorded a separate chapter in Part 3 to highlight their power alongside their simplicity and ease of implementation. (Traditional Six Sigma continues to use weak quality tools, while cost and cycle time tools are hardly even mentioned.)

3. *Major Line Functions.* The major line functions in a company are design, manufacturing, and all service operations. In Part 4, a full chapter is devoted to each function so that readers can concentrate on that function that is of special interest to them. (Traditional Six Sigma has only manufacturing as its major scope, and even there its coverage is poor.)

4. *Results.* In the final analysis, results are the outputs of the disciplines. Results are divided into a few highly relevant primary parameters and several secondary parameters that embellish the primary ones. Each parameter is given a quantitative rating to track a company's results.

The Self-Assessment/Audit

One of the great benefits of *The Power of Ultimate Six Sigma* is a self-administered audit that can measure the business health of any company. The standards are high enough for a reach-out and yet low enough so that companies with low scores won't give up in frustration. The audit can also be used by a company to pace its longitudinal progress year-by-year. Traditional Six Sigma companies have no audits, other than a narrow attempt at just product quality.

Case Studies of Benchmark Companies

Each area-by-area chapter is further illustrated with a case study of a benchmark company that is deemed to be "best in class" and whose success factors are worth emulating.

Conclusion

The final message that readers of this book will take away with them is one of new hope, new horizons for corporations. The Ultimate Six Sigma journey promises to take today's businesses:

- From anemic (or even negative) profits to a 2:1, 3:1, or 4:1 profit improvement.

- From sleazy business practices to a "true north" of business ethics and integrity.

- From a narrow concept of the traditional customer to the discharge of social responsibility to the larger community.

- From a detached view of social ills to a business Marshall Plan to tackle the needs of the world's poor—at a profit!

Acknowledgments

Before acknowledging the people who have inspired me in writing this book, I'd like to mention the confluence of three world events that have enabled me to expand the horizons of *The Power of Ultimate Six Sigma*.

First, the need to combat the terrorism of September 11, 2001, beyond a military solution has reinforced my conviction that only corporations, joined in a business Marshal Plan, can solve the world's social ills and yet make a profit. A major tool is micro loans, where more than 100 million of the world's poor people have been placed on their economic feet, with 90 percent of the loans paid back. I'm delighted that through the pioneering work of the World Zoroastrian Organization and its champion Dinshaw Tambole, my wife and I have funded four destitute families in India to become successful entrepreneurs. If each corporation can replicate such help, the war on poverty can still be won!

Secondly, my crusade against the rapacious, mess of financial analysts and the inordinate greed of CEOs, have at long last received media attention. Hopefully, I have added my humble voice to the chorus of business ethics and reform.

Thirdly, the dismal profit performance of many Fortune 500 companies has energized me to focus on 200 disciplines in this book to turn a sow's ear of losses into a silk purse of profitability.

And, now, for the guiding lights of my life and work. Foremost are my parents, whose lives were a perfect Six Sigma of excellence and service to humanity. To them I owe everything. A second influence is Bob Galvin, Chairman Emeritus of Motorola. As the world's foremost industrial leader, he inspired all of us to rise to our full potential.

A third inspiration is Dr. C. Jackson Grayson—advisor to three U.S. Presidents, and Chairman of the flagship American Productivity and Quality Center. His encouragement has been the genesis of this book.

Another towering influence was my late "guru" Dorian Shainin, the world's foremost quality problem-solver. I'm grateful for the powerful support of Arthur Nielsen, Jr., Chairman Emeritus of A.C. Nielsen; editors Neil Levine and Mike Sivilli of AMACOM Books; Harvey Kaylis, President, Mini Circuits; and Mike Katzorke, Vice President, Cessna Aircraft.

Among my colleagues at Motorola, I salute Oscar Kusisto, Vice President and a true leader; Bill Schmidt, my touchstone and sympathetic critic; Adolph Hitzeberger and Carlton Braun, part of our Young Turk brigade; and Bill Wiggenhorn, President of Motorola University.

It is difficult to mention many of my four hundred clients in my consultations around the world. But, I am delighted to acknowledge Bill Beer, President of Maytag Appliances, who adapted my Ultimate Six Sigma to launch his "Maytag Constitution." Willy Hendrickx, Frans Wouters, and Sid Dasgupta—Directors of Philips Electronics, who flooded forty Philips plants with my techniques; and Ted Tabor and Carl Saunders of Caterpillar in advancing my methods in seven Caterpillar plants.

My special thanks to Ratan Tata, Chairman of Tata Industries, India's largest company, for introducing my Ultimate Six Sigma in his plants. The most notable was the brilliant Six Sigma results achieved by his Vice President, Y. Nath and his Director, Ramesh Parkhi at Tata's TELCO plant.

Also, a warm thank you to my esteemed associate, Jean Seeley, whose professionalism and speed produced this manuscript in record time.

Finally, I am grateful to my family—my daughters Safeena and Shenaya, and my sons, Adi and Xerxes—for their faith and confidence in their father. But above all, to my beloved wife, Mehroo, for the sustained outpouring of her love, and unstinting support of nearly half a century.

Part One

The Power of Ultimate Six Sigma
Evolution and Infrastructure

The Power of Ultimate Six Sigma: A Reach-Out Purpose—Business to Solve the World's Ills at a Profit

The ultimate cure for global terrorism is to solve the desperate needs of mankind. This can only be done by business, bonded together in a business Marshall Plan, with profit at the end of the rainbow.
—KEKI R. BHOTE

The Deep-Rooted Tentacles of Terrorism

September 11, 2001, proved to be the opening shot against terrorism heard around the world. The United States has won the first round of that war. The Taliban has been liquidated; al Qaeda has been marginalized. Afghanistan has been liberated militarily, if not politically. Yet the war on terrorism is far from over.

We are engaged in another titanic struggle against terrorism, just as we were engaged in the second half of the twentieth century in a cold war against Soviet communism. What is common to all terrorists is that they feed at the same trough of disillusionment, discontent, and despair—namely, hunger, illiteracy, disease, pollution, and above all, the lack of jobs—*meaningful* jobs.

Until the yawning gap between the corrupt, rapacious, dictatorial rulers of lands where terrorism breeds and the hordes of the dispossessed is tackled, terrorism cannot be snuffed out. In the final analysis, the solutions are not the result of the force of arms; rather, they are economic. It is jobs, jobs, and jobs—and only meaningful jobs will do.

Needed—A Business Marshall Plan

The uplifting task is monumental. The United States, as the only superpower in the world, cannot do it alone. The European Union is too mousy to help. Governments collectively cannot address these economic problems. They are too bureaucratic and economically isolationist. The United Nations cannot engage in the task. It is too impotent structurally and too strapped financially. The World Bank and the International Monetary Fund cannot take on the burden. They can only advise.

There is only one global institution—*business*, motivated by capitalism and fueled by profit—that can mount a frontal attack on these scourges of mankind. Business alone has the know-how, the skills, and the drive to rise to the challenge. But business must enlarge its horizons, moving beyond its tunnel vision of shareholder value to the larger tableau of stakeholder value, embracing customers, employees, suppliers, and investors, and on to the panorama of the ultimate purpose of business—societal value—*the betterment of mankind, with profit at the end of the rainbow.* This is not just Pollyanna optimism. The movement to involve business in tackling social ills, while earning the right to a profit, is already under way in the fields of education, food, health, social infrastructure, and above all, in business as a helping hand for the dispossessed to start their own businesses.

Education

Consider these trends in the education sector:

- Private schools are outperforming failing public schools, both in terms of student achievement and parent satisfaction. Even the U.S. Supreme Court has approved the voucher system and given a boost to the enlargement of private schools.

- Leading companies such as IBM Corp., Motorola, and GE are transforming high school and college curricula to better equip graduates for jobs in industry.

- Collectively, industry is spending more on education and training than the total budgets of all the universities in America. That is not altruism. That is good return on their investment.

Hunger

Several enterprising companies are engaged in the genetic engineering of food products to provide added nutrition to millions of people at lower cost. Companies such as Archer Daniels Midland are striving to become the food basket to the world.

In addition, the Green Revolution, spurred on by the contributions of corporate agricultural technology, has transformed countries such as India, once on the edge of famine, into food-exporting nations.

Disease

There are examples of business coming to the rescue in situations or emergencies where access to medicine and medical treatment is lacking:

- Doctors Without Borders, a worldwide organization supported by businesses in the medical field, sends out thousands of doctors to the poorest countries to treat patients who have no recourse to health care.

- Leading drug companies are finally distributing medication at low cost to countries afflicted with dread diseases such as AIDS, accepting the business principle of a lower profit for larger volumes.

Infrastructure

While the debate rages about the world's dependence on oil, there is a silent break-through under way where wind power is blossoming from a cottage industry to a regional and national grid for the generation of power. It is one of the cheapest sources of energy, with hundreds of thousands of entrepreneurs creating their own windmills and dotting the entire landscape.

As another example, the bottleneck of clogged roads in developing countries is also being blasted away by private companies. Where governments have been too poor and too corrupt to construct roads, private companies are getting the job done at low cost to the public and at a profit to themselves.

Training for Jobs

I revisited India recently and discovered that where there were sleepy villages and widespread unemployment only ten years ago, the number of private enterprises offering training in software, and jobs to follow, are transforming the rural landscape. Second only to the United States, India is already a leading country for software development in the world.

The Organization for Educational Resources and Technological Training (ORT) is one of the world's largest nongovernmental education and training organizations. It spans five continents and more than 100 countries. It trains more than 290,000 students each year in diverse fields such as computers and software, team development, environmental preservation, and mentoring.[1] More important, it goes beyond just job counseling to find jobs for its students.

Microloans for the Poor to Start Their Own Enterprises[2]

Fed up with government-to-government aid programs that are siphoned off into the pockets of corrupt officials or wasted in bureaucratic bungling and turf wars, countries all over the world—from Bangladesh to Brazil, from Mexico to Kyrgyzstan—are moving toward microloan programs advanced by private organizations. These micro-loans, which can range from $10 to $500, are made to the poor—seamstresses, "pud-dle jumper" rickshaw drivers, farmers, and the like—to help them start their own microbusiness. These are the little folk that a regular banker would not even allow into his office! And yet these loans—at no interest—are paid back with a more than 90 percent recovery rate and then recycled into new loans.

James Wolfensen, president of the World Bank, states: "This is not just about resources. It is about building on and then replicating, for example, microcredit for women or community-driven development where the poor are at the center of the solution, not at the end of a handout."

The London-based World Zoroastrian Organization (WZO)[3] has funded over a thousand poor rural folk in Western India with loans from $300 to $2,000 for farm-ing, trucking, or even small-scale urban businesses. In addition, WZO gives technical help, financial advice, and emotional support to these people until they pull them-selves up by their bootstraps. The most encouraging statistic is an 88 percent loan retirement rate, with the same funds being recycled for the next wave of applicants.

Furthermore, there is no need to throw vast amounts of money into microloans. In the Fergana Valley that borders Uzbekistan, Kyrgyzstan, and Tajikistan,[4] tens of thousands of farmers have been helped by ACTED, which provides funds for plant-ing new crops, improving animal husbandry, and rebuilding irrigation networks with a paltry budget of $100,000. That is less than 80 cents per farmer rehabilitated!

As reported in the May 11, 2002 issue of *The Economist*, in Bangladesh alone, 80 percent of the poor families in one of the poorest countries of the world have bene-fited from microloans from 600 microfinance institutions.

These examples of private enterprises supporting business development in devel-oping countries are just a small and little-publicized start. Think of what can happen if individuals, partnerships, cooperatives, and corporations could launch similar initia-tives of free enterprise.

Business—Reform and Cure Thyself!

The road to a social utopia, led by business and paved with promise, is nevertheless pockmarked with land mines manufactured by business itself. Enron, Arthur Ander-sen, and WorldCom are not the exception to skullduggery, they are the rule. Senator Joseph Lieberman, one of the most pro-business members of Congress, states:[5]

> *We've seen too many companies bending rules, pushing through loopholes, defin-ing ethical deviation down, and replacing honesty with hokum and hype. In the process, they don't just distort our values. They distort the markets, they taint the system, and they threaten the free flow of capital to other deserving industries.*

Of course, not all companies can be tarred by unethical corporate greed. But a few examples illustrate why, in a recent Gallup Poll, business leaders scraped the bottom of the barrel in integrity, even lower than the politicians!

Examples of Business Behaving Badly

- *Misuse of Retirement Funds.* Corporations have used employee 401(k) retirement funds freely for wheeling and dealing, while freezing employee stock within the company.

- *Audit Firms Permitted to Double Up as Consultants.* This is a case of asking the cat to take care of the milk.

- *Financial Analysts Misusing Insider Knowledge.* Stock analysts using their inside knowledge to trade in the stocks on which they pontificate in public is a classic case of conflict of interest that verges on boilerplate operations. The attorney general of New York is conducting a major investigation of this scandal that is approaching Enron proportions.

- *Stock Options for Executives Not Treated as Expense.*[6] When options are not subtracted from current earnings, unlike wages and other benefits, the result is a gross exaggeration of profits that misleads shareholders. Alan Greenspan has said that the tax treatment of options inflated growth in earnings of large corporations by two and a half percentage points a year between 1995 and 2000. Had stock options been treated as expenses, the boom in profits for American companies would have ended by 1997.

- *Overcharging.* Several "respected" companies, such as GE, have been dragged into court for gouging the U.S. Defense Department for hundreds of millions of dollars in unwarranted overcharges.

- *Financial Statements That Are Opaque.*[7] When financial statements are not transparent, that means:

    1. More information is buried in the footnotes than in the body of the statement.

    2. Disaggregation disclosures are inadequate to predict earnings and cash flow.

    3. Estimates, assumptions, and off-balance sheet risks are sketchy.

    4. Little information is disclosed on a company's success factors and nonfinancial performance measures.

■ *Accounting Fraud.* The practice of listing expenses as capital gains to boost profits is now so widespread that the entire accounting profession and its conniving auditors are no longer trusted. This is one of the reasons for the panic in the stock market that has lost almost $1 trillion of equity shares.

■ *Excessive Senior Executive Pay.* The ratio of the Japanese CEO's total compensation to the lowest line worker's compensation is 10:1 to 30:1. The German ratio is 30:1 to 60:1. The U.S. ratio is more than 500:1. In the 1990s, the average CEO pay of the top 350 U.S. companies rose 535 percent, while the average worker pay rose only 32 percent. The combination of bonuses and stock option plans for top managers is five to ten times their salaries in leading U.S. firms. And to add insult to injury, these additional forms of compensation are offered to them at the same time that these executives are showing losses and laying off workers! Table 1-1 highlights the inherent unfairness of these statistics. John Cavanagh, president of the Institute for Policy Studies (IPC), a Washington D.C. think tank, states:

It is a flaw in the American dream that one group should be getting such a grotesquely skewed portion of the pie while most Americans get next to nothing. It degrades our democracy.

Table 1-1. A CEO windfall: "a drag on democracy."

- The average CEO at one of the 350 biggest U.S. corporations receives, in salary and bonuses, $12.4 million per year.
- The average CEO at a large Internet company receives, in salary and stock options, $15.4 million per year.
- The average factory worker receives $23,433 per year.
- The ratio of CEO compensation to factory worker compensation is 523:1, the highest of any industrialized nation in the world.
- In the 1990s, average CEO pay rose 535 percent, while average worker pay rose 32 percent.
- In an August 2000 Business Week/Harris Poll, 73 percent of the respondents indicated that the compensation of top officers of large U.S. corporations was "way too much."

Source: "Executive Excess 2000: Seventh Annual CEO Compensation Survey" (Washington, D.C.: IPC, August 30, 2000).

This is not an anticapitalist tirade. No engine for world development has been as effective as capitalism. But it cannot be unfettered, unbridled, undisciplined—a law unto itself. Hopefully, Enron, Arthur Andersen, WorldCom, and others have shown that there is a grievous price to be paid for violating the public trust—a hit in the pocketbook from, of all people, its stockholders and its customers!

The Need for "Power of the Ultimate Six Sigma"

Having shown the need for a business Marshall Plan to lift the scourge of poverty from one-third of mankind, and having traced an outline of required reforms if business is to rise to this global challenge, we can now use the power beacon of the Ultimate Six Sigma to light the path to total business excellence. Let's start with the urgent need for the Power of Ultimate Six Sigma, which stems from businesses needing to improve their profits, their quality standards, and the tools they use to solve quality problems. There are six needs.

Need 1: Anemic Profits

Corporate America, especially the technology sector, is in a deep funk. Faced with that unheard-of phenomena—negative profits—corporations thrash around with layoffs and haphazard and mindless cost-cutting in a desperate search for that will-o'-the wisp: shareholder value. But their panic-stricken efforts have resulted in neither profits nor customer loyalty, nor shareholder value!

This book offers a detailed blueprint, in fifteen chapters, to dramatically improve profits and at the same time capture customer loyalty, employee loyalty, and supplier/distributor loyalty. It highlights 200 disciplines that provide the high-octane fuel to make the profit engine purr!

Need 2: Quality—An Uncertain Trumpet

Barry Goldwater, the Republican curmudgeon, once said that the pursuit of liberalism was no virtue and the pursuit of conservatism no vice. To paraphrase Goldwater, the pursuit of quality for the sake of quality alone is no virtue, while the pursuit of quality for customers and long-term profit is no vice. Traditional Six Sigma is focused almost entirely on quality alone. Yet history is replete with companies nearly shipwrecked on the rocks of a narrow quality focus while little attention is paid to customers and business imperatives. Here are a few examples:

- *Florida Power and Light (FPL): Quality Structure That Ignored Customers.* FPL won the famed Deming Prize for quality, but shortly thereafter, it almost went bankrupt. As the company became preoccupied with people preparing quality charts and tied up in meetings, customer complaints were ignored. FPL had to be rescued by a new management team that applied the wrecking ball to its top-heavy quality structure that had ignored the customer.

■ *Wallace Company: Quality Laurels and Chapter 11*. This oil equipment company was among the first companies to win the Malcolm Baldrige National Quality Award. It became a quality role model. But two years later, as the cost of its quality obsession soared, it filed for Chapter 11 bankruptcy. (This triggered a joke in the media that winning the Baldrige Award was a sure ticket to bankruptcy!)

■ *United Parcel Service (UPS): Fast Delivery Results in Loss of Market Share*. UPS linked its quality efforts to fast delivery. Detailed time-and-motion studies became its definition of quality. Yet UPS steadily lost market share because what its customers really wanted was more access to drivers to get answers to questions and to seek advice on the best routing.

These three examples illustrate, in stark terms, the danger of pursuing quality isolated from the customer, isolated from employees, and isolated from bottom-line results. The inoculation against this virus is the Power of Ultimate Six Sigma!

Need 3: Discarding Fads, Potions, and Nostrums of the Quality Movement in the Last Fifty Years

This disillusionment with quality is by no means new. The history of the quality movement in the last fifty years has had a program-of-the-decade flavor. As companies seek quality salvation, each new fad replaces a discarded one. Sampling plans, Zero Defects, Quality Circles, Statistical Process Control (SPC), Total Quality Management (TQM), and the Hyped Six Sigma of many a consulting firm are tombstones on the sorry road to quality!

Need 4: 1980s to 1990s: The Age of Standards—Boondoggle and Retrogression

A whole plethora of bureaucratic quality standards has been foisted upon a reluctant industry.

ISO-9000 was launched in 1987 as a worldwide standard by a consortium of forty-five countries participating in the International Standards Organization (ISO). It is an elementary quality system—the least common denominator of mediocrity of these squabbling nations. Even with periodic improvements, ISO-9000 has set back the quality movement by twenty years. As its critics say, if you want to freeze unacceptable defect levels, ISO-9000 will enable you to do so consistently!

QS-9000 is the standard developed in the 1990s by the Big Three automotive companies for their first-tier suppliers. It is an improvement over ISO-9000, but it is still couched in bureaucratic speak and contains little guidance on how to help hapless suppliers achieve even modest levels of quality.

In a classical example of bureaucratic creep, the ISO series of standards has grown from the lone ISO-9000 to 12,000 standards, designed by more than 200 technical committees! Has any congressional investigation questioned the benefit-to-cost ratio of this unseemly proliferation?

Need 5: Quality Systems—Hesitant Steps on the Road to Quality Perfection

Formal quality systems evolved, to a greater or lesser extent, from the haphazard quality manuals of individual companies. Chief among them are:

- *The Deming Prize.* This quality system emphasizes statistics, but is not focused on leadership or on the principal stakeholders—customers, employees and suppliers.

- *The Malcolm Baldrige National Quality Award.* While its guidelines are better than ISO-9000 or QS-9000, the Baldrige Award is far from being a world-class quality system. Its guidelines touch only superficially on the customer and on leadership. And they fall short in the all important "how to" of tools to achieve quality breakthroughs. Furthermore, the ambiguities of language associated with this quality system would make a lawyer look like a novice!

- *The European Quality Award.* With a focus on business results, this quality system is an improvement over Baldrige, but is nowhere near world-class quality requirements.

Table 1-2 is a subjective but relevant score of the effectiveness of various quality standards and systems. It is based on my consultations with more than 400 companies all over the world.

In conclusion, there is a compelling need for a world-class system that only the Power of Ultimate Six Sigma can provide.

Need 6: Tools—Driving a Nail in the Wall Without a Hammer

Bill Conway, the former chairman of the Nashua Corporation, received a delegation of vice presidents from the Ford Motor Company who wanted to explore the reasons for Nashua's outstanding quality success. He told his listeners: "I'm going to select two of you for a contest. The winner will get a free vacation in Hawaii. The loser will get nothing. The contest involves driving a nail into the wall behind me. Each of you will get a nail. One will get a hammer; the other—nothing. Who will win?" Tragically, industry

Table 1-2. Relative effectiveness of quality standards/systems.

Quality Standard/System	Effectiveness (Scale: 1 = least effective; 100 = most effective)
ISO-9000	5
QS-9000	15
Deming Prize	30
Malcolm Baldrige Award	35
European Quality Award	40
Motorola Six Sigma (see Chapter 2)	50
Hyped Six Sigma (see Chapter 2)	30
Ultimate Six Sigma (see entire book)	90

tries to solve its chronic quality problems with weak tools—hammering with a wet noodle instead of a sledgehammer! A catalogue of these wet-noodle tools follows:

■ *The Seven Tools of QC are of Kindergarten Effectiveness.* The Japanese have packaged a set of quality techniques, labeled the seven tools of quality control (QC), to solve quality problems in production. They include PDCA (Plan, Do, Check, Act), data collection, graphs, histograms, cause-and-effect diagrams, and control charts.

■ *The Seven Quality Management Tools (Another Wet-Noodle Hammer).* The Japanese have amazing penchant for making simple things complicated. These tools are useless in problem solving. They include Affinity Diagram, Interrelationship Diagram, Tree Diagram, Matrix Diagram, Matrix Data Analysis Plot, Process Decision Program, and Arrow Diagram.

■ *Computer Simulation.* The computer age is upon us in earnest. We seem to have developed a blind faith in the computer's ability to do anything, to solve any problem, instead of relying on the God-given computer between our ears—the brain. For problem solving, a computer must be programmed with the mathematical equation that governs the relationships between the dependent variable and the independent variables. Without that formula, the computer is reduced to a guessing game, at best. This is especially true when interaction effects are present between variables. Unfortunately, in complex products and processes, not even an Einstein can develop a formula that fits.

■ *Traditional/Hyped Six Sigma DMAIC Methodology.* The Six Sigma methodology most widely used—and the one promoted in run-of-the-mill books—is known as DMAIC (define, measure, analyze, improve, and control). DMAIC is nothing but a warmed-over version of PDCA (plan, do, check, act) that has been peddled as a problem-solving tool for more than forty years. DMAIC is muddled in definition, imprecise in measurement, impotent in analysis, incapacitated in improvement, and rudderless in control. Other than that, it is okay!

Table 1-3 lists a subjective—but realistic—score of the effectiveness of various problem-solving tools—again, based on my problem solving for companies in four continents.

As with systems, there is a need to jettison the tired tools of the twentieth century and embrace the powerful tools of the twenty-first century, such as Design of Experiments (Shainin/Bhote), which is detailed in Chapter 9.

Table 1-3. Relative effectiveness of problem-solving tools.

Problem-Solving Tools	Effectiveness (Scale: 1 = least effective; 100 = most effective)
Seven Tools of QC	3
Seven Management Tools of QC	2
Computer Simulation	15
Traditional/Hyped Six Sigma Methodology (DMAIC)	15
Design of Experiments (DOE):	
• Classical (brief treatment in Chapter 9)	30
• Taguchi (brief treatment in Chapter 9)	20
• Shainin/Bhote (Chapter 9)	100

Objectives of the Ultimate Six Sigma

The Ultimate Six Sigma process has several reach-out objectives for industry. The objectives are to:

- Develop techniques/disciplines that can truly impact corporate profitability, not just fool around its edges.

- Implement a practical, how-to guide to propel a company to quickly achieve the benefits (discussed in the next section) of the Ultimate Six Sigma.

- Develop a comprehensive infrastructure that goes well beyond the narrow confines of quality (the small Q) to encompass all areas of business excellence (the Big Q).

- Maximize all stakeholder loyalty—customer loyalty, employee loyalty, supplier loyalty, distributor/dealer loyalty, and investor loyalty.

- Maximize business results: profits, return on investment, asset turns, inventory turns, and sales/value-added per employee. Furthermore, go beyond just the financials.

- Minimize people turnover and bring joy to the workplace, especially to the line worker.

- Go beyond the propaganda and "results with mirrors" of the hyped Six Sigma consulting companies to usher in Ultimate Six Sigma—which is low in implementation costs and high in business results.

- Provide keys to critical success factors in each of twelve areas:

1	Customer loyalty and long-term retention
2	Leadership (i.e., providing vision and inspiration, which facilitates employees reaching their full potential)
3	Organization (i.e., revolutionizing the ways people are hired, trained, evaluated, compensated, and promoted)
4	Employees (i.e., empowering them on the road to industrial democracy)
5	Supplier partnerships (i.e., improving customer quality, cost, and cycle time while enhancing supplier profits)
6, 7, 8	Powerful new tools (i.e., for achieving quality, cost, and cycle time breakthroughs)

9	Design (i.e., maximizing customer value and "wow")
10	Manufacturing (i.e., transforming a sunset obsolescence into a sunrise enlightenment)
11	Support services (i.e., converting a black hole of little accountability in the business/white collar world to service with maximum productivity)
12	Quality of results (i.e., achieving order of magnitude improvements)

■ Conduct periodic audits and self-assessments to achieve continuous, never-ending improvement. Use these audits as a guide to the disciplines and techniques needed for quick action.

Benefits of the Ultimate Six Sigma

Table 1-4 compares the results of a traditional company versus those following a hyped Six Sigma practice versus the results from a full Ultimate Six Sigma implementation.

Table 1-4 shows lucidly that:

■ The Ultimate Six Sigma company can attain one to two orders of magnitude improvement over a traditional company.

■ The hyped Six Sigma companies have not published results in most parameters vital to any business—a further indication of its "all show and little substance" hollowness.

Table 1-4. Results: traditional vs. hyped Six Sigma vs. Ultimate Six Sigma companies.

Area	Metric	Results		
		Traditional Co.	Hyped Six Sigma Co.	Ultimate Six Sigma Co.
Business/ Financials	Profit on Sales	4%	6%	>10%
	Return on Investment	8%	12%	>50%
	Asset Turns	2	Unknown	4
	Inventory Turns	10 to 15	Not measured	>100
	People Turnover/ Year	20% to 10%	Not measured	1% to 2%
	Productivity: Value Added/ Employee/Year	$100,000	Not measured	>$600,000
Customer Loyalty	Retention	<75%	Not measured	>95%
	Longevity (years)	<5	Not measured	>10
	Stakeholder Satisfaction	<50%	Not measured	> 90%
Quality/ Reliability/ Cycle Time	Cost of Poor Quality (COPQ)	8% to 20%	Not measured	1% to 2%
	Outgoing Quality (ppm)	10,000 to 30,000	1,000 to 3,000	<100
	c_{pk}	1.0	1.33	>2.0
	Field Reliability (ppm/yr.)	30,000 80,000	Not measured	<500
	Cycle Time (multiples of theoretical cycle time)	10 to 100	Not measured	1.5 to 2.0

CHAPTER 2

From the Infirmity of the Hyped Six Sigma to the Power of Ultimate Six Sigma

We are witnessing Six Sigma Houdinis, who can conjure up
the magic of transforming any old quality level to an ideal of
Six Sigma!   —KEKI R. BHOTE

Six Sigma: A Bright New Flame or a Sputtering Fire?

Six Sigma's popularity is catching fire throughout our industrial world as no other movement has done in recent memory. Leading companies are seeking to increase their lead with Six Sigma. Others are scrambling to get on board with whatever Six Sigma driftwood they can find. And consulting companies with a half-baked knowledge of the real Six Sigma are peddling their snake oil to gullible corporations, desperate for results.

Will the fire of Six Sigma continue to burn bright into the future, or will it be snuffed out along with the banked ashes of total quality management (TQM), business process reengineering (BPR), MRPII, value analysis, scientific management, and other claimants to the throne of innovation in the last century? The answer depends on how Six Sigma is truly understood and effectively implemented. For instance:

17

- If its emphasis is on quality alone, to the exclusion of customers and profits, the company will achieve neither quality nor profits.

- If its emphasis is on profits and shareholder value alone, to the exclusion of stakeholder value, it will achieve neither profits nor stakeholder value.

- If its emphasis on an elitist organization of black belts and master black belts, it will become a victim to the disease of Taylorism.

- If it listens to the hyped Six Sigma siren song of the consulting companies, it will continue to flounder in mediocrity.

- If, however, the principles of the Power of Ultimate Six Sigma are implemented with a focus on the customer; on leadership; on releasing the inherent, creative talents of employees; and on the use of powerful and little-known tools of the twenty-first century, the dawn of a bright new era of total business excellence can be ushered in, along with a sharp increase in corporate profitability.

The danger from the machinations of the hyped Six Sigma advocates is so real and so widespread that it's necessary to contrast vividly its fundamental weakness *vis-à-vis* the towering strengths of the Ultimate Six Sigma.

The Evolution of Six Sigma

Process capability, called c_p, is defined as S/P for a given parameter, where:

S = the specification width (highest minus the lowest *allowable* reading)

P = the process width (highest minus the lowest *observed* reading)

c_{pk} is process capability, corrected for a noncentering of the process average, $\overline{X}$, relative to the design center (or target value). If $\overline{X}$ and the design center are the same, $c_{pk} = c_p$; if not, a slight formula correction lowers c_{pk} relative to c_p. Traditionally, process width is also measured in sigma terms, where sigma (Greek letter σ) is the standard deviation of a group of data, for a given parameter, from its average $\overline{X}$.

- Until the 1970s, a process width of $\overline{X} \pm 3\sigma$ was larger than a specification width of $\overline{X} \pm 2\sigma$. This resulted in a defect level of 4.5 percent, but was considered "good enough" quality. This meant a c_{pk} of 0.67.

- In the 1980s, process widths were targeted to equal specification widths, with both at $\overline{X} \pm 3\sigma$. This resulted in a lower defect level of 0.27 percent or 2,700

Table 2-1. Quantitative relationship between Sigma, percent (or ppm/ppb) defective, and c_{PK} (for process width of $\overline{X} \pm 3\sigma$).

Specification Width	Amount Defective Outside Specification Width		
	%	PPM/PPB	c_{PK}
$\overline{X} \pm 2\sigma$	4.56	45,600 ppm	0.67
$\overline{X} \pm 3\sigma$	0.27	2,700 ppm	1.00
$\overline{X} \pm 4\sigma$	0.0063	63 ppm	1.33
$\overline{X} \pm 5\sigma$	0.00057	0.57 ppm	1.67
$\overline{X} \pm 6\sigma$	0.0000002	0.02 ppm (2 ppb)	2.00

parts per million (ppm) and was considered a "reach out" quality level, with a c_{PK} of 1.0.

- In the 1990s, with global competition driving quality toward zero defects, process limits at $\overline{X} \pm 3\sigma$, and specification limits at $\overline{X} \pm 3\sigma$ (i.e., a c_{PK} of 1.33), the defect level is further reduced to 63 ppm. As an example, QS-9000, the quality system of the automotive industry, requires a minimum c_{PK} of 1.33 for key parameters from its suppliers.

- In the 2000s, world-class companies are striving for process widths reduced to $\overline{X} \pm 3\sigma$, relative to specification limits of $\overline{X} \pm 5\sigma$, resulting in defect levels as low as 0.57 ppm (i.e., a c_{PK} of 1.67).

- The full impact of Motorola's famous Six Sigma launch is a process width reduced to $\overline{X} \pm 3\sigma$, relative to a specification width of $\overline{X} \pm 6\sigma$, lowering the defect level to a microscopic two parts per billion (ppb)—or a c_{PK} of 2.0. For all practical purposes, that is *zero defects*. This is the statistical meaning of Six Sigma.

Table 2-1 depicts these relationships.

Enlarging the Concept of Six Sigma

At Motorola, we extended the concept of the statistical Six Sigma in two significant ways from a single parameter:

1. To *all* parameters in a product and converting the total number of defects into a percentage, or ppm, and using an expansion of Table 2-1 to calculate the corresponding sigma level.

2. Adding the total number of defects at each of several checkpoints on an entire production line and dividing these defects by the number of units produced. This figure, called the total defects per unit (TDPU) would be converted into a percentage or ppm and an extension of Table 2-1 used to calculate the corresponding sigma levels.

As an example, if a production line manufacturing cellular phones checked 100,000 units in its final station and found 5 defects, the defect level would be 0.005 percent, or 50 ppm or 4.1σ. If the same production line had 10 checkpoints and found 5 defects at each checkpoint, there would be 50 defects in 100,000 units or 0.05 percent or 500 ppm and only 3.48σ.

The Hyped Six (Sick) Sigma Heresies

This Motorola ideal of an enlarged Six Sigma was watered down by several consulting companies with questionable integrity. Their approach deserves the appellation: "the hyped Six Sigma." They have so emasculated the definition of Six Sigma that any quality level, high or low, could masquerade as Six Sigma.

Heresy 1: Allowing the 1.5 Sigma Shift

The hyped Six Sigma approach asserts that it is too difficult to hold the average, $\overline{X}$, at the target value (i.e., design center) of a parameter's distribution because of inherent shifts in materials and processes, etc. So it blithely allows a 1.5 sigma shift of $\overline{X}$ from the target value. This increases the defect level from 2 ppb to 3.4 ppm—a quality adulteration of 1700:1!

True practitioners of problem solving know that it is relatively easy to correct for an $\overline{X}$ shift from a target value through a minor adjustment or tweaking and eliminate the 1.5 sigma noncentering. Yet the Six Sigma hypers brazenly perpetuate the fraud of sprinkling holy water on a 3.4 ppm defect level—a 1,700 times deterioration—and baptizing it as Six Sigma!

Heresy 2: Diluting the Defect Level and the Associated Sigma Level with Parts Counts

The sigma level, artificially boosted by the 1.5 sigma shift, is given a further boost by the hyped Six Sigma people who brazenly divide the actual product defect ppm level by the number of parts in a product and equate the artificially low defect level to a fictitiously high sigma level. As an example, if a product containing 100 parts has a defect level of 10,000 ppm, or 1 percent or a true sigma level of 0.86, this unnecessary 1.5 sigma shift would artificially raise the sigma level from 0.86 to 3.75. Now, if the parts count of 100 were taken into consideration, the artificial defect level would be further reduced from 10,000 ppm to 100 ppm on this product and the sigma level raised from 0.86 to 3.75 and on to a most respectable 5.2!

The higher the parts count in a product (and complex products can have more than 50,000 parts), the greater is the likelihood that a poor quality product will fly under the radar detection screen and pass off as a perfect Six Sigma product. In fact, engineers in hyped Six Sigma companies do not want to lower the parts count in their products for fear of lowering their sigma performance. In a few cases, they even attempt *to add* to the parts count (and increase costs) to make their sigma score look good! And yet a customer rightly feels that his received quality has not improved and that his manufacturer's claim of Six Sigma perfection is a fraud.

Heresy 3: "Feuding" with Opportunities Per Part to Reduce Defect PPMs Even Further

But this is not the end of the con game. Beyond the 1.5 sigma center shift dilution and the parts count "dilution squared," there is a further "dilution cubed." This is done by dividing the defect level of Heresy 2 by the number of opportunities each part can have for defects. In the previous example, if each of the 100 parts has five opportunities for defects, the true defect level of 10,000 ppm would be artificially and progressively reduced first to 100 ppm by parts count and then reduced to 20 ppm, by opportunity, while the sigma level would be fictitiously increased from 0.86 to 3.75 to 5.2 and on to an incredulous 5.6!

Table 2-2 shows the progressive magnitude of the dilution. What an easy rubber yardstick for the Six Sigma hypers to juggle!

Heresy 4: Defining an Opportunity for Defects

There is yet another fudge factor in the hyped Six Sigma sleight-of-hand. It has to do with how different people may count an opportunity for defects on a part. As an example, does a resistor with two leads have one opportunity for defects or two—because it has two leads, each of which supposedly has an opportunity for a defect? Does a microprocessor with 80 leads have one opportunity or 80 opportunities for defects? The hyped Six Sigma con artists choose the latter to make themselves look good with a fictitiously high sigma level. Yet, does the customer give a hoot as to how many parts he has in his product or how many opportunities each part has for generating defects?

"Hyped Six Sigma" companies have become so obsessed with the minutiae of Six Sigma measurements, especially in support services, that they can eventually bankrupt the companies they heroically try to reform.

Table 2-2. The anemic Six Sigma: the "hyped" approach's preposterous reduction in defect levels and increases in σ levels.

Configuration Based on:	True Defect Level (PPM)	True Sigma Level	"Hyped Six Sigma" (Fictitious) Defect Level (PPM)	"Hyped Six Sigma"* (Fictitious) Sigma Level (σ)
Total Product (TP)	10,000	0.86σ	10,000	3.75σ (Dilution #1)
100 Parts/Product	10,000	0.86σ	100	5.2σ (Dilution #2)
Opportunities/Parts	10,000	0.86σ	20	5.6σ (Dilution #3)

* Allows a 1.5σ shift of X from target value. The product in this example is a cellular phone.

As a result of these heresies, advocates of the hyped Six Sigma can conjure up any sigma level that suits their political purpose—using Machiavellian gamesmanship. But, in the final analysis, they get hoisted on their own petard. Customers dissatisfied with the same tired defect levels on their products, but which are dressed up in fancy "hyped Six Sigma" attire, vote with their feet and their pocketbooks to dump such companies and switch to their competition.

The Ultimate Six Sigma

In sharp contrast to the hyped Six Sigma, the Ultimate Six Sigma points to "true north" in the world of business:

■ It goes way beyond conventional quality systems (e.g., ISO-9000, Malcolm Baldrige National Quality Award, and total quality management), practiced by companies with a "follow the leader" sheep mentality, to the pursuit of total business excellence.

■ It goes way beyond traditional product quality and reliability to breakthroughs unparalleled in levels, yet matched by increased customer retention, value, and "wow," as well as a doubling of corporate profit.

■ It goes way beyond token decreases in cycle time to 10:1 and even 50:1 decreases, with resultant increases in inventory turns of 10:1 and 20:1.

■ It goes way beyond the narrow scope of traditional Six Sigma (as detailed in the section on the Objectives of the Ultimate Six Sigma in Chapter 1).

A Synopsis of Hyped Six Sigma Weaknesses and Ultimate Six Sigma Strengths

Having outlined the collusion in the very definition of hyped Six Sigma and sketched the salient features of the Ultimate Six Sigma, a short synopsis of the inherent weaknesses of the hyped Six Sigma practices and the corresponding robustness of the Ultimate Six Sigma, as detailed in subsequent chapters, is in order. The object is to prevent readers and innocent companies from falling for the publicity and self-promotion of the hyped Six Sigma consultants and their black belt claims.

Table 2-4 is a capsule summary of the two approaches, first by features and secondly by area.

Results: From Mediocrity to World Class

If the game of bowling were played using industry norms, the bowling pins would be removed so that there was no target to shoot at, team interactions would be discouraged, and the score would be kept by the supervisor who would demand that each person do better.

The hyped Six Sigma results are couched in similar fashion. There are no firm targets for quality (except for a fraudulent 3.4 ppm), reliability, cycle time, customer retention/longevity, ^Cp_K, cost/productivity, and innovation.

By contrast, the Ultimate Six Sigma not only measures each of these parameters, but it expresses five levels of achievement for each—ranging from a primitive company's results to world-class levels. These are detailed in Chapter 15—on results.

The Origin, Development, and Renewal of Motorola's Six Sigma

This chapter concludes with the story of Motorola, the pioneer of the Six Sigma process. It provides the perfect backdrop to the development of the Ultimate Six Sigma methodology in succeeding chapters.

The Japanese Challenge

The genesis of Motorola's Six Sigma was the intense challenge of Japanese competition. Japanese companies were eating our lunch in several businesses in the 1970s and getting ready to eat our dinner as well. "Meet the Japanese Challenge" became the

Table 2-4. The hyped Six Sigma versus the Ultimate Six Sigma: a comparison by features and by area.

(You can fool some of the people all of the time, and all of the people some of the time, but you can't fool all of the people all of the time.)

Characteristic Features	Hyped Six Sigma	The Ultimate Six Sigma
Profit on Sales	3% improvement	6% to 10% improvement
Return on Investment	2:1 to 3:1	5:1 to 10:1
Black Belt Organization	Elitist: 1 in 100	Everybody a black belt
Objective	Profit	Satisfaction of all
Scope	Confined to product	stakeholders
Defect Goal	3.4 PPM (but achieved	Excellence in all areas of
	with mirrors!)	a business
Field Failure Goal	No metric	True defect levels:
Implementation Cost	$40,000-$50,000 per	< 10 PPM
	student	10 to 100 PPM/year
Training Time	6 months	< $2,000 per student
Curriculum	>90% not needed	1 week
	or used	Focus on simple, useful
System Scoring/Audits	None	tools
Culture	No change	Comprehensive self-
		assessment
		Hiring, evaluation,
		compensation, promotion
		practices transformed

Area-by-Area

Customers	Customer satisfaction	Customer loyalty
Management	Micromanagement	Inspiring leadership
Organization	Vertical, bureaucratic	Horizontal, team-centered
Employees	Passive, alienated	Contributing, empowered
Quality	Design of Experiments	10 powerful tools of the
	(DOE) (classical only)	21st century
Cost	Not considered	7 power tools of the last
		century

Cycle time	Not considered	10 powerful tools of the 21st century
Suppliers	Pro-forma quality audits	Commodity teams; active, concrete help in quality, cost, cycle time
Design	Classical DOE	Product characterization/ optimization/robustness
Manufacturing	Elementary 5-step problem solving	MEOST, Precontrol, Positrol, Process Certification
Support Services	Process mapping	VE, force field analysis, job redesign, 10-step roadmap
Results	No targets for reliability, cycle time, customer retention, innovation	Comprehensive targets for business, customers, quality/reliability

company's call to arms. Bob Galvin, the chairman of the board at Motorola, decided that he would fight Japanese competitors with the same weapon they had used to capture market share in the United States—namely, quality.

10:1, 100:1, 1000:1 Quality Improvement

In 1981, Bob Galvin established a quality improvement goal of 10:1 in five years. Motorola's previous quality record had been considered respectable, improving at 10 percent per year. But Galvin's goal was to improve it—not by 50 percent or 100 percent, but by 1,000 percent in five years! Many skeptics declared it an impossible goal. But, by 1986, most of Motorola's divisions had met that goal. This author, who was then the group director of Motorola's Automotive and Industrial Electronics Group, achieved the 10:1 improvement in three years. However, when we benchmarked ourselves against the Japanese, we found that they were still ahead in quality. So, in 1987, Galvin raised the height of the bar with a further 10:1 improvement, but this time it had to be achieved in two years. And in 1989, he again furthered our sights for a third 10:1 improvement by 1991. Starting in 1981, Motorola had to improve quality by an incredible 1000:1 in ten years.

The goal was not completely achieved throughout Motorola's worldwide operations, but the average improvement was 800:1, starting from an already-respectable quality base in 1981. The entire progression to these lofty quality heights was given the appellation Six Sigma—less as a statistical term, more as a rallying cry for perfection.

The Pot of Gold

Many in the media were critical of Motorola's "obsession" with quality. "Wouldn't there be a severe cost penalty for such a magnitude of quality improvement?" they smirked. But Motorola never lost sight of its customers or the bottom line in this quality pursuit. Since 1979, Motorola had been tracking its cost of poor quality, which includes warranty, scrap, repair, analysis, inspection, and test costs, along with the cost of carrying inventory. In ten years, it saved more than $9 billion by reducing this cost of poor quality. That was the pot of gold that enabled Motorola to recapture customers previously lost to the Japanese through lower prices. That was the pot of gold that gave our Motorola employees higher incentives and wages. That was the pot of gold that allowed the company to keep its loyal investors—with Motorola stock having appreciated 24:1 in thirteen years. Several years later, a leading news journal asked: "Mr. Galvin, you have led the company to many quality peaks and have won many honors, including the Malcolm Baldrige Award. What is it that you regret the most in your quality drive?" Bob Galvin's amazing answer: "I did not set high enough goals!"

Success Factors in Motorola's Six Sigma Drive

Success has many fathers; failure is an orphan. Nevertheless, there are several reasons for Motorola's spectacular quality achievement that are worth highlighting.

Success Factor 1: Bob Galvin's Inspiring Leadership (see Chapter 5)

Success Factor 2: Twenty-first Century Tools Forged in the Twentieth-Century Crucible

I took responsibility and leadership in researching and implementing powerful new tools to achieve breakthroughs in Motorola's 10:1, 100:1, and 1000:1 quality improvement drive. The tools, their application, and their implementation are described in Chapters 9, 11, and 14.

As a result, Motorola benefited by orders-of-magnitude improvements in quality, more than $30 billion in cost reduction, and a greater than 10:1 reduction in manufacturing cycle time.

Success Factor 3: Total Customer Satisfaction

In the 1980s, Motorola revolutionized its main objective and changed its focus from profit to total customer satisfaction.

Success Factor 4: Empowerment of People

Motorola had always enjoyed a worldwide reputation as a "people caring" company. But in its Six Sigma era, the caring became even more explicit. The jewel in the crown was Motorola's total customer satisfaction (TCS) competition (see Chapter 7).

Success Factor 5: Win-Win Partnerships with Suppliers (see Chapter 9)

Tackling the Quality of Education in the Nation's Schools

Stepping outside the confines of industry and into the untested waters of social responsibility, Motorola undertook to inject quality into the curricula and teaching methods of high schools and universities. The importance of quality had only been vaguely understood in these institutions and the word *customer* was off their radar screen.

I was personally involved in introducing Six Sigma to a prestigious university in the Chicago area and was amazed by the magnitude of the challenge. In general, I have found, in my subsequent consultations, that certain quality effectiveness scores—which I've listed in Table 2-5—subjective though they are, can be applied to different institutions. To schools, as they say in show business: "You have a long way to go, baby!"

Table 2-5. Quality effectiveness scores, by type of organization.

Institution	Quality Effectiveness (Scale: 1 = least effective; 100 = most effective)
Manufacturing	70
White Collar	45
Service	25
Government	20
Schools	15
Hospitals	10

Sharing Motorola's Success with the Outside World

In line with the Baldrige Award requirement, Motorola shared its success factors with hundreds of companies all over the globe and placed its Six Sigma innovation on the world map.

My March to the Ultimate Six Sigma

Yet, after having earned the plaudits of a grateful America for launching its Six Sigma, the question arose at Motorola: "What do we do for an encore?" Bob Galvin, Motorola's chairman, suggested that a few of us research extending the frontiers of product quality to all areas of a company—including the quality of leadership, the quality of employees, the quality of organization, and the quality of business processes.

As a result, I started working with Dr. C. Jackson Grayson—a great American who had served in the cabinet of two U.S. presidents and who persuaded the Congress of the United States, along with the American Society for Quality, to create the Malcolm Baldrige National Quality Award. Our goal was to go beyond the Baldrige Award, which was becoming somewhat ossified. Dr. Grayson, who is now the chairman of the American Productivity & Quality Center (APQC) in Houston, was most gracious with his suggestions and encouragement. My research with Dr. Grayson was the foundation of the Ultimate Six Sigma.

After forty-two years of an exciting and fulfilling career at Motorola, I decided to retire and formed my own consulting company, Keki R. Bhote Associates. My goal has been to help companies worldwide solve and prevent chronic quality problems, using the enormously successful Shainin/Bhote Design of Experiments that we had launched at Motorola in 1982. While this goal was achieved in many of the more than 400 companies where I consulted, I came to the conclusion that companies needed to operate on a broader canvas. That meant they had to look beyond just quality perfection and reach instead for business perfection and for real profit improvement, not profit tokenism.

Motorola's Six Sigma was good. Hundreds of companies had come to learn about it and many copied it in various stages of implementation. But we needed to take Six Sigma to graduate school. This became even more urgent because the hyped Six Sigma consultants were retrogressing their clients from college to high school! Six Sigma was degenerating into another quality fad. And so I escalated my research into methods for going beyond Six Sigma. My clients liked the expansion and urged me to formalize it. My work came to the attention of Jim Nelson, the far-seeing publisher of Strategic Directions of Switzerland. He encouraged me to write two booklets as part of a huge opus: *The Total Quality Portfolio*. My contributions were:

"Plan for Maximum Profit: The 12 Critical Success Factors That Guarantee Increased Profits from Total Quality"[1]

"Quality Project Alert: The Early Warning Signals for Any Quality Initiative in Danger of Costing More Than It Earns"[2]

The favorable reception accorded to these two volumes, and the enthusiasm of my clients, provided the launching pad for the Ultimate Six Sigma and this book.

CHAPTER 3

The Scope, Structure, and Methodology of the Power of Ultimate Six Sigma

Human progress is seldom linear. Often it is reversible. But it comes through, bright and shining, at the final gatepost. . . .
—OLD PROVERB

Scope of the Power of Ultimate Six Sigma

A recent movie title, *Eyes Wide Shut*, may well capture the present myopic vision of corporate management. Unfocused in its view of customer insights, unfocused in its understanding of true leadership, unfocused in its ability to empower its employees, unfocused in its ability to build bridges of partnership with its suppliers, and unfocused in its knowledge of the disciplines needed for quality, cost, and cycle time improvement, yesterday's corporate tycoons are stuck in their pygmy tracks of sorry performance and even worse results.

The scope of this book is to 1) change corporate vision from "eyes wide shut" to "eyes wide open," from anemic profits and embarrassing losses to robust and sustained profits, and 2) to build on the conceptual framework of the Ultimate Six Sigma by developing a firm, practical roadmap that companies can readily and quickly implement. It concentrates on the disciplines and techniques that must be harnessed. In short, it moves from the IQ (intelligence quotient) of my previous book to the AQ (action quotient) of this updated one.

Figure 3-1. The structure of the Ultimate Six Sigma.

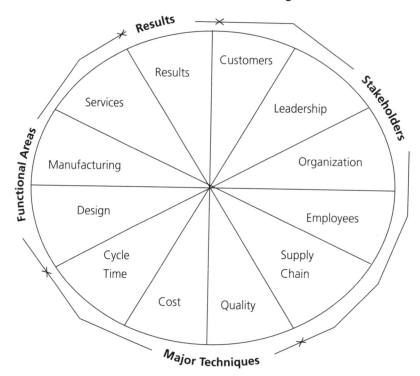

A Strengthened Structure of the Ultimate Six Sigma

This chapter is the last in the introductory Part 1. The organization of the rest of this book focuses on four elements: 1) stakeholders, 2) major techniques, 3) functional areas, and 4) results. The linkage between these four elements is shown in Figure 3-1 and represents the overall structure of the Power of Ultimate Six Sigma as put forth in this book.

- *From Shareholder Value to Stakeholder Value.* Going beyond the obsession with the financial analyst and the investor, Ultimate Six Sigma embraces customers, corporate leadership, organization infrastructure and culture, employees, and supply chain partnerships (including first, second, and third-tier suppliers; distributors; dealers; retail chains; installers; and servicers).

■ *Major Techniques.* Three major techniques are necessary for each area of a company to achieve effectiveness—quality, cost, and cycle time. The quality techniques go far, far beyond those used in traditional Six Sigma companies or those used by master black belts, black belts, and green belts. The cost reduction techniques, which are almost nonexistent in traditional Six Sigma companies, include innovations that are new or unused in more than 80 percent of companies. The cycle time reduction techniques, again unknown in most traditional Six Sigma companies, go well beyond obsolete practices such as MRPII and short-interval scheduling.

■ *Applications in Major Line Functions.* The major functional areas within a company—design, manufacturing, and services (including support services such as sales/marketing, accounting, human resources, and field operations) are now oriented toward "how to" execution.

■ *Results.* It is important, in the final analysis, to develop metrics by which results can be assessed. The primary metrics include not only financials but also the important constituencies of customers, leadership, and employees. The secondary metrics—a longer list—embellish and circumscribe the primary metrics.

The conclusion of this Ultimate Six Sigma process is a message of new hope and new horizons for the beleaguered corporations of today.

Methodologies: A "How to" of Practical Implementation

The succeeding chapters (Chapters 4 through 15) constitute a roadmap by which a company can, in stages, aspire to the Ultimate Six Sigma. Each chapter contains the following highlights:

1. *A Brief Background.* The importance of the Ultimate Six Sigma process and underlying principles are stressed, along with the inadequacies of the current practices in most companies.

2. *Details of the Disciplines Required for Successful Implementation.* I have found a distressing lack of familiarity with many of the disciplines/techniques/tools in every one of the twelve areas covered by Ultimate Six Sigma. Unless their power is recognized and a conscious, deliberate decision is made to rapidly deploy them, companies will fall further and further behind their competitors or languish in the mediocrity of

the traditional Six Sigma approaches and their black belt limitations. Each discipline is explained (or references are given for further detailed study). Several companies have used consultants to initiate these disciplines, but care must be exercised that the consultant has depth of knowledge and proven success to steer them.

3. *A Case Study of a Benchmark Company for the Particular Area.* It is always helpful to know that the disciplines/techniques discussed in the book are not just theoretical ideals. Consequently, a company that is truly a benchmark for the disciplines implemented in each area has been selected to illustrate successful implementation. The selection is based partly on reputation and partly on my own experiences with more than 400 consultations, but always on performance excellence.

4. *Self-Assessment Audit and Scoring System—A Company's Health Chart.* A salient feature of the book is a self-assessment—or external audit—by which a company can determine its Ultimate Six Sigma "health." None of the traditional Six Sigma practices have anything even remotely connected with an audit. (The Malcolm Baldrige National Quality Award guidelines do constitute an audit, but it is so elementary by comparison and so convoluted in language that it is not even worth an expenditure of valuable company time.) In addition, the audit can be used, longitudinally, to measure yearly progress in a company's march to business excellence.

Scoring System of the Self-Assessment

The self-assessment/audit is based on a listing of the most important and practical disciplines needed by each of three types of companies and includes an implementation timetable for each company type. The system for scoring a company's success on the road to Ultimate Six Sigma is outlined here.

1. *Areas.* The maximum possible score in the audit is 1,000 points. Each of ten areas—organization/culture; employees; supply chains; quality, cost; cycle time; design; manufacturing; services; and results—carries a total of 80 points. The exceptions are customers and leadership, each of which is assigned 100 points because of their greater importance and impact on the entire company. This is because no company can exist without customers and no company can long survive without leadership. (A company can change these point weightings in each area depending on the importance it attaches to that area. It can even change the total score of 1,000 points. But it is recommended that all divisions/businesses within a company adopt a uniform scale or score in order to compare different divisions or to measure the performance of each division over time.) Table 3-1 is a capsule summary of the audit in the twelve areas and their key characteristics, each with its maximum assigned score.

(text continues on page 39)

Table 3-1. Power of the Ultimate Six Sigma: a self-assessment chart/audit and scoring system.

Area	Key Characteristics	Importance (Points)
1. Customers	1.1 Customer Differentiation	10
	1.2 Customer Loyalty Metrics	30
	1.3 Customer "Wow"	20
	1.4 Customer Cultivation	25
	1.5 Company Infrastructure for Customer Loyalty	15
	Customers: Total	100
2. Leadership	2.1 Personal Philosophies/ Values	50
	2.2 Enabling People to Reach Their Full Potential	50
	Leadership: Total	100
3. Organization	3.1 Dismantling Taylorism	5
	3.2 Assault on Bureaucracy	20
	3.3 Revamping the Organizational Structure	15
	3.4 Revolutionizing Management Practices	30
	3.5 Egalitarianism	10
	Organization: Total	80
4. Employees	4.1 Motivation	10
	4.2 Job Redesign	5

(continues)

Table 3-1. (continued.)

Area	Key Characteristics		Importance (Points)
	4.3 Creating an Empowering Climate		35
	4.4 Team Competition		5
	4.5 On the Road to Empowerment		25
		Employees: Total	80
5. Supply Chain	5.1 Company Policies		15
Management	5.2 Partnership Supplier Selection		20
	5.3 Supply Chain Infrastructure		25
	5.4 Supplier Development		20
		Supply Chain Management: Total	80
6. Quality	6.1 Customers		10
	6.2 Leadership		5
	6.3 Organization		10
	6.4 Employees		10
	6.5 Supply Chain Management		5
	6.6 Design		15
	6.7 Manufacturing		5
	6.8 Services		10
	6.9 Results		10
		Quality: Total	80

7. Cost Reduction	7.1 Customers	5
	7.2 Leadership	5
	7.3 Supply Chain Management	20
	7.4 Tools	35
	7.5 Design	5
	7.6 Manufacturing	10
	Cost Reduction: Total	80
8. Cycle Time Reduction	8.1 Supply Chain	10
	8.2 Design	15
	8.3 Manufacturing	30
	8.4 Employees	5
	8.5 Customer/Supplier	5
	8.6 Support Services	15
	Cycle Time Reduction: Total	80
9. Design	9.1 Organization for New Product Development	5
	9.2 Management Guidelines	15
	9.3 "Voice of the Customer"	10
	9.4 Design Quality/Reliability	15
	9.5 Design Cost Reduction	15
	9.6 Design Cycle Time Reduction	10

(continues)

Table 3-1. (continued.)

Area	Key Characteristics		Importance (Points)
	9.7 Creativity and Innovation		10
		Design: Total	80
10. Manufacturing	10.1 Manufacturing Resurgence		10
	10.2 Quality Improvement in Manufacturing		40
	10.3 Cycle Time Improvement in Manufacturing		15
	10.4 General		15
		Manufacturing: Total	80
11. Services	11.1 NOAC Principles/Practices		20
	11.2 NOAC Structure		20
	11.3 NOAC Implementation		15
	11.4 NOAC Improvements; "Out-of-Box" Thinking		25
		Services: Total	80
12. Results (Primary)	12.1 Customer		20
	12.2 Leadership		20
	12.3 Employees		20
	12.4 Financials		20
		Results: Total	80
		GRAND TOTAL	1,000

2. *Key Characteristics.* Each area contains several key characteristics that cover the scope of that area. Table 3-1 also shows the number of key characteristics in each area and the points attached to them.

3. *Disciplines.* As the heart of the Power of Ultimate Six Sigma, disciplines propel a company to rapid implementation. There are sixteen disciplines in each area, with the exception of the customer and leadership areas where, because of their greater importance, there are twenty disciplines. In all, therefore, there are 200 disciplines that are vital to the success of a company's march to the Ultimate Six Sigma. Each discipline carries a maximum of five points. A rating scale of 1 to 5 is assigned to each discipline, with 1 being the lowest rating and 5 the highest.

4. *Rating of Each Discipline.* Table 3-2 shows the criteria by which the auditor rates each discipline. A score of 1 to 5 is used, depending on the degree to which the discipline is implemented.

5. *Timetable for Implementation by Company Type.* A distinctive innovation in the drive to the Ultimate Six Sigma is a suggested timetable for implementing each discipline by three types of companies:

- *Type A companies* are those forward-looking companies, big or small, that already have a modicum of exposure to some of the 200 disciplines and want to reach out for Six Sigma perfection as early as possible. Each discipline is launched without any procrastination and a conscious effort made to complete it within a two- to three-year target. Results of Type A companies should be reflected in tangible benefits—both primary and secondary—which are listed in Chapter 15.

- *Type B companies* are generally smaller companies that may not have the resources to marshal an immediate effort. They may not have the same

Table 3-2. Rating of each discipline.

Rating	Criteria
1	No knowledge of the discipline
2	Only a conceptual awareness of the discipline
3	Discipline started, but with less than 50% implementation
4	Discipline implemented 50% to 80%
5	Discipline implemented more than 80% with reflected business results

Table 3-3. Characteristics of companies with varying priorities on the road to the Ultimate Six Sigma.

Company Characteristic	Company Type		
	A	**B**	**C**
Desired Sigma Goal	Six Sigma	Five Sigma	Four Sigma
Scope	All Stakeholders	Customers, Employees	Customers
Company Size	All sizes	Small	Large
Passion to Improve	Strong	Moderate	Low
Cultural Resistance	Low	Moderate	High
Leader-to-Manager Ratio	>20:80	10:90	1:99
Familiarity with Disciplines/ Techniques	Moderate	Low	Low
Time to Implement (Years)	2 to 3	3 to 5	5 to 10

stretch goals or the same passion to improve. Their unfamiliarity with the disciplines/techniques may require a longer gestation period. And their total implementation may take longer, say, three to five years.

- *Type C companies* are comfortable with the *status quo* and feel less of a need to reach out. These companies are generally large and bureaucratic, with a preponderance of managers over leaders (see Chapter 5). Their short-term success may inhibit their appetite for improvement. Their pace of reform is slow, taking five to ten years to achieve even modest sigma levels.

Table 3-3 is a list of characteristics by company type.

6. *Total Rating: A Measure of a Company's Business Health.* Table 3-4 adds up the ratings of the disciplines, key characteristics, and areas to arrive at a total score for the company audit. It also shows how the total score can be interpreted in terms of an equivalent business health and an equivalent sigma level.

Table 3-4. Total rating: a corresponding business health and equivalent sigma level.

Total Company Rating	Equivalent Business Health	Equivalent Sigma Level
800–1,000	Robust health	6 Sigma
600–799	Good health, but periodic physical checkups urged	5 Sigma
400–599	Poor health; continued monitoring needed	4 Sigma
200–399	Major surgery required	3 Sigma
Below 200	Terminally ill	2 Sigma

Part Two

The Power of Ultimate Six Sigma
From Shareholder Value to Stakeholder Value

CHAPTER 4

From Mere Customer Satisfaction to Customer Loyalty

You may think that you make products, but you really make loyal customers. You may think that you make sales, but you really make loyal customers. —MARK HANAN AND PETER KARP

The Inadequacy of Catering to Just Customer Satisfaction

While many companies have jumped on the customer satisfaction bandwagon, most of them don't realize that the customer train has left the station without them.

Here are the facts on the depressing negatives of mere customer satisfaction:

■ According to a Juran Institute survey, more than 90 percent of the Fortune 200 companies are convinced that maximizing customer satisfaction maximizes profitability and market share. Yet *fewer than 2 percent* are able to measure bottom-line improvements from documented increases in levels of customer satisfaction.

■ Anywhere from 15 percent to 40 percent of customers who say they are satisfied defect from a company each year.

- In the U.S. auto industry, the average repurchase rate of satisfied customers from the same car company is *less than 30 percent.* The corresponding figure for the appliance industry is *below 45 percent.*

- The defection rate of people over age 65 is 40 percent; for those over age 35 it is 60 percent; for those between ages 20 to 35 it is more than 85 percent.

Clearly, there is little correlation between customer satisfaction and customer loyalty.

By contrast, here are the facts on the enormous positives of customer loyalty:

Fact 1   There is a very close correlation between customer loyalty and profitability.

Fact 2   A 5 percent reduction in customer defection can result in profit increases from 30 percent to 85 percent (as shown in Figure 4-1).

Fact 3   If customers increase their customer retention (the opposite of customer defection) by 2 percent, it is the equivalent of cutting their operating costs by 10 percent.

Fact 4   Loyal customers provide higher profits, more repeat business, higher market share, and more referrals than do "just satisfied" customers.

Fact 5   It costs five to seven times more to find new customers than to retain customers.

Fact 6   One lifetime customer is worth more than $850,000 to a car company (an example is given later in this chapter).

The *sine qua non* of corporate concern, therefore, should be a paradigm shift:

- From customer satisfaction to customer loyalty, customer retention, and customer longevity

- From zero defects to zero customer defections

Examples of the Highest Loyalty Leading to Meteoric Financial Success

There are shining examples of companies that have put customer loyalty on a pedestal and—as a result—reaped amazing financial success. Each of them exceeds 95 percent customer retention per year. They include Leo Burne H, MBNA Corp., John Deere, State Farm, and Lexus, among others.

Figure 4-1. Profit increases with a 5 percent reduction in customer defections.

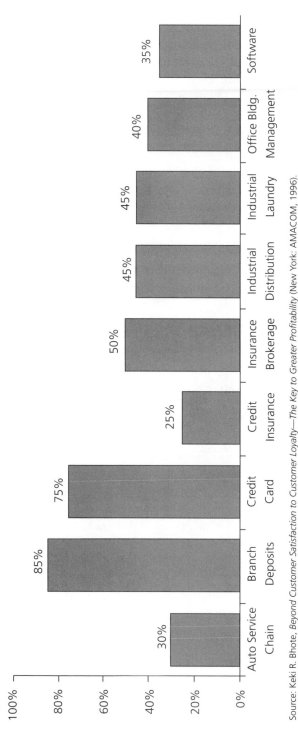

Source: Keki R. Bhote, *Beyond Customer Satisfaction to Customer Loyalty—The Key to Greater Profitability* (New York: AMACOM, 1996).

With the importance of customer loyalty—towering above customer satisfaction—firmly established, we can move on to the practical implementation of customer loyalty. For a more detailed background and conceptualization of customer loyalty, two references are recommended:

The Ultimate Six Sigma—Beyond Quality Excellence to Total Business Excellence[1]

Beyond Customer Satisfaction to Customer Loyalty—The Key to Greater Profitability[2]

For any company, large or small, the emphasis must be on the practical and the doable, and there are five essential disciplines:

1. Reduction of the Customer Base and Differentiation

2. Measurement/Quantification of Core Customer Defections

3. Assessment of Customer "Wow!"

4. "Taking the Customer's Skin Temperature Every Day"

5. Establishment of the Company Infrastructure for Customer Loyalty

Discipline 1: Reduction of the Customer Base and Differentiation

Traditional Approach. The more customers, the better. Growth becomes a mantra.

The Ultimate Six Sigma Discipline. Not all customers are worth keeping, just as not all suppliers, distributors, or product lines are worth keeping.

During a consultation with a company that was losing money, I asked its CEO how many of his 800 customers were profitable. "About 200," he replied. "Then why do you keep most of the rest?" I parried. His straight-faced answer: "To keep the plant busy!"

Unless a company is in the charity business for its customers, the indiscriminate pursuit of all customers is plain dumb.

Figure 4-2 illustrates how A. T. Kearney[3] uses a metal analogy to differentiate and segment a customer base into four categories:

■ *Platinum customers* constitute 10 percent of the total customer volume of a company but constitute 30 percent of its profit. Cling to these crown jewels—

Figure 4.2. Platinum, gold, silver, bronze, and tin customers: their differentiation and contribution to profitability.

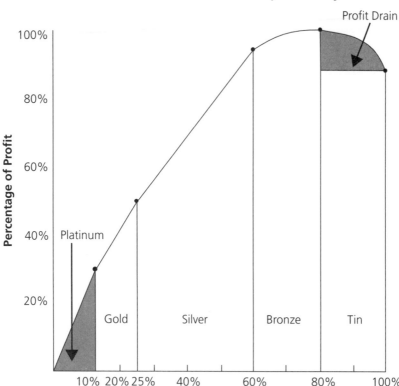

they are the most loyal of customers and the most difficult for competition to dislodge.

■ *Gold customers* span 15 percent of the company's customer volume and provide 20 percent of its profits. They are almost as important as the platinum customers, but are not part of the strategic alliances created with the latter. Together, the platinum and gold customers are labeled *core customers* who require continuous, never-ending attention and care.

■ *Silver customers* account for 35 percent of the customer base and about 40 percent of the company's profits. Maintain relationships with these customers, but there is no need for assiduous cultivation.

■ *Bronze customers* number 20 percent by customer volume but barely 5 percent of the company's profits. For these customers, the company is on a slippery slope from black ink to red ink. Be prepared to cut loose from them.

■ *Tin customers* total 20 percent by customer volume and actually drain profits by 15 percent. Dump them. (Often, sentimental ties or the future potential of converting them into profitable customers may hold a company back from terminating them. At the very least, an attempt should be made to increase prices to facilitate their exit or enhance profitability.)

It is estimated that a *customer base reduction of 30–40 percent* can be accompanied by a *20–30 percent improvement in profits.*

Discipline 2: Measurement and Quantification of Core Customer Defections

Traditional Approach. More than 99 percent of companies do not measure the cost impact of the defection of their core customers. Even worse, their accounting departments, which continue to live in the nineteenth century, do not even know how to estimate the financial loss from such defections. The stark result is that these companies miss the boat on the most prolific technique, bar none, to improve their profits.

The Ultimate Six Sigma Discipline. Contrary to the conventional wisdom, customer defection is actually easy to quantify. The loss need not be 100 percent accurate with accounting certitude. (Accountants are exactly wrong rather than approximately right!)

Example

What is the cost to a car company of a single defector who is so turned off that he will never buy from that company again? Assume that the defector has forty years of adult life left; that the average cost of the car is $30,000; and that the customer will buy ten such cars in his working life. He is likely to tell twenty of his friends and relatives about his unhappiness with the company. Assume that three of the twenty people he tells heed his advice and won't buy another car from the company, either!

The loss to the company, therefore, is not $30,000 but 10 x $30,000 x 3—or $900,000. Add the loss of servicing, parts, and financing and the costs exceed $1 million.

The Multiplier Effect

The previous example can be replicated for any company, any industry. The numbers may not pass a strict accounting muster, but the multiplier effect of the loss of a single core customer cannot be denied. It must be measured. It must be quantified. With a typical customer defection rate of 15 percent to 40 percent, the potential loss of such defections run into millions of dollars for a large company.

It is for this reason that warranty costs are just the tip of the huge iceberg of profit loss. The cost of a potential defecting customer is often at least ten to a hundred times the paid-out costs of a warranty claim.

Discipline 3: Assessment of Customer "Wow!"

Traditional Approach. In assessing what the customer wants, it is not the "voice of the customer" that is heard, but the "voice of the engineer" who thinks he knows more about the customer's needs than the customer. The result is that 80 percent of new products end up on the ash heap of marketing.

The Ultimate Six Sigma Discipline. Two disciplines are used to capture the "voice of the customer"—mass customization and quality function deployment.

Briefly, mass customization recognizes that each customer is unique and has highly individualized requirements. Each customer today wants exactly what he wants, where he wants it, when he wants it, at the price he wants. It turns topsy-turvy Henry Ford's famous choice of "any color you want as long as it is black!" (Mass customization is explained in some more detail in Chapter 9.)

Quality function deployment (QFD) is more suited when there is a large number of core customers with common requirements. The specific discipline is the House of Quality, where customer attributes and competitor perceptions are translated into engineering specifications. If done correctly, QFD can perform a new design in half the time, at half the cost, with half the defects and half the manpower required in older designs. After ten years, however, the bloom is off the QFD rose because of the lower and lower commonality of customers and their higher and higher individualization.

Concentration on All Elements of Customer "Wow"

Traditional approaches focus on performance and/or quality as customer priorities. However, there are twenty characteristics of a product or service that are of interest to customers. For products, Figure 4-3 depicts a network of elements that combine to create "wow" in the customer's mind. Figure 4-4 is a similar network for services.

Two factors are most important to customer "wow." First, the design should introduce features unanticipated by the customer, but whose creation results in a rush of customer delight. A second is an inviolate rule that my students in graduate school have dubbed Bhote's Law. It states: "It is that element missing from a product

Figure 4-3. A network of elements of customer "wow" for products.

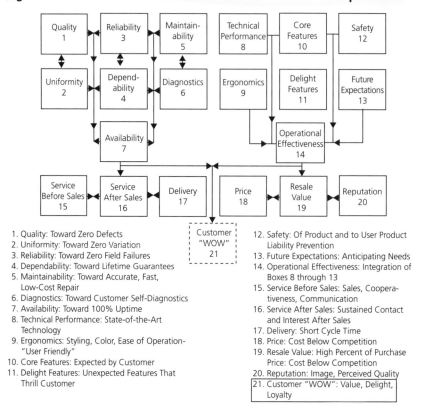

1. Quality: Toward Zero Defects
2. Uniformity: Toward Zero Variation
3. Reliability: Toward Zero Field Failures
4. Dependability: Toward Lifetime Guarantees
5. Maintainability: Toward Accurate, Fast, Low-Cost Repair
6. Diagnostics: Toward Customer Self-Diagnostics
7. Availability: Toward 100% Uptime
8. Technical Performance: State-of-the-Art Technology
9. Ergonomics: Styling, Color, Ease of Operation- "User Friendly"
10. Core Features: Expected by Customer
11. Delight Features: Unexpected Features That Thrill Customer

12. Safety: Of Product and to User Product Liability Prevention
13. Future Expectations: Anticipating Needs
14. Operational Effectiveness: Integration of Boxes 8 through 13
15. Service Before Sales: Sales, Cooperativeness, Communication
16. Service After Sales: Sustained Contact and Interest After Sales
17. Delivery: Short Cycle Time
18. Price: Cost Below Competition
19. Resale Value: High Percent of Purchase Price: Cost Below Competition
20. Reputation: Image, Perceived Quality
21. Customer "WOW": Value, Delight, Loyalty

or service which is important to a customer that a company must pursue with laser-like precision and intensity."

A Company Effectiveness Index (CEI): Measured by a Core Customer

With the constant desire for quantification and a scoring system, on the one hand, and a complex array of parameters to assess performance on the other, how can a single numeric score—say, from 1 to 100 points—be assigned to subjective evaluations of companies by core customers, or of company leadership by its employees, or of internal suppliers by internal customers within a company?

Several years ago, I formulated a matrix that can achieve a quantified score, regardless of the number of attributes or parameters being measured. Table 4-1 is an example of a company effectiveness index, assessed by a major (core) customer. In

Figure 4-4. A network of elements of customer "wow" for services.

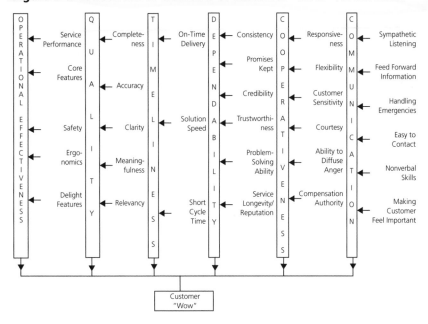

column one are listed the various customer requirements, as selected by the customer. The second column assigns an importance (I) to each requirement, as determined by the customer, on a scale of 1 to 5, with 1 being the least important and 5 the
most important. In the third column is the rating (R), again determined by the customer, of the company's performance for each requirement and using the same scale
of 1 to 5. In the fourth column, the figure (I) in the second column is multiplied by the
figure (R) in the third column to determine the company's score—(S) = (I) x (R)—for
each requirement.

To determine the overall CEI, the importance numbers in column two are totaled
to (Y), and the scores in column four are totaled to (T). The overall company effectiveness index is then calculated using the simple formula T/5Y x 100, which is
expressed as a percentage. (The 5 in the formula comes from the maximum rating of
5 for each requirement.) The maximum CEI is 100 percent. A CEI rating below 20
percent would denote a terminally ill company. Between 20 percent and 40 percent,
a company would be in intensive care. Between 40 percent and 60 percent, it would
require hospitalization. Between 60 percent and 80 percent, it would need periodic
checkups. A CEI above 80 percent would indicate a company in robust health.

The same CEI can be expanded to determine how the customer compares the
company against its best competitor. Column five is the customer's rating of the com-

Table 4-1. Customer effectiveness index (CEI): a general model for products, as measured by a core customer.

Requirement	Importance (I) Scale: 1-5	Co. Rating (R) Scale: 1-5	Co. Score (S) (S) = (I) x (R)	Competitor Rating (CR) Scale: 1-5	Competitor Score (CS) (CS)=(I) x (C)
Quality (upon receipt)					
Reliability (within warranty)					
Durability (lifetime)					
Serviceability					
Uptime (% use)					
Technical Performance					
Features (that sell)					
Safety					
Human Engineering					
Reputation					
Sales Cooperativeness					
Price					
Resale Price					
Delivery					
TOTAL SCORE	SUM OF (I) = (Y)		SUM OF (S) = (T)	-	SUM OF (CS) =C

Customer Effectiveness Index (CEI) expressed as a percentage:

a) For Company = $\dfrac{T}{5y}$ x 100   b) For Competitor = $\dfrac{U}{5y}$ x 100

petitor's performance (CR) for each requirement on the same scale of 1 to 5. The sixth column multiplies the numbers in columns two and five to determine a competitor's score for each requirement: (CS) = (I) x (CR). For the overall CEI of the competitor, the scores in column six (CS) are totaled (U). The overall competitor CEI is U/5Y x 100, expressed as a percentage.

The same principles and type of index can be used for any subjective evaluation, such as leadership (see Chapter 5) and for the service industry, support services in the manufacturing industry, and internal customer/supplier links.

The elegance of the company effectiveness index is the remarkable way in which it simultaneously analyzes:

- The relative importance customers attach to their priority requirements

- The strength and weakness of the company for each requirement as determined by the customer

- The strength and weakness of the company for each requirement *vis-à-vis* its best competitor, again as determined by the customer

Discipline 4: "Taking the Customer's Skin Temperature Every Day"

Traditional Approach. There are undoubtedly companies that believe that this would be a better world if there were no customers! But even good companies do not cultivate customers. Close personal relationships are rare. Top management visits to customers are rarer still, and after the sale is made the customer is relegated to history.

The Ultimate Six Sigma Discipline. By contrast, in the Ultimate Six Sigma, the relationship is guided by the famous founder of the Matsushita empire, Konosuke Matsushita, who insisted that his sales force "take the customer's skin temperature every day!" This entails:

1. Creating a firm win-win partnership with core customers, based on ethics, mutual trust, and mutual help

2. Keeping a finger on the pulse of every core customer—his requirements, hopes, concerns, and irritations—not once, and not through a routine survey or associated statistics, but in a continuum of time

3. Building close personal relationships and bridges with key customer personnel, not in a fawning manner, but in terms of building a ladder of mutual trust

A Design of Experiments that I conducted for AT&T determined that the most important difference between the company's successful and unsuccessful salespeople was the length of time they spent with customers. Effective salespeople were in close contact with their customers; less successful salespeople made only pro forma visits.

4. Having top management visit customers to get firsthand and direct feedback—without the distorting filter of a protective bureaucracy.

Bob Galvin, Motorola's retired chairman, would visit each of his top-ten customers, spending a whole day not with his counterpart CEOs, but with the troops that were the real users of Motorola products. One of the key points they stressed was that Motorola was good at telling customers what they needed, but poor at listening to what they wanted. As a result, each Motorola executive is now required to meet regularly with ten of his top customers—an invaluable source of customer input.

5. Never forgetting about the customer after the sale is consummated. It costs five to seven times more to find new customers than to retain present customers. Even if future sales are not generated, these customers can be an invaluable source of referrals and word-of-mouth advertising.

A survey looked into why customers don't go back to the same dealer that they bought their last car from. The survey revealed that: one percent had died; 3 percent had moved to another town; 5 percent shifted because of price; 9 percent bought another car brand; 14 percent switched because of poor service. What happened to the remaining 68 percent? They switched because "the dealer didn't give a damn after the sale!"

Discipline 5: Establishment of the Company Infrastructure for Customer Loyalty

Traditional Approach. Since most companies are not even aware that customer loyalty is such a prolific profit generator, they have no organizational structure to address it. In fact, a survey conducted by the REL Consultancy Group on customer retention[4] revealed these shocking findings:

■ Sixty-one percent of companies surveyed felt that customer defections would have an insignificant impact on sales.

- Over 33 percent made no attempt to identify defecting customers.

- Twenty-five percent did not ask defecting customers their reasons for leaving.

- Thirty-three percent took no action on defecting customers.

The Ultimate Six Sigma Discipline. In order to sustain a customer loyalty culture, it is necessary to build a viable company infrastructure: This requires four disciplines—meaningful metrics, a top-level steering committee, a chief customer officer, and a customer defection management SWAT team.

Meaningful Metrics

Metrics are the essential starting point to establish a customer loyalty baseline. Among the most important are:

- Reduction of total customer base (with retention of primarily platinum and gold customers)

- Defection rate (i.e., defecting customers as a percent of the total number of customers)

- Amount and continuity of core customers (e.g., by number, by dollars, by time)

- Repeat purchases by core customers

- Referrals by core customers

- Correlation of customer retention and profitability

Customer Loyalty Steering Committee

There is no business purpose more important than customers and no parameter more profitable than customer loyalty. This makes a top management steering committee essential. It should consist of the CEO as chairman and his direct reports as members. The steering committee's tasks include:

- Establishing targets for minimum retention rates and longevity of core customers

- Appointing a customer czar and a customer defection SWAT team

- Reviewing progress against targets

- Tying senior management incentives to increasing retention rates

- Promoting synergy between the customer, employees, and the supply chain

========== CASE STUDY ==========

LEXUS—A BENCHMARK COMPANY IN THE
AREA OF CUSTOMER LOYALTY

In the automotive market, where customer loyalty to a car manufacturer has evaporated, one car brand—Lexus—stands head and shoulders above the rest of the pack.

Results

■ While the retention rate for the average U.S. car company is below 30 percent, the retention rate for Lexus—Toyota's luxury car—is 75 percent (i.e., 94 percent per year in a typical four-year life with a single owner). The corresponding retention rate for BMW is 43 percent and for Mercedes, 42 percent.

■ Lexus accounts for only 2 percent of Toyota's sales but 33 percent of its profits.

■ Its trade-ins are the highest in the industry. In fact, customers have difficulty buying a used Lexus.

Strategy

■ Lexus studied the total car owner cycle—from shopping, buying, driving, and servicing to trade-in—to optimize value to the customer at each step.

■ It aims for Cadillac and Mercedes customers, two companies with high brand loyalty.

■ It believes that the key to customer loyalty lies in a *loyal partnership with its dealers*.

■ It focuses on fewer than 200 dealerships as compared with a market saturation of up to 600 dealerships among other car companies. The greater volume per dealer affords lower markups and higher profits.

Profitable Service

■ Service charges for Lexus cars are lower than the competition because of high service volume.

■ Post-warranty service captures 80 percent of its customers versus industry figures of 30–40 percent.

■ Lexus offers intensive training of service personnel—more in one month than in eighteen months with Cadillac.

■ Fewer dealer locations are compensated with free loaners and free pickup and delivery for servicing customers from their homes.

■ Lexus proves that a dealer with lower retention rates on customer-paid service loses $500,000 per year versus a comparable dealer with higher service loyalty.

■ It has teams of service consultants sent to dealers who underperform on service profitability.

■ It teaches dealers how to failure-analyze defection rates.

■ It is the only car company that tracks service retention rates for every dealer, every day.

■ It has the best parts inventory management, with higher parts availability and lower inventory costs—an average of $100,000 as compared with the industry average of $200,000.

Chief Customer Office (CCO)

This person must be the embodiment of the mind, heart, and soul of the customer within the company. The CCO should be next in rank only to the CEO—ahead of the chief operating officer (COO) or the chief financial officer (CFO). Avoid selecting a lightweight to do this heavy customer lifting.

Customer Defection Management SWAT Team

Included in this vital team should be the company's best marketers and problem solvers. It cannot be an *ad hoc* group but a permanent entity, because customer loyalty—like quality—has no finish line. The team's task is to gather, analyze, and reduce core customer complaints.

Another useful task of the SWAT team is to monitor changing needs and priorities of the core customers—their experiences with the company's product, services, sales/dealer/installation personnel; their future expectations, their referrals to other potential customers; and their involvement—in the case of OEM customers—in new designs.

Self-Assessment/Audit on Customer Loyalty: Implementing Disciplines by Company Type and Months to Complete

1. *Self-Assessment/Audit.* Table 4-2 is a self-assessment/audit that a company or its external Ultimate Six Sigma auditors can conduct to gauge how well it has progressed to a state of business health (and equivalent sigma levels) in the area of customer loyalty. It has five key characteristics and twenty important and essential disciplines with 5 points each for practical implementation. The total score for this area is 100 points. The term *customer* in this context refers mainly to core customers.

2. *Implementation Disciplines by Company Type.* As explained in Chapter 3, the disciplines can vary depending on three different company types (see also Table 3-4 for the distinguishing characteristics of each company type).

Type A company disciplines apply to those companies, big or small, that truly want to reach out for Six Sigma as quickly as possible, preferably within two to three years, and wish to move to maximum customer retention.

Type B company disciplines apply to smaller companies that also want to improve, but are limited by lack of resources and unfamiliarity with the disciplines/techniques needed for customer retention. The pace is slower—three to five years.

Type C company disciplines apply to companies whose short-term success may inhibit their appetite for improvement. They are not especially customer-focused. The goals are more modest and the pace slower still—four to eight years.

3. *Time Required for Implementing Each Discipline.* Finally, Table 4-3 lists the time required (in months) for each discipline to be completed, depending on the company type. Because customer loyalty is vital to profitability, the timetable for all company types should be accelerated. In general, Type A companies have both the need and the will to effect disciplines rapidly. Type B companies need more time to ponder and digest a discipline. Type C companies are the slowest to grasp the merits of a discipline and may never implement some of them.

Table 4-2. Customers: key characteristics, essential disciplines, audit score, and time to complete—by company type (100 points).

Key Characteristics	Essential Disciplines	Rating 1-5 * (See Table 3-2)	Months to Complete, By Company Type		
			A	B	C
1-1 Customer Differentiation	1. Customer base reduced; mainly platinum, gold, and silver customers (minimum 30%).		3	6	12
	2. Impact of reduced customer base on profit increase calculated (minimum 10%).		6	12	-
1-2 Customer Loyalty Metrics	1. Customer defection rate quantified.		3	6	12
	2. Amount and continuity of customers (by number, by dollars, and by time) quantified.		4	8	15
	3. Repeat purchases by customer quantified.				
	4. Value added to customers, as perceived by them		12	24	-
	5. Favorable referrals by customers		6	12	18
	6. Correlation of customer loyalty (retention) and profit made.		12	18	-
1-3 Customer "Wow!"	1. Mass customization employed to individualize customer requirements.		12	24	-
	2. Quality function deployment used to translate voice of commonalized customers into engineering specification.		8	15	-

(continues)

Table 4-2. (continued.)

Key Characteristics	Essential Disciplines	Rating 1-5 * (See Table 3-2)	Months to Complete, By Company Type		
			A	B	C
	3. Product/service design concentrates on features that create unanticipated customer delight/"wow."		12	24	48
	4. Top Management focused on those important elements of customer enthusiasm missing from its product/service		12	18	36
1-4 Customer Cultivation	1. A firm win-win partnership forged with customer, based on ethics, mutual trust, and mutual help.		12	18	36
	2. Customer's changing needs, expectations, concerns, and emotions continuously monitored.		12	15	24
	3. Amount of time spent with customer and developing close personal relationships maximized.		6	9	18
	4. Top management visits to customers conducted regularly to get unfiltered, firsthand feedback.		3	6	12
	5. Firm rule established to "never forget the customer after the sale has been consummated."		3	3	6

Key Characteristics	Essential Disciplines	Rating 1-5 * (See Table 3-2)	Months to Complete, By Company Type		
1-5 Company Infrastructure for Customer Loyalty	1. Top management steering committee established.		6	12	18
	2. Chief customer officer (CCO) position, next in importance only to the CEO, made operative in fact.		3	6	18
	3. High-level customer defection SWAT team made operative to resolve all potential customer defection issues.		3	3	6

Notes: The term *customer* in this table refers mainly to core customers.
* 1 = lowest rating, 5 = highest rating

CHAPTER 5

From Blinkered Micromanagement to Leadership with Panoramic Vision

We measure the effectiveness of the true leader not in terms of the leadership he exercises but in terms of the leadership he evokes; not in terms of his power over others, but in terms of the power he releases in others; not in terms of the goals he sets and the direction he gives but in terms of the plans of action others work out for themselves with his help; not in terms of decisions made, events completed, and the inevitable success and growth that follow from such released energy, but in terms of growth in competence, sense of responsibility, and in personal satisfaction among many participants. Under this kind of leadership it may not always be clear at any given moment who is leading. Nor is this important. What is important is that others are learning to lead well.

—ROBERT W. GALVIN

A glaring and persistent weakness among traditional Six Sigma practices is to make no distinction between management and leadership and—worse—make little effort to explore either in search of Six Sigma perfection.

The Demise of Management, The Birth of Leadership

Ask any group of people within a company for its perception of the percentage of executives that are managers versus leaders. The answer ranges from 90–99 percent for managers, but 10 percent to one percent for leaders! Why is it that *manager* is a dirty word and *leader* an ennobling entity? The answer may lie in the personal philosophies and unchanging values that distinguish managers from leaders. The differences are awesome and are highlighted in Table 5-1.

It must be stated, at the outset, that while leadership is generally associated with the top echelons of a company, it also extends to every level of corporate rank. It even extends to an individual contributor who, though he may have no one reporting to him, is often looked upon as a true leader by his colleagues and may have an influence far greater than a boss with statutory authority.

Furthermore, it is not an axiom that leaders are born, not made. Leadership does not come naturally to more than a few gifted people. But it can be acquired through discipline, conscious, persistent effort, and practice.

Let's elaborate on some of these philosophies and values.

Ethics: A Bedrock of Relationships, An Anchor of Stability

Every major religion of the world has an ethical code that is amazingly common to all of them. Ethics are the compass that points mankind morally to "true north." It has governed relationships among people, societies, religions, and countries for more than 8,000 years of civilization. It represents an anchor of faith and stability in a changing and uncertain world.

Yet corporate ethics seem to be an oxymoron! Stories of company after company cited for financial skullduggery, bribes, kickbacks, and environmental pollution fill the news media. These firms may get by, even win out in the short run; but they lose their corporate souls and their very existence in the long run. The collapse of Enron, Arthur Andersen, and WorldCom should serve as a wake-up call to unethical companies. Sooner or later they will be hit in the pocketbook, either with a sharp drop in stock prices, or loss of customers, or both. By contrast, a corporation with sterling ethics and uncompromising integrity is not only successful over time, but is held up by the public as a role model.

"It is a fairly new realization for corporations," says crisis communications consultant Karl Fleming, president of Prime Time Communications, "but the *right ethical decision* is also the *right business decision*." Bennett Davis[1] states:

Table 5-1: Personal philosophies/values: managers vs. leaders.

Personal Philosophies/Values	Manager	Leader
1. Ethics	Corporate ethics—an oxymoron	Vital; uncompromising integrity
2. Trust in employees	Minimal and not reciprocated to that trust	Abiding trust, which encourages people to live up
3. Help/Guidance	Limited and begrudging; results in stunted growth of people	Abundant; enabling people to reach their full potential
4. Freedom	Restricted; micromanagement	Employees given freedom to reach goals their own way—including making mistakes
5. Superordinate Values	Finessed situationally	Constant, unchanging
6. Vision	Tunnel vision; blinkered	Leading on a path never traveled; true belief and missionary passion
7. Inspiration	Little to no followership	Charisma engenders committed, loyal followership
8. Authority/Power	Derived by organizational position	Gives up power—and, paradoxically, gains real power
9. Governing Style	Boss	Coach, consultant, teacher, guru
10. Emotional Quotient (EQ)	Little empathy, warmth, humility, or social skills	Empathetic, warm, humble, and high in social skills

A confluence of events has rewritten the rules of the marketplace, regardless of whether companies understand this or not. Every corporation is now being channeled into ethical probity by four factors:

First, the public is beginning to judge companies by their social performance—their impact on the environment and their role in aggravating or relieving social problems—as much as by their financial performance.

Second, consumers have become shell-shocked by a continuous barrage of reported shenanigans, both governmental and corporate—from Watergate to Big Tobacco—indirectly killing millions of people the world over right up to the present day.

Third, crusading special interest groups are exerting enormous pressure— from challenging even venerable institutions like the International Monetary Fund and the World Bank to judgments against cartels—on firms to toe the ethical line on human, social, and environmental problems.

Fourth, the competitive, unsparing, and technologically sophisticated media are motivating companies to be more honest. A company's ethical lapse can now be flashed to news outlets and brokerage houses globally, before a CEO can hurry back from lunch!

The collapse of Arthur Andersen and WorldCom may point the way to the best punishment of corporate fraud—a fatal hit in the pocketbook. What is needed is for such a company's customers to band together and cease doing business with it. That will send the strongest message to other companies to toe the ethical line. Stockholders fleeing such companies is another deserved punishment.

In this pivotal area of ethics, managers are not necessarily unethical, but they succumb to the siren song of the company's bottom line, rather than ethical probity, when they come to a fork in the road. On the other hand, a true leader will never compromise an all-consuming integrity to stoop to the lucre of an unethical decision. Like a sturdy oak, the leader stands tall in the eyes of employees.

Trust: The Self-Fulfilling Prophecy

When a teacher looks upon a student as stupid, the student responds by fulfilling the lowest expectations of the teacher. By contrast, when a teacher has faith in a student, trusts him, and encourages him to constantly improve, the student rises to the challenge. This is the principle of the self-fulfilling prophecy.

In the corporate world, unfortunately, trust is a rare attribute. Managers don't trust their people. In return, the people don't trust their managers. Companies don't trust unions. Unions don't trust companies. Companies don't trust governments. Governments don't trust companies. Companies don't trust their suppliers and customers. The suppliers and customers don't trust the companies. Granted, trust is not a light switch that you can turn on instantly and fill a relationship with the warm glow of trust. Granted, trust is fragile and one false move can undo it. It is going to take months, even years, for the public to trust CEOs, following their outrageous ethical lapses. Trust has to be nurtured patiently. It is a step-by-step interactive process. In the final analysis, it has to be earned.

The manager has little trust in his employees' ability and effort. He supervises sullen employees whose work attests to his low expectations. As a result, the employees' trust in the manager is equally low. True leaders trust their people, have faith in their creativity, and encourage them to grow to their full potential. Bob Galvin, chairman emeritus of Motorola, relates that his father, Motorola founder Paul Galvin, "subjected me to a fierce discipline. He trusted me!"[2] Trust begets trust. It generates a strong compulsion in the one trusted to live up to that trust.

Help and Guidance for Employees to Reach Their Highest Potential

Lack of trust limits a manager's desire to help his people. Insecure that staff members may learn so much that his own position is threatened, he renders only token help. The result is a stunted growth of his people.

Given trust as a prerequisite, a leader enthusiastically helps his people to grow. This is especially emphasized in Japan, where the CEO's primary role is "the care and feeding of the young." The type of help is not a straitjacket master-to-apprentice regimen. Rather, it is guidance with a loose rein. That guidance may be technical, administrative, strategic, or in the arena of human relations. It is said that the average person exercises only two percent of the potential of the God-given computer between his ears—the brain. A genius exercises it up to 10 percent. A leader knows that given his trust, support, encouragement, training, and help, there is no earthly barrier to human potential!

Freedom to Explore and to Make Mistakes

A manager, preoccupied with self-preservation and a sense of omnipotence, tends to micromanage people, breathing down their necks, directing them at every turn, and—sometimes—even castigating them for mistakes while taking credit for their success.

The leader, recognizing that he is not God and does not have all the answers, gives his people freedom to explore their own pathways, their own solutions, even make their own mistakes. Paul Galvin, the founder of Motorola, says: "Do not be afraid to make mistakes. Wisdom is often born of such mistakes. You will know failure. Determine now the confidence required to overcome it. . . . Reach out. . . ."[3] Freedom, however, does not mean anarchy. The leader has the duty to lead, set the direction, establish goals, and monitor results. But having done that, he gets out of the way! Jack Welch, the legendary former chairman of General Electric Company, sums up leadership in his 3Ds—direct, delegate, and disappear!

Pivotal Values—Superordinate and Unchanging

Every corporation formulates a set of values, beliefs, and principles that serve as an internal "constitution." Managers may pay lip service to such a set of values. They may even display it as a wall hanging. But, in reality, the manager finesses these values situationally—that is, he does whatever the situation calls for. He bends and shades these values, if needed, to maximize that sacred cow—shareholder value.

A leader looks upon pivotal values as the Rock of Gibraltar—constant and unchanging. Examples are uncompromising integrity, respect for the dignity of the individual, and customer "worship." The leader also emphasizes a few simple values that give clear direction and purpose to a group's work. He knows that people can only focus on just a very small number of such values. As an example, President Ronald Reagan stressed, over and over, a few crucial values: less government; lower taxes; stronger defense; the Soviet Union as an evil empire. He took the people with him to a "morning in America," "to that shining city on a hill." Begrudgingly, historians are reassessing him as a great leader, a great president.

Radar Vision and Missionary Passion

A manager, tied down by hundreds of operational duties and daily firefights, has no time or little appetite for developing a vision for the future. His view is blinkered, his thinking short-term, his approach pedestrian. Rodman L. Drake, managing director of a management consulting firm, was amazed when he queried a number of CEOs as to where they would like their companies to be five years from now; most of them could not formulate or even express that vision.

A leader, in sharp contrast, has a clear sense of that vision. Bob Galvin defines a leader in succinct terms as "one who takes a company on a road that no one has traveled before. It's a manifestation of the grander changes in direction, whatever they may be—geographic, product, market, or the way of doing things." And that clear, farsighted vision is accompanied by true belief and missionary passion.

Inspiration and Followership "to the Ends of the Earth"

In the annals of time, all the great leaders—political, military, religious—have one thing in common: their ability to inspire people, to bind them into a common objective, consensus, and commitment, and earn their unquestioning loyalty.

The manager, with a lack of trust, a lack of vision, and a lack of passion is incapable of arousing that fervor among his "troops." Reminiscent of this managerial style is a pathetic managerial quote: "There go my people. I must follow them, for I'm their leader!"

The leader, on the other hand, marshals all his personal philosophies and values and converts them into a radiant charisma that so fires up people with crusading enthusiasm that they would follow him to the ends of the earth.

Authority/Power
Managers derive their power through the organizational chart. Leaders gain real power by surrendering formal power.

Governing Style
The manager swings his weight as the boss. The leader is a coach in the best traditions of the world of sports.

Emotional Quotient
Psychologist Daniel Goldman has stated that "emotional intelligence is the overlooked but essential ingredient of leadership. It is the primary factor that distinguishes great leaders from average ones."[4] Presidents Franklin Roosevelt and Ronald Reagan are shining examples of emotional intelligence. Call it EQ (emotional quotient) as distinguished from IQ and AQ (action quotient). EQ encompasses empathy, warmth, humility, listening skills, and other social skills.

The Enlightened Role of Leadership—Unleashing the Human Spirit

Fortified by high-minded personal philosophies and values and principles, leaders are revolutionizing the roles of traditional top management in a number of profound ways that change the very psyche of an organization.

From Taylorism to Releasing the Locked-Up Genie of Worker Creativity
For the better part of the twentieth century, management was a prisoner to the theories of Frederick Winslow Taylor, who compartmentalized the roles of management (who did the thinking) and workers (who did the manager's bidding). Managers designed systems, procedures, and policies to ensure that the workers became as robotic and reliable as the machines they ran. These systems, which were intended to ensure control and conformity, instead inhibited creativity and initiative. The workers became passive. Worse, Taylorism created antagonism among the workers, even subversion!

In recent years, managers have softened the polarization of Taylorism, but they still cling to top-down planning and control with a strategy-structure-systems model that chains lower levels in the organization to the captivity of conformance and cynicism. It perpetuates employees using only 10–20 percent of their capacity at work, as contrasted with the 80–90 percent with which they energize their home lives.

Enlightened leaders dismantle the strategy-structure-systems model to unleash the human spirit and make initiative, creativity, and entrepreneurship priorities for their employees. Göran Lindahl, ABB Ltd.'s executive vice president, has stated: "My first task is to provide the framework to help engineers and other specialists develop as managers; the next challenge is to loosen the framework to let them become leaders . . . where they set their own objectives and standards. When I have created the environment that allows all managers to transform themselves into leaders, we will have a self-driven, self-renewing organization."[5]

Driving Out Fear—A Prerequisite

Fear among employees to speak out is one of the most corrosive outcomes of an autocratic management. Dr. W. Edwards Deming says that its cost to a company is appalling. The fear of being upbraided or fired will cause employees to withdraw into a cocoon of noninvolvement. Removing fear—which is something that can only be verified by employees alone—is the first step in releasing the genie of employee creativity.

Renewal and Innovation to Infuse a Corporation with New Energy

Another essential element of a leadership role is renewal of the corporation—call it a periodic corporate blood transfusion. Renewal recharges the company's tired batteries and infuses it with energy. It starts with "abandoning yesterday" and freeing resources assigned to things that no longer contribute to results. It is closely coupled with innovation and its windows of opportunity that assess:

- A company's unexpected successes and failures and those of its competition

- Incongruities between industry efforts and the values and expectations of its customers

- Demographic shifts such as collapsing birthrates and changes in disposable-income spending

- Economic returns for consumers twenty to thirty years from now (as opposed to short-range returns)

- Global competitiveness with labor costs playing an ever-decreasing role

- The growing incongruence between economic globalization and the political nation-state[6]

Innovation is also encouraged by industry leaders among their employees. The most famous example is 3M's "skunk works," where employees are given time and freedom to innovate with no controls other than to produce a viable, salable product within one year. "In fact, 3M generated $5.6 billion in sales in 2000, fully one-third of its revenues from goods that didn't exist four years earlier."[7]

Creativity—A Building Block of "Reaching Out"

Creativity is inherent in all human beings. Among the most creative are children—until the education system and the rules and regulations of the adult world knock the starch out of this early creativity, sentencing people to a lifetime of humdrum conformity. Yet creativity can be learned, just as leadership can be learned. Another important role for the leader, then, is to encourage creativity in all employees through deliberate training—by encouraging them to think "outside of the box"; by stimulating the challenge of policies and practices that are purely for internal control as opposed to benefiting the customer; by promoting the freedom to experiment; and by celebrating and rewarding creative breakthroughs.

Training—The Key to Continuous Learning

Graduating from school or college is only a passport to learning. It is said that the half-life of an engineer's usefulness is only five years after graduation (perhaps even less as new technological breakthroughs succeed old technological breakthroughs with dizzying speed), so it becomes imperative for engineers to stay current. The great W. Edwards Deming said: "If you do not learn something new every day, you might as well fold your tent on Mother Earth." Most people, however, need an external stimulus to learning. A leader's role is to provide that stimulus through training—university training, corporate classroom training, and on-the-job training. Progressive leaders are allocating 3 percent to 5 percent of a company's payroll for training. Some are making it mandatory that every single employee be trained for a minimum of forty hours per year. Collectively, these leaders spend more on corporate training than the entire budgets of all the universities in America.

Goals—Few, Reach-out, and Continuous

Another distinctive responsibility of leaders is to select just a few goals crucial to the enterprise and then establish truly challenging targets with an ambitious timetable. If people are given mediocre goals, they will persist in the same old-fashioned ways of reaching them. But with reach-out targets, they will have to shift conventional paradigms and explore entirely breakthrough approaches. (See the case study of Bob Galvin's Motorola as a benchmark in leadership later in this chapter.) Furthermore, these stretch goals should not be a one-time event, but repeated continuously and systematically.

Quality of Work Life—Creating Joy in the Workplace

Recognizing that employees spend nearly 50 percent of their waking hours at work, true leaders concentrate on improving the quality of work life for their people. Leaders recognize that some drudgery and boredom is inevitable, both in manufacturing and in business processes, but they attempt to inject a degree of job excitement by facilitating both horizontal and vertical job enrichment, creating teamwork, giving powerful tools to workers (see Chapters 9, 10, and 11) so that they experience the thrill of solving problems by themselves, and making "each employee" a manager in his own area. The result is an atmosphere of joy in the workplace that is heartwarming to behold.

Job Security—A Passport to Productivity

In the light of the hundreds of thousands of employees laid off during the 2001 recession and the aftershocks of September 11, job security has become a dreaded casualty. No company, in good conscience, can give an ironclad guarantee against layoffs and downsizing.

The hallmark of a true leadership, however, consists of launching several measures that mitigate the need for layoffs. These measures may include:

- An understaffing policy of 10–20 percent compensated (if necessary) with overtime

- A push-pull practice with subcontractors and suppliers (i.e., outsourcing and insourcing)

- Sizable reductions in job classifications, obsolete work rules, and restrictive job definitions so that downsizing is not needed in the first place

- Retraining, including outside schooling

- Job rotation (e.g., from manufacturing to sales, from production to maintenance, even from company to community work)

Gain Sharing—Fair and Equitable

One of the distinctive differences between a truly successful company and a mediocre one is the differentials in gain sharing between senior managers and those employees who have earned it by their tangible contributions to profitability. The average company, if it considers gain sharing at all, grants those employees who have directly contributed to the company's bottom line a grudging 10 percent of base pay. By contrast, leaders in progressive companies grant 25–80 percent of base pay to their deserving employees. They recognize that if it is fair to give executives incentive pay, it is equally fair to give their line workers, who have earned it, a comparable incentive pay.

Closing the Yawning Gap Between the CEO and the Line Worker

A Yankelovich poll[8] of American and Japanese workers asked for reactions to the statement, "I have a need to be the best I can, regardless of pay." Surprisingly, the

American worker outscored the Japanese. However, when asked, "Who would benefit from an increase in worker productivity?" the answers flip-flopped. Ninety-three percent of the Japanese workers felt they would benefit. Only 9 percent of the American workers felt they would gain. This is not surprising. The Japanese workers' bonus amounts to three to six months of extra pay per year. The workers bonus varies from zero to 10 percent per year in most American companies. There are honorable exceptions, of course, where a combination of incentives and employee stock ownership plans (ESOP) for workers result in 60–80 percent of base pay. The benchmark is Lincoln Electric Company with incentives that are 95 percent of base pay!

By contrast, the American CEO receives a total compensation that's more than 100 to 500 times that of a factory worker while the Japanese ratio is 10:1 and the German ratio is 30:1. The combination of bonuses and stock option plans for top management is five to ten times their salaries in leading U.S. firms. (See Chapter 1, Table 1-1 for even more statistics on how U.S. companies overcompensate executives.) This "irrational exuberance" of CEO greed has not only not been lost on the public, but it has reached the halls of Congress, where legislation to curb and punish this unseemly CEO appetite is in process.

Results as a Prerequisite

Obviously, worker incentives, bonuses, gain sharing, and stock options cannot be a socialistic giveaway. They must be earned, with significant financial gains to the company as a result of worker productivity. Table 5-2 indicates that the incentives/bonuses of companies that put people first are easily paid for by the productivity gains, measured in multiples over their industry averages.

Table 5-2. Bonuses paid vs. productivity gains in leading "people first" companies.

Company	Bonus as % of Base Pay	Productivity Gain Over Industry Average
Lincoln Electric Co.	95%	3.5:1
Andersen Windows	70%	2:1
Steelcase, Inc.	60%	2.5:1
Worthington Industries	80%	3:1
Nordstrom, Inc.	80%	3:1
Nucor Corp.	75%	4:1

From Corporate Leader to Civic Leader

In the final analysis, a true leader's role is not only within his corporate domain, but also in discharging his social responsibility to the public—to the community, state, nation, and even beyond, to the world. This starts with creating the conditions by which the public perceives the company to be a model employer, with a waiting list of people seeking its employment. It continues with educating the public, and especially students, on the positive and dynamic role of free enterprise in shaping the world's future. It goes on to render service to the community in terms of charity, civic causes, education, and urban development. The creative juices of business leaders are also in demand in a new frontier where the opportunity exists to tackle chronic social problems, convert them into business opportunities, and still making a profit (see Chapter 1).

A Leadership Effective Index (LEI): Measured by Employees

Chapter 4 developed a company effectiveness index (CEI) by which a core customer could assess the effectiveness of a company with a single point score that embraces several requirements of the customer and the extent to which those requirements are being met by the company. The CEI condenses several parameters, both objective and subjective, into a quantifiable metric.

Table 5-3 is a similar matrix by which the leadership of a company can be assessed with a single point score. There are twenty leadership attributes, each of which is given an importance (from 1–5), with 1 being the least important and 5 the most important. A similar rating of 1–5, with 1 being the lowest rating and 5 the highest rating, is given by the "customers" of that leadership—namely, the employees. In addition to the employees' assessment, alternative assessments could be done by the CEO's direct reports, the board of directors of the company, or all three.

CASE STUDY

A BENCHMARK COMPANY IN THE AREA OF LEADERSHIP— MOTOROLA'S BOB GALVIN

James O'Toole,[9] noted authority on leadership and vice president of the Aspen Institute, names the modern-day CEOs who are the corporate equivalents of the four presidents memorialized on Mount Rushmore. They are Herman Miller's Max De Pree, Corning's James Houghton, Scandinavia Airlines' Jan Carlzon, and Motorola's Bob Galvin. According to O'Toole:

Thanks to Galvin's understated leadership, Motorola has probably done the best job of any large U.S. corporation at institutionalizing change. It became the first large company in America to enable its workers to be leaders themselves. Power is widely shared without degenerating into anarchy. . . . The results of Motorola's system are well known: perhaps the highest quality products in American industry, regular introduction of innovation, and of course, high profits.

Bob Galvin has been my mentor, inspiration, and guiding light in the fifty years of my discipleship under him. This case study is but a pale reflection of the floodlight he has shone on the trail of world leadership. His personal philosophies and values as a true leader mirror those listed in Table 5-1:

■ *Ethics.* Bob Galvin's uncompromising integrity is a legend at Motorola. He would not countenance any bribe, any kickback, to any customer or government official in any country in the world, no matter how prevalent and accepted a practice it might be in that country or how serious a business loss it might entail. A high Chinese government official told me that of all the foreign companies in China, Motorola was the most respected for its honesty, integrity, and transparency. In another incident, a few senior controllers transferred sales from one month to the next to increase sales for the next month. Bob Galvin, discovering this irregularity, ruled that he would not fire these long-time employees, but ordered each one to contribute $1,000 to his favorite charity, by way of punishment. The story went around Motorola's plants worldwide. That is the stuff of ethics!

■ *Trust.* Galvin always had an abiding faith in his people, which in turn engendered a compelling challenge among his "associates," as he calls them, to rise to his level of trust, to earn it. When he introduced the first 10:1 quality improvement goal, he claimed he did not know how this challenging five-year target—which no industry had achieved or even undertaken—would be met. But he had such faith in his people and their ingenuity that he was confident that they would find a way. And they did. Not once, not twice, but three times, with a 10:1, 100:1, and an almost 1000:1 improvement in ten years!

■ *Help and Guidance, or Cloning and Cultivating Leaders.* Galvin deeply believed that there was no limit to the human potential—not just for the brainy and privileged few, but for all, no matter how low their starting point. "We've been about the job of evangelizing, teaching, and causing more and more people to realize that leading—taking us elsewhere—is also part of their job," Galvin has said. That's why James O'Toole calls him a "leader of leaders."

(continues)

■ *Freedom, or Asking "Why Not" Rather Than Why.* "My normal mode," Galvin says, "is to rarely be prescriptive, because I often don't know the prescriptive answers to questions. . . . My disposition has been more characterized by 'why not' than by 'why.' More often I'd say, 'Why not do it your way?'" He gives his people freedom, the space to spread their wings. He reinforces his father Paul Galvin's famous quote, which is bannered all over Motorola: "Do not be afraid to make mistakes. Wisdom is often born of such mistakes." Yet he expects that this freedom should result in meeting or exceeding shared goals.

■ *Vision and Renewal: The Twin Spirits of Leadership.* Galvin defined a leader as someone who takes his people into unknown, untried, and unexplored areas with uncanny vision. He feels that vision and renewal are intertwined. His vision is of a Motorola that can grow ten times and more in the next twenty-five years. The key to that vision is renewal—the driving thrust of Motorola. Thrust to Bob has a special meaning. "It does not mean mission or strategy. It speaks to genuine energy. To me, the great energy of the institution is the energy of renewing." This means change—rapid and large change—with reach-out improvements, five to ten times in magnitude. Renewal also includes recommitting to values such as displaying respect for the dignity of the individual and total integrity.

Motorola's meteoric rise is a tribute to this vision and renewal. As vital opportunities presented themselves—from battery eliminators to car radios to walkie-talkies (the basic communication link in the fields of World War II); from televisions to semiconductors and microprocessors; from pagers to cellular phones; from communication links in outer space to exploration beyond the solar system—Motorola's commitment to renewal has served it well.

■ *Inspiration and Followership.* Within Motorola and among the hundreds of organizations that he has addressed, Bob Galvin is called a second Winston Churchill, not only for his silver-tongued oratory but also for the uplifting inspiration of his message. More important, he genuinely attracts followership. He is a role model for American industry. Among Motorolans he is an icon. One facet of that worship is the fact that Motorola—a multinational company with plants in some of the countries with the strongest labor unions—has no unions anywhere in the world. Despite repeated attempts by unions to organize its employees, Motorola remains a nonunion tower of strength because its people know the implementation of Galvin's conviction that "the company can do more for its employees than any union ever can."

■ *Selflessness.* In an interview with Bill Ginnodo, editor of Commitment Plus, Bob Galvin has a final word for aspiring leaders. "Be selfless; it takes a lot of confidence to be selfless."[10]

Table 5-3. A leadership effectiveness index (LEI) as measured by employees.

Leadership Attributes*	Importance 1–5 (I)	Rating (R) 1	2	3	4	5	Score (S) S = (I) x (R)
A. Personal Philosophies/Values							
1. Ethics: uncompromising integrity							
2. Trust in employees							
3. Active help in developing employee potential							
4. Freedom to employees to pursue corporate goals							
5. Small set of superordinate, unchanging values							
6. Vision to explore uncharted paths							
7. Inspiring employees with enthusiasm and passion							
8. Relinquishing formal power—leading by example							
9. Coach, teacher—not boss							
10. High EQ (emotional quotient): empathy, warmth, humility							
B. Enabling People to Reach Their Full Potential							
1. Taylorism dismantled to free the human spirit							
2. Driving out fear among employees							
3. Energizing the company with renewal and innovation							
4. Stimulating creativity and "out-of-the-box" thinking							
5. Training for all employees and monitoring results							
6. Enhancing quality of work life with job enrichment							
7. Strengthening job security with minimum layoffs							
8. Equitable gain sharing for all employees							
9. Reducing the remuneration ratio of top management:line workers							
10. Fulfilling social/civic responsibilities to the public							

*These ratings and scores are determined by 1) employees through company attitude surveys, 2) the CEO's direct reports, 3) the board of directors of the company, or 4) all of the above.

Total Score = $\dfrac{\text{Sum of (S)}}{\text{Sum of (I)} \times 5} \times 100 = \%$

Self-Assessment/Audit on Leadership: Implementing Disciplines by Company Type and Months to Complete

1. *Self-Assessment/Audit.* Table 5-4 is a self-assessment/audit to determine a company's business health in the area of leadership. It has two key characteristics and twenty essential disciplines for practical implementation, with a maximum of 5 points each, for a total of 100 points.

2. *Implementation Disciplines and Commentary on Completion Time by Company Type.* Even though leadership can be learned, the transition from management to leadership isn't easy. Hence, it takes longer (in numbers of months) to implement leadership principles than technical disciplines. In fact, for Type C companies that are mired in the *status quo* and unwilling to change their Theory X management styles, some of these disciplines may never be implemented, the more the pity.

Table 5-4. Leadership: key characteristics, essential disciplines, audit score, and time to complete each discipline—by company type (100 points)

Key Characteristics	Essential Disciplines	Rating 1–5*	Months to Complete, by Company Type		
			A	B	C
1-1 Personal Philosophies/ Values	1. Corporate *ethics* and uncompromising integrity practiced by company leadership and transmitted to all employees.		24	36	—
	2. Leaders show *abiding trust* in their employees, who reciprocate that trust and rise to fulfill that trust.		24	36	—
	3. Leaders actively *help their employees* through counseling and guidance to reach their highest potential.		30	48	—
	4. Leaders give their employees *freedom* to follow their own pathways to corporate goals.		12	24	48
	5. Leaders have establishd a small set of *superordinate, unchanging values* to guide the corporation to "true north."		6	12	18
	6. Leaders display *vision* to lead the company along unexplored paths with a sure sense of direction.		12	24	—
	7. Leaders *inspire their people* with their enthusiasm and passion, so employees implicitly follow their lead.		24	36	—
	8. Leaders *relinquish formal power and gain real power*—by example.		30	48	—
	9. Leaders act like coaches, not autocratic bosses.		18	36	—
	10. Leaders imbued with *emotional quotient (EQ)*— empathy, warmth, humility, and high social skills.		24	48	—

(continues)

Table 5-4. (Continued.)

Key Characteristics	Essential Disciplines	Rating 1–5*	Months to Complete, by Company Type		
			A	B	C
1-2 Enabling People to Reach Their Full Potential	1. Leaders have *dismantled Taylorism* to free the human spirit.		24	36	—
	2. Leaders have *driven out fear* among their employees.		12	24	36
	3. Leaders energize the corporation *with renewal and innovation.*		12	24	36
	4. Leaders stimulate *creativity* and "out of the box" thinking among their employees.		12	24	36
	5. Leaders focused on *training* for all employees, with a minimum of 3% of payroll and monitoring payback.		6	12	24
	6. Leaders have improved the *quality of work life* with job enrichment, team work, and problem-solving tools.		9	18	36
	7. Leaders have enhanced *job security* through actions to circumvent and minimize layoffs.		12	18	36
	8. Leaders have made *earned gain sharing* more equitable and fair for all employees.		9	18	36
	9. Leaders have appreciably reduced the total *remuneration ratio* of top management to line workers by a minimum of 5:1.		12	24	—
	10. Leaders have fulfilled their *civic and social responsibilities* to the public by being a model employer, initiating community service, and tackling social ills, with profit as the result.		36	—	—

*The rater grades each discipline as a scale of 1–5, with 1 being the lowest rating and 5 the highest.

Organization: From the Straitjacket of Taylorism to the Freedom of a Culture of Entrepreneurship

We will win and you will lose! Your failure is an internal disease. Your companies are based on Taylor's principles. Worse, your heads are Taylorized, too. You believe that sound management means, on one side, executives who think; and on the other, men who can only work. But we know that only the intellects of all employees can permit a company to live with the ups-and-downs of global challenges. Yes, we will win and you will lose. For you are not able to rid your minds of obsolete Taylorism that we never had. . . .

—KONOSUKE MATSUSHITA, FOUNDER OF THE
MATSUSHITA INDUSTRIAL EMPIRE, ADDRESSING THE WEST

I'm not going to have monkeys running the zoo. . . .[1]

—FRANK BORMAN, FORMER CHAIRMAN OF
EASTERN AIRLINES, DISCUSSING WORKER PARTICIPATION

The Long Road from Taylorism to Empowerment

The yawning organizational divide, represented by these contrasting statements, has shrunk in recent years. Matsushita's "in your face" words belie the fact that Japan remains one of the most authoritarian industrial regimes in the world. Worker participation is never allowed to break through the glass ceiling of senior management. And America (Frank Borman not withstanding) no longer thinks that workers should check their brains at the guard door while entering because they won't need them inside! Taylorism has declined in the past twenty to twenty-five years. Management today genuinely wants worker involvement. But for the most part, it doesn't know how. Organizing teams and directing its members to participate is reminiscent of King Canute of old England ordering the waves never to touch his royal feet at the seashore!

Traditional Approach. Forming quality circles and adopting *kaizen* were not successful, given the rugged John Wayne individualism of Western culture. The introduction of total quality management (TQM) in the 1980s improved quality but not the business bottom line. Business process reengineering[2] (BPR) improved business but was viewed by workers as a euphemism for downsizing and layoffs—a deterrent to morale.

The Ultimate Six Sigma Discipline. This chapter builds the organizational infrastructure needed to create a milieu in which self-motivation can be sparked and sustained. For a radical change in a corporate culture—from one of stifling drudgery to one of true empowerment—employee values and beliefs must be changed. For employee values and beliefs to be changed, management systems and practices must be changed first. Table 6-1 depicts a logical ten-step process in creating the freedom of a culture of entrepreneurship.

Step 1: Eliminate Mind-Numbing, Energy-Sapping Bureaucratic Rules and Regulations

A litmus test on rules, regulations, and policies is:

- If they benefit a customer and capture his loyalty, keep them.

- If they are only for internal control, challenge them and even throw them out.

Numerous examples abound of bureaucratic practices that are waiting to be "busted up":

- Get rid of the executive parking spots, the executive lunchroom, the executive washroom, and the executive limos since they only serve to puff up managers with self-importance and—by inference—demean the workers.

- Avoid endless meetings. I have a rule where a company's effectiveness is inversely proportional to the number of meetings it holds! If meetings are

Table 6-1. A ten-step process for creating a culture of entrepreneurship.

1. Eliminate mind-numbing, energy-sapping bureaucracy.

2. Tear down and rebuild the organizing infrastructure.

3. Change requirements for hiring employees.

4. Train, train, train all employees.

5. Revamp performance appraisal.

6. Change the rules of compensation.

7. Design meaningful and egalitarian gain sharing.

8. Redesign promotion criteria.

9. Promote team synergy.

10. Facilitate total involvement.

necessary at all, have stand-up meetings with no chairs. You'll be amazed at how short and focused they'll be!

■ Drastically reduce policy manuals. Nordstrom, Inc., the $2 billion retailer, has just a one-sentence policy manual: "Use your own best judgment at all times!"

■ Throw off the chains of long, written procedures—especially the tyranny of ISO-9000 and other standards that are a decided drag on productivity and have actually set back quality two decades.

■ Cut e-mail, which is rapidly becoming junk mail, by 75 percent.

■ Discourage employees from staring at their computer terminals like isolated robots and encourage face-to-face interactions as a healthier way to build relationships.

■ Shorten or eliminate most reports—written or e-mail. The Ten Commandments take only half a page; the Declaration of Independence, three-quarters of a page, and Lincoln's Gettysburg Address is one page. Most of your company's reports are to protect the originator's rear end.

■ Raise spending authority for employees from zero or minuscule levels that reek of mistrust to levels that are tangible evidence of management's confidence in employee responsibility. This is especially important for those employees that come in constant contact with customers. Immediate financial settlements by such customer-contact employees can diffuse customer anger and convert the latter into loyal customers.

■ Above all, reduce the compensation ratio between top management and direct labor. It is at least 100:1 and as much as 500:1 in the United States (and rising) compared with 30:1 in Germany and 10:1 in Japan. With one exception, nothing demotivates people as much as when they see their real contributions reduced to a pittance of a pay raise while senior management dishes out huge salary increases, bonuses, incentives, and stock options to itself. The exception is even more corrosive. Top management feeding at the corporate trough with obscene increases while actually laying off workers. Lee Iacocca, when criticized by the media for his $20 million total compensation in 1986 while he cut pay for other employees, had a blatant response: "That's the American way. If little kids don't aspire to make money like I did, what the hell good is this country!" Yet the trend in the United States is moving exactly the wrong way. If corporate America does not heed the lessons of history, it is doomed to repeat it and perpetuate Taylorism.

Step 2: Tear Down and Rebuild the Organizational Infrastructure

A second important step on the road to empowerment is to revamp the organizational structure:

■ From the vertical organization to the horizontal organization

■ From recentralization back to decentralization

■ From the tall organizational pyramid to the flat pyramid

From the Vertical Organization to the Horizontal Organization

Figure 6-1 is a typical example of a vertical organization with separate departments, each protected by "territorial" walls and "moats" or "white spaces" between them. The engineering manager doesn't talk to the manufacturing manager who, in turn, doesn't talk to the materials manager; and none of them want to communicate with the quality manager; and so on. This lack of cooperation forces vertical communication—from a department to the general manager and down again to another department. In real life, though, problems and customers are no respecters of organizations. They cut across departments horizontally.

Dr. Kaoru Ishikawa, the Japanese quality guru, once remarked during a visit to

Figure 6-1. Traditional organization: vertical management with white spaces.

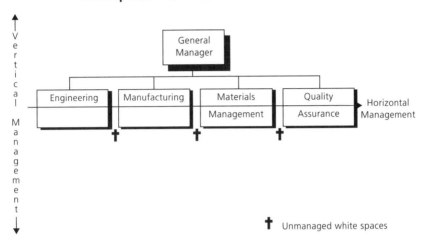

America that the U.S. organization was flawed. It had good vertical management, but no horizontal management. He used the analogy of a piece of cloth with vertical threads but no horizontal threads. It would not be very strong.

So how is a cross-linking horizontal management to be achieved? Behavioral scientists have stressed, on an effectiveness scale from 1 to 1,000 (with 1 being the least effective and 1,000 being the most effective) that holy pronouncements on mission statements and the like have an effectiveness of one. Management exhortations for improvement have an effectiveness of ten. Training has an effectiveness of 100. But the team concept has an effectiveness of 1,000! So a cross-linking horizontal organization is achieved by cross-functional, interdisciplinary teams brought together to solve problems and break down departmental walls and vertical silos.

In in his book *Thriving on Chaos*, Tom Peters states that "the self-managing team should become the basic organizational building block to win against other world economic powers." Figure 6-2 is an example of an organization chart that has switched from departments to teams (except for a few support services that act as coaches and guides). Gone are the traditional engineering, sales, marketing, purchasing, manufacturing, and other departmental hierarchies. They are subsumed in process-oriented teams such as the strategic development process, the product development process, the order fulfillment process, and the customer service process.

From Recentralization Back to Decentralization

A promising organizational development around World War I, led by General Motors and DuPont, was to decentralize large companies into divisions for greater autonomy

Figure 6-2. A business process reengineering organizational chart.

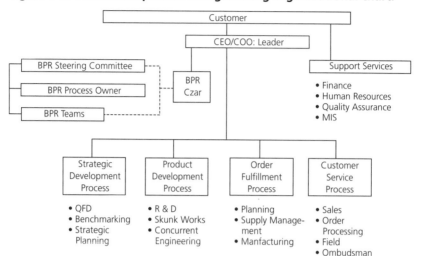

and efficiency. But the virus of bureaucracy attacked corporate divisions with equal vigor, causing organizational bloat. For example, if a company does 100 units of work an hour and each of its workers does ten units an hour, it would need eleven people—ten workers and one supervisor. If the demand grew to 1,000 units of work an hour, it would need not just 110 people but 196! Why? There'd be 100 workers, supervisors, one manager, one assistant manager, eighteen personnel administrators, nineteen long-range planners, twenty-two in audit and control, and another twenty-three in facilitation and expediting![3]

Furthermore, the end of World War II saw creeping recentralization, with finance, purchasing, human resources, public relations, and quality regaining central control in the name of a new centralizing god—operations research. Even the chairman, CEO, CFO, and other functions became the "office of the CEO," with two or three persons in each office instead of one. Adding to this organizational sprawl was the matrix organization, with each person now being subjected to the push-pull of two bosses—a functional boss and a departmental boss.

What is needed, therefore, is a return to true decentralization and a simultaneous shrinkage of both corporate and divisional staff. With the information technology (IT) explosion, a direct link between senior management and the worker can be established, bypassing the ranks of middle manager, foreman, and supervisor. Using the tools of value engineering, zero base assessment, and process redesign, it is possible to cut headquarters staff by at least 75 percent. Consider these examples:

■ An A. T. Kearney study[4] of forty-one large companies compared the financials of successful versus unsuccessful companies. Successful companies had 500 fewer corporate staff specialists per 1 billion in sales.

■ Topsy Turvy,[5] an $80 million-per-year company producing women's hair products, has only three employees.

■ Mars, Inc., a $7 billion company, has only a thirty-person headquarters staff.

From the Tall Organizational Pyramid to the Flat Pyramid

A third feature of organizational restructuring is flattening a total organizational entity with several layers of management levels between the CEO and the line worker (as many as fourteen to eighteen layers in large companies, and seven to eleven in smaller ones) to a maximum of five layers for large companies and three for a single plant.

Example
A young engineer newly hired in a large company was seven layers down in the managerial hierarchy. Twenty-five years later, he had risen to becoming a quality director, but he was now eight levels down from the CEO. That is bureaucracy's appetite-Sumo wrestler style!
 The largest organization in the world, bar none, is the Catholic Church with 800 million members. It has only five layers. For 1,500 years and more, it has vetoed more layers and runs one of the tightest organizational "ships" in history.

Typically, a manager can control six to eight direct reports. The objective of the flat pyramid is to increase that span to fifty or to a hundred and more so that it becomes extremely difficult to micromanage people, directing every step and breathing down their necks at every turn. The enlightened manager has to let go, loosen the reins, learn to trust employees, and give them the freedom and space they need—as long as corporate goals are fulfilled. The manager's role becomes that of a counselor and guide. Once more, consider some examples:

■ Motorola's showpiece plant at Easter Inch in Scotland started with 1,700 people and three levels, including the line worker. It now has 4,000 people with only four levels.

■ The A. T. Kearney study, referred to earlier, found that the successful companies had three to nine fewer management layers than the unsuccessful ones—an average of 7.2 versus 11.1.

■ A Motorola organizational restriction is to discourage any plant in a single location to go beyond a 300-person headcount because of the loss of cohesion and *esprit de corps* that larger plant sizes could endanger.

Step 3: Change Requirements for Hiring Employees

With the bust up of bureaucracy and the crafting of a viable organizational infrastructure in place, the next step is a radical departure in the way recruitment for future employees is conducted. President Eisenhower once said, "War is too important to be left to the generals." As president of my Glencoe school board, I can make a parallel statement: "Education is too important to be left to educators." And, by extension, it can be said that corporate recruitment is too important to be left to the human resources people and their psychologist testers. They can do the initial screening, but it is the line people who best know what kind of people they need.

Step 4: Train, Train, Train All Employees

Training is the next organizational milestone on the road to empowerment. In many ways, the outcome of training—namely, the elevation of worker skills—is the key differential between a company that wins and a competitor that loses. Yet that lesson has hardly been learned in the West, with the possible exception of Germany. Consider the following:

■ The U.S. government contributes—via tax incentives—3,200 times as much to companies, through technology, as it does through employee training.

■ Large Japanese companies provide one year of training to their new recruits before they are actually put on the job. As a result, their line workers take on the tasks of the technicians, and the technicians take on the tasks of the engineers, leaving the latter free for research and development.[7]

■ The Japanese bring that tradition to their transplants. Nissan Motor is the benchmark. The automaker spent $63 million training 2,000 workers before its plant in Smyrna, Tennessee started operations.[8]

There is a giant caveat, however: Training without evaluation of its effectiveness is worse that no training. Classroom training is not enough; evaluation of the instructor by students is not enough; supervisor/manager assessment is—as we say in mathematics—necessary but not sufficient. There should always be independent, quantitative audits of benefits (in terms of quality, cost, and cycle time improvements) conducted within three months and then again a year after such training.

Step 5: Revamp Performance Appraisals

W. Edwards Deming long railed against current systems of performance appraisal that grade employees on a curve (see Figure 6-3)—say, on a scale of 1 to 10, with 1 being the worst grade and 10 being the best.[9] Deming stated that 5 percent of the people are the truly outstanding performers and candidates for advancement. Another 5 percent are the laggard performers and should be terminated or transferred to other jobs. The great majority, 90 percent of the people, are doing the best they can under an organizational system that is defective. Measuring these people, then, does not really measure their performance; the appraisal is actually measuring the noise in the system instead of the signal (to use an electronic term, the signal-to-noise ratio). Furthermore, these semiannual or annual performance appraisals end up doing psychological harm to the person being rated, and it may take months to recover from them.

That doesn't mean that there should be no performance evaluation at all. One should be instituted. But it should be nonscalar, constant, nonthreatening, and it should be a "360-degree evaluation" as well as team evaluation.

Figure 6-3. Performance Rating on a Curve.

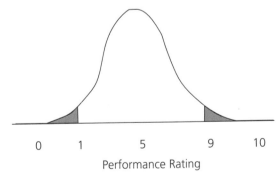

Step 6: Change the Rules of Compensation

Along with radical changes in the way people are hired, trained, and evaluated, there should be corresponding changes in the way people are compensated for their work.

Table 6-2. Old, rigid vs. new, enlightened pay practices.

Old Practice	New Enlightened Practice
• Small, *pro forma* merit increases based largely on cost-of-living.	• No *pro forma*, "automatic" merit increases each year.
• No or small bonuses for employees as a whole.	• Large bonuses/incentives based on performance.
• Small differential in increases between poor and outstanding performers.	• Large differential in pay increases between poor and outstanding performers.
• Staff people command higher salaries than line people for comparable levels.	• Line people have equal or higher salaries than staff people for comparable levels.
• Salaries based on hierarchical position and number of people managed.	• Salaries based on performance/results, with an individual earning more than his manager made possible.
• Performance criteria fuzzy.	• Performance criteria based on results in quality, cost, cycle time, innovation, and teamwork.

Table 6-2 clearly shows the difference between old, rigid practices governing pay and newer, enlightened practices. In the final analysis, fair and meaningful pay is an important part of employee recognition.

Step 7: Design Meaningful and Egalitarian Gain Sharing

Gain sharing as a key element of a culture change has been covered in Chapter 5 on leadership and need not be repeated in this section. Generally speaking, however, in designing effective incentive systems—be they bonuses or stock ownership programs—a few guidelines need to be stressed.

Guidelines for Maximum Effectiveness

■ The base pay should be somewhat higher than comparable jobs in other companies in the vicinity.

- Multiple skills, creating flexibility within a team and between teams, deserve graduated incentive pay.

- Incentives should be based on team performance against goals.

- Incentives should also be tied into profit on sales and return on investments (ROI), business by business, with a floor—i.e., a minimum level for the incentive gate to open—for each of these two metrics. (The danger, of course, is that true profits can be inflated by slick and fraudulent accounting practices. Hopefully new, punitive laws may put an end to these shenanigans.)

- The formula for calculating incentives should be simple and understood by all.

- A targeted incentive should be 20 percent of base pay, provided the profit/ROI gates are open.

- The incentives should be paid out at least every quarter, preferably monthly.

- Employee stock option plans (Enron notwithstanding!) are better than cash payouts because they encourage employee ownership and give employees a stake in the company as well as a long-term outlook.

Step 8: Redesign Promotion Criteria

Promotions, even more than salaries and gain sharing, are the most tangible forms of recognition. There are two tracks for promotion. One is managerial, the other professional/technical. Most people consider the managerial track as the only way up the corporate ladder, believing that position, rank, and the number of people managed are the *sine qua non* of advancement.

This is not necessarily true. In today's fast-changing technological world, professional contributors can be more important than managers. Progressive companies recognize this and provide a professional track for promotions that attest to the professional's importance and prestige. Staff scientists in such companies can be worth their weight in gold and recognized as such. A second consideration is that the managerial track is not only more crowded but also much narrower today because the ranks of middle managers are being squeezed out—on the one hand by empowerment at the bottom rungs of the corporate ladder, and on the other hand by the power of information technology directly available to top management.

Past Performance Is Not a Valid Reason for Promotions

In the past, there has been a tendency to reward high performers with promotions. There may be several personal attributes causing that high performance, but these attributes may not be those required for the promoted job. This is captured in the famous Peter Principle, where a person gets promoted until he reaches his own level of incompetence.

Promotion Based on Potential for Leadership

Instead of past performance, which, of course, should be amply rewarded with bonuses, stock options, and other compensation, the criteria for promotions are very different. The litmus test is: Does the person have the potential for moving from a manager (or individual contributor) to a leader? The subject of leadership qualities is thoroughly covered in Chapter 5, but briefly, an assessment can be made by asking the following questions:

- Does the person have the personal philosophies and values required of leaders?
- Is the person highly people-oriented, willing to coach and help people reach higher and higher levels of potential?
- Is the person entrepreneurial?
- Is the person innovative, generating a stream of ideas?
- Is the person capable of creating fun and joy in the workplace?

Steps 9 and 10: Team Synergy and Total Involvement

Team synergy is achieved when each team member feels he has gained from the team's activities and results and recognizes that interdependence (rather than independence) is sought. Total involvement becomes operative when no team member feels left out.

CASE STUDY

A BENCHMARK COMPANY IN THE AREA OF ORGANIZATION—CHAPARRAL STEEL10

Big Steel in the United States has long moaned about steel dumping from overseas steel companies and about how there is no level playing field because of the low labor cost abroad. They have sought and now gained protection from the Bush Administration—a move likely to perpetuate their inefficiency and likely cost more job losses among the consumers of their products than would be saved for Big Steel.

   Yet a few minimill steel companies such as Chaparral Steel and Nucor Corporation have captured over 33 percent of the steel market. They have excellent profits, based on a 4:1 productivity increase over industry averages, and they pay their workers incentives averaging 75 percent over base pay. Their cost per ton of steel is lower than Third World countries and is half of the costs of a typical Japanese mill. So much for the myth of uncompetitive American labor costs!

Chaparral Steel has torn down its vertical silos of departmental isolations and dismantled its bureaucracy. Its research operation no longer lives in an ivory tower but is on the shop floor, where ideas for improvement and technological breakthroughs are jointly evaluated by engineering, production, and maintenance and put to the test immediately using the factory as the real laboratory. In many cases, core customers are drawn into these evaluations.

Chaparral has only three management levels between the CEO and the worker—a vice president, superintendent, and foreman. The foreman has a great deal of freedom to make important decisions. The company has no quality inspectors. The line workers are responsible for their own quality. "They act like owners," and the company has a reputation for the best quality in the marketplace.

Chaparral gives people freedom to perform. Its security guards, as an example, enter data into computers, double up as paramedics and ambulance drivers, and are reaching to do some accounting functions. Its teams and their facilitators do their own hiring and training, their own safety checks, their own upgrading of old equipment and prove in (turnkey) of new equipment.

A unique feature at Chaparral is its "sabbatical," where teams are given time off from their regular work to tackle special innovation projects. In the process, they visit customers, universities, suppliers, and researchers and benchmark other companies.

Over the years, I have developed my golden rule: "If you are selling in a particular country or region, it is most logical and economical to manufacture in that country or region." Chaparral is a heartwarming case study that demonstrates the validity of that golden rule.

Self-Assessment/Audit on Organization: Implementing Disciplines by Company Type and Months to Complete

1. *Self-Assessment/Audit.* Table 6-3 is a self-assessment/audit to determine a company's business health in the area of organization. It has five key characteristics and

(text continues on page 99)

Table 6-3. Organization: key characteristics, essential disciplines, audit scores, and time to complete each discipline—by company type (80 points).

Key Characteristics	Essential Disciplines	Rating 1-5*	Months to Complete, By Company Type		
			A	B	C
1-1 Dismantling Taylorism	1. Taylorism—the evil of managers thinking and workers treated as a pair of hands—has been eliminated.		12	24	—
1-2 Assault on Bureaucracy	1. Only those rules and regulations that benefit the customers have been retained; those solely for internal control have been jettisoned.		6	12	24
	2. Employee spending authority has been raised as an expression of trust, especially for customer contact employees.		12	18	24
	3. The organization has reduced executive perks that are interpreted as demeaning to workers.		12	24	36
	4. The number of meetings, memos, e-mails, policy manuals, and procedures has been reduced by at least 50%.		4	9	12
1-3 Revamping the Organizational Structure	1. *Team.* The organizational structure has been converted from department-oriented vertical management to				

	horizontal management with the team as a basic building block.	18	24	—
	2. *Decentralization.* The organization has moved from a top-heavy centralized entity to a decentralized one, with a minimum reduction of 80% in corporate staff and support services.	15	24	48
	3. *Delayering.* The company has flattened its organization pyramid by reducing the number of management layers between the CEO and line worker to a maximum of 5, even for the largest companies.	12	18	—
1-4 Revolutionizing Management Practices	1. *Hiring* criteria have emphasized team player potential, customer sensitivity, alignment with corporate values, and a desire to learn.	12	18	24
	2. *Training* has been extended to all employees, for a minimum of 40 hours/year/employee and a minimum expenditure of 3% of payroll.	12	24	36
	3. *Training results* have been audited to ensure minimum benefit-to-cost ratio of 10:1	24	36	—
	4. *Performance appraisal* has been shifted from one made by the supervisor to an internal			

(continues)

Table 6-3. (Continued.)

Key Characteristics	Essential Disciplines	Rating 1-5*	Months to Complete, By Company Type		
			A	B	C
	customer evaluation, as well as a 360-degree evaluation by customer, manager, peers, and employees.		18	24	—
	5. *Compensation* policies have been changed from small *pro forma* merit raises with small differentials between employees, to no merit raises but with large incentives/ bonuses based on performance.		24	36	—
	6. *Promotion* policies have been changed from those based on past performance to those based on growth and entrepreneurship potential.		12	18	36
1-5 Egalitarianism	1. *Total Compensation.* The differentials between CEO/top management and the worker have been held to a maximum 50:1 ratio.		24	—	—
	2. *Zero Bonuses.* A firm policy of no bonuses or stock options for top management in a year of profit loss or layoffs.		24	—	—

* The rater grades each discipline on a scale of 1–5, with 1 being the lowest rating and 5 the highest.

sixteen essential disciplines required for practical implementation, with a maximum of 5 points each, for a total of 80 points.

2. *Implementation Disciplines and Commentary on Time Required for Completion by Company Type.* Changing an organizational culture is one of the most difficult transitions for any corporation. It involves not only leadership at the top, but the need to change peoples' values, so it is always hampered by a resistance to change. It is for this reason that the months to implement the individual disciplines in Table 6-3 appear to be stretched out into years. This is especially true for Type C companies that are big, inflexible, and unwilling to depart from conventional thinking. In fact, they are not likely to ever introduce some of the disciplines listed.

CHAPTER 7

Employees: Industrial Autocracy Toward Industrial Democracy

There is no asymptotic barrier to the human potential, given
leadership encouragement, trust, support, training, and coaching to all employees. . . .   —KEKI R. BHOTE

Our people were labeled 'ordinary,' but they have achieved
extraordinary results.   —OSCAR KUSISTO, MOTOROLA VICE PRESIDENT

From "How to" to "Want to" in Motivation

The subject of worker motivation has elicited a mountain of management interest
and produced a mouse of results. Some of the recent movements such as total quality management and business process reengineering have failed to light a motivation flame in the workers' hearts. Quality systems such as ISO-9000 and the
Malcolm Baldrige National Quality Award bypass motivation altogether as a key
consideration.

Traditional Six Sigma practices pay scant attention to the worker, let alone motivation wellsprings. As an example, the whole black belt apparatus of goal champions
and master black belts is an elitist system that selects one out of a hundred people for
special status and attention while ignoring the potential of ninety-nine others.

Past managerial efforts have concentrated on "how to motivate" the worker
rather than encouraging a "want to motivate" attitude by the worker. Motivation cannot be extrinsic; it must be intrinsic.

101

A Synopsis of Motivation Theories

Motivation theories abound on the "want to" approach—that is, on needs that produce motivation. These needs range from Abraham Maslow's hierarchy of human needs to Douglas McGregor's Theory X and Theory Y. One of the best examples is Scott Myers's concepts on maintenance and motivation needs.

Scott Myers's Maintenance and Motivation Needs[1]

In an adaptation of Herzberg's theories, M. Scott Myers developed a three-ring concept of worker needs as shown in Figure 7-1. Maintenance needs in the outer ring are physical (e.g., food and shelter), economic (e.g., a paycheck, job security), status (e.g., dignity of the individual, perks, prestige), and social (e.g., the need for interaction with fellow employees). These maintenance needs, similar to Herzberg's contentment factors, cause dissatisfaction when absent but do not, on the other hand, produce motivation when present. At best, they maintain the *status quo* and possibly prevent employees from leaving the company. The inner ring contains the same motivation factors—growth, achievement, responsibility, and recognition—formulated by Herzberg. But the innermost ring, at the very core of motivation, is the job itself—and how to make it interesting, challenging, exciting.

Job Redesign—the Centerpiece [2]

If, indeed, the job is the core of motivation, the challenge is how to make a dull, boring job, one that characterizes a production assembly line and many other routine tasks in a company, interesting and even exciting.

Behavioral scientists tell us that in order to inject fun into work, you must capture three psychological states that have always made sports fun:

Meaningfulness	Workers must perceive their jobs as worthwhile and important.
Responsibility	Workers must believe that they are personally accountable for the results of their efforts.
Knowledge of Results	Workers must be able to determine, on a regular basis, whether the results of their efforts are satisfactory.

In the presence of these three psychological states, the worker feels good about himself when he performs well. They produce the all-important internal motivation. If even one of these psychological states is missing from the job, the internal motivation is reduced.

Figure 7-1. Employee needs: maintenance and motivational.

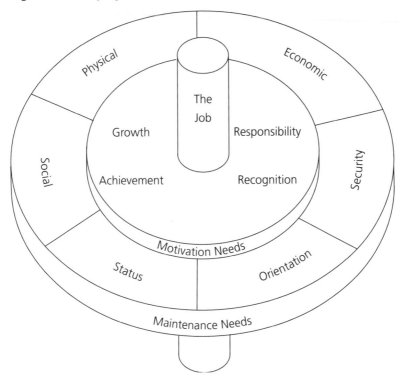

The Full Model of Job Redesign

The concepts of psychological states and job dimensions, essential to job interest, challenge, and fun, can be meshed to form a powerful model for redesigning jobs. Figure 7-2 is a schematic representation of how a job can be redesigned to produce true internal motivation.

At the right of Figure 7-2 are the five goals that companies and workers share: high internal motivation, high quality, high job interest and satisfaction, low absenteeism, and low people turnover.

To achieve these goals, fun must be injected into the job through the three psychological states: meaningfulness of work, responsibility for outcomes, and knowledge of results. This, in turn, requires that the five core job dimensions, previously outlined, must be present in the job.

Finally, in order to establish these five core dimensions, five *implementing concepts*—combining tasks; forming natural work units; establishing client relationships; creating vertical job enrichment; and opening feedback channels—must be designed into the job for optimum results.

Figure 7-2. The full model of job redesign.

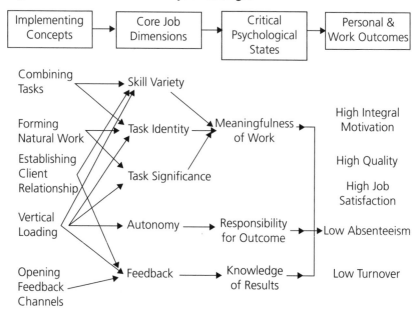

Injecting Fun and Excitement Into a Dull, Mind-Numbing Assembly Line Job

For most professionals, the job itself provides adequate interest, challenge, and stimulation. But what about the many routine jobs in industry—such as an assembly line, cleaning services, clerical, data entry, and so on—where brawn is substituted for brain. What "pride of workmanship," which management bemoans workers of today are losing, can an assembler have putting in bolts on the wheels of cars as they move past him on a car line, hour after hour, day after day, week after week, month after month?

Unfortunately, such jobs are necessary. What can be done, however, is to redesign them using the template of Figure 7-2. Such a job redesign of a typical assembly line is outlined in Table 7-1.

Conventional managers may argue that all of these actions take away "holy" production time. But they don't realize that direct labor constitutes only 3 percent of a company's sales. A 20 percent loss of production time is only 0.6 percent of sales, whereas efforts to reduce the cost of poor quality (COPQ), improve total productive maintenance (TPM), reduce cycle time, and improve customer retention may accumulate to almost 50 percent of sales!

(text continues on page 107)

Table 7-1. Redesigning a dull assembly line job to create a spark of interest, fun, and excitement.

Implementing Concept	Actions
1. Combining Tasks	• Obtain material.
	• Arrange/fill bins.
	• Check tools.
	• Learn multiple skills, with incremental pay for each new skill.
	• Administer self-inspection (using Poka-Yoke, as covered in Chapter 9).
	• Self-test.
	• Conduct routine preventive maintenance.
2. Natural Work Units	• Establish focus factories (see Chapter 11).
	• Divide work by customer, rather than by product line.
	• Work on all subassemblies of a product line instead of specific subassemblies of several product lines.
	• Form teams; convert the supervisor into a facilitator.
3. Client Relationships	• Establish contact with external customers and external suppliers where possible, including visits.
	• Solicit and obtain support from white-collar services.
	• Identify and build relations with professional experts.
	• Determine requirements of internal customers (Chapter 14) and get feedback from them on progress.
	• Specify requirements to internal supplier (Chapter 14).
4. Vertical Job Enrichment (The Most Important Aspect of Job Redesign)	• Help formulate work hours, including flex hours.

(continues)

Table 7-1. (Continued.)

Implementing Concept	Actions
	• Help determine overtime, incentives, alternatives to layoffs.
	• Determine line balancing/sequencing.
	• Conduct time and motion studies (better than external industrial engineers).
	• Form problem-solving teams.
	• Formulate written/audio/video instructions where needed.
	• Highlight critical quality, cost, cycle time parameters.
	• Work on methods improvement.
	• Help design work station layout.
	• Help reduce setup/changeover time (see Chapter 14).
	• Learn and implement the powerful tools of the 21st century (Chapters 9, 10, 11) to solve chronic problems and make presentations of results to management.
	• Suggest and help build simple sensors (e.g., Poka-Yoke) to prevent operator-controllable errors.
	• Assist in Positrol, Process Certification, and Pre-control (see Chapter 9).
5. Feedback	• Get immediate nonthreatening feedback from Poka-Yoke sensors.
	• Get periodic feedback for the team from internal customers.
	• Get guidance and coaching from the manager at least once per week.
	• Design and maintain scoreboards for charting progress and for maximum visibility.
	• Understand and interpret P&L statements and the balance sheet (see the section on Open Book Management.)

Job Security vs. the Damocles Sword of Layoffs

Although job security as a "passport to productivity" was covered in Chapter 5, an additional point needs emphasis. One of the roadblocks to worker motivation and to teams signing up for empowerment is their genuine fear that the resultant productivity improvements will usher in layoffs, retrenchment, downsizing.

Providing a Climate for Worker Productivity

Worker productivity cannot flourish in a repressive, overbearing, bureaucratic culture. It cannot thrive in a vacuum. It must be preceded by genuine, enlightened management policies that include:

- *Driving Out Fear.* This concept was discussed in Chapter 5 on leadership. The only way to assess whether fear to speak out has been genuinely eliminated, or at least severely attenuated, is to ask for direct worker feedback through surveys.

- *Strengthening Job Security.* This subject was also dealt with in Chapter 5 on leadership. Here, too, management must provide the assurance that productivity contributed by workers will not be allowed to result in a loss of their jobs. Furthermore, if layoffs are absolutely unavoidable, they should start with the ranks of management and support staff and reach the worker last.

- *Lifting Dead-Weight Bureaucratic Rules.* Chapter 6 on organization listed several mind-numbing, energy-sapping bureaucratic rules that should be eliminated for worker creativity and productivity to flourish.

- *Distributing Pay and Gain Sharing Equitably.* Pay is not a motivator. It is an output, not an input for worker productivity. Merit increases should not be *pro forma* (see Chapter 6), though pay for performance is a practice whose time has come. This means large pay increases must be commensurate with earned productivity gains. It means an equitable distribution of gain sharing between managers and workers.

- *Practicing Management by Walking Around (MBWA).* This is a highly recommended practice for a manager to get away from his ivory castle and visit his people. The manager needs to mingle with and listen to his employees with empathy; encourage their ideas with suggestions or even error cause removal (ECR)—where potential problems can be pointed out; conduct rap sessions; cheer them; and celebrate their success.

  I was consulting with a plant of about 300 people, where most of them did not know who the plant manager was, had never seen him, or couldn't recognize him by sight. The plant manager, in turn, did not know any of his employees other than his immediate staff. Needless to say, the plant was almost terminally ill, in terms of business health.

By contrast, the famous vice chairman of Motorola, Bill Weisz, instituted a discipline where every manager had to visit his line workers for at least two hours each week to jump-start an MBWA policy.

■ *Mentoring.³* Another discipline, widely practiced by the Japanese, is to have a senior manager act as counselor and coach to a few workers. (They call it the godfather system.) This mentor can smooth the way through an organization's minefields, facilitate quick learning, and enhance productivity for the enterprise, while helping the worker in career development.

■ *Providing Appropriate Tools.* It is imperative that workers be given powerful but easy tools to solve problems and to improve productivity. If they are given the tired tools of the twentieth century, such as PDCA, Ford 8-D, the seven tools of quality control (QC), or DMAIC (design, measure, analyze, improve, and control) that are empty shells and a skeleton framework, they will get frustrated and suffer from "give-up-itis." This is why movements like *kaizen* and quality circles, while encouraging from the perspective of people involvement, are ineffective for problem solving, cost reduction, and cycle time reduction. By contrast, the tools described in Chapters 9, 10, and 11 are an order-of-magnitude or two more effective.

Team Competitions—Another Gold Mine

The team concept, as the basic building block of an organization, is now so pervasive in a few companies that they have proliferated them, with scores of teams in each plant, hundreds in each major division, and thousands in a corporation as a whole.

Typically, each team—generally, cross-functional—is organized on a purely volunteer basis. However, the desire to join a team is so compelling that very, very few workers are holdouts. The team elects its own leader (with the supervisor graduating into a facilitator), gives itself a catchy name, and chooses its own goals (generally, improvements in quality, cost, cycle time, innovation, or some other problem that is of concern to the team or the business in which it operates). The teams are then given time—three to six months or more—to achieve their goals. They are rewarded with bonuses, usually twice a year, with presentations to the plant management.

On the Road to Industrial Democracy

In the past to twelve years, three positive innovations have been launched in empowerment practices—all leading to the ultimate vision of industrial democracy. They have several features in common, not the least of which is a compelling desire by the workers to play a significant role in the success of the organization and in their own success—emotional, managerial, and financial.

Open Book Management— "Lightning in a Bottle!"

Open book management can be defined as a way of running a company that gets everyone to focus on helping the business make money, "by giving every employee a voice in how the company is run, and a stake in the financial outcome, good or bad."[4]

"If you could tear apart an open book company and compare it with a conventional business, you'd see three essential differences," says John Case, author of *Open Book Management: The Coming Business Revolution*:

> 1. *Every employee sees—and learns to understand—the company's financials, along with all the other numbers critical to tracking the business's performance. (That is why it is called open book.)*
>
> 2. *Employees learn that, whatever else they do, part of their job is to move those numbers in the right direction. . . .*
>
> 3. *Employees have a direct stake in the company's success. If the business is profitable, they get a cut of the action. If it's not, they don't. . . .*[5]

THE MOTOROLA TCS COMPETITION

Motorola is, undoubtedly, a benchmark in the arena of team competition. Worldwide, it has more than 6,000 teams in friendly competition, which it calls its Total Customer Satisfaction (TCS) Competition. Each major plant has fifty to a hundred teams. The few best teams are selected to represent the plant in a regional meet; the best of these move on to presentations at the sector level; and the finalists from the sectors then make presentations at corporate headquarters in Schaumburg, Illinois, where the CEO evaluates the results for two full days. Six gold medals and twelve silver medals are awarded to the winners.

There has been some media criticism about this TCS competition: that it promotes competition, rather than cooperation; that for every winning team there are many losing teams; that there is too much hoopla; and that the teams spend too much time with glitzy showboating. But it is the best example of converting dull work into fun; of generating unbelievable enthusiasm; of giving workers, who've never made a speech in their lives, an opportunity to appear before senior management and speak with amazing aplomb. And the bottom line is the savings to Motorola of $2 billion to $3 billion a year—a return on investment of 15:1.

The underlying principle of open book management is that "the more employees know about a company, the better they will perform," and the more tangible will be the benefits to the company. Don't use information to intimidate, control, or manipulate people. Use it to teach people how to work together to achieve common goals and thereby gain control over their lives. When you share the numbers and bring them alive, you turn them into tools people can use to help themselves as they go about their business every day."

Open Book Implementation

While there are as many variations in open book implementation as there are companies practicing it, a few common themes characterize most of them:

1. *Show all employees the financials.* Put up scoreboards so that key financials can be tracked weekly and teach everyone how to read or interpret:

- P&L statements and the balance sheet

- After-tax profits, retained earnings, debt-to-equity ratios, cash flow

- Inventory turns, asset turns, and overhead chargeout rates

- Revenues per employee

2. *Teach the basics of business.* It is amazing how little most workers know about business. Some believe that revenues are the same as profits! (When I was teaching a graduate student class at a prestigious University in Chicago, the students' thought that the average profit on sales that companies make was 40 percent!) In teaching the basics:

- Start with personal finances

- Use simple case studies and business games

3. *Empower people to make decisions based on what they know.* Plenty of companies give lip service to the concept of empowerment. They call meetings and set up project or cross-functional teams—so many teams that a wag once remarked that companies could be mistaken for bowling leagues. But since they don't share financial information, employees do not know how their work affects the bottom line. To rectify the situation:

- Call biweekly meetings, where income and cash flow statements and forecasts are discussed so people can take back the information to their own units.

- Turn the company into a collection of smaller companies, along the lines of focus factories.

- Turn departments into business centers with their customers—internal or external—as their focus, and hold them responsible for their own finances, as well as hiring and disciplinary decisions.

4. *Ensure that everyone—everyone!—shares directly in the company's success and in the risk of failure.* This is not just a profit-sharing system, determined each year after

the fact, at the discretion of management, and where employees don't know how the company is doing and don't have a clue about how their own work affects what they receive as a bonus. Rather, in the open book system:

- Annual targets are set for profits and return on assets. If the employees hit both targets, employees collect payouts ranging from 10–50 percent of their total compensation. And they can track progress against these targets, month by month.

- Open book management can work without employee stock ownership, but it works better when employees own stock in the company. Equity encourages long-term thinking, for staying the course, and for sacrificing instant gratification in order to build for the future.

Companies Incorporating Open Book Management

The originator of open book management was Jack Stack, president and CEO of the Springfield ReManufacturing Company (SRC) in Springfield, Missouri. His missionary zeal brought several convert companies—mostly small ones, at first—to SRC to study the company's miraculous turnaround. These included Cin-Made, Chesapeake Packaging, Foldcraft, Web Industries, Jenkins Diesel Power, and others. The impact of more than 3,000 visitors and 300 presentations by SRC has brought in the big boys: FedEx, Wal-Mart, Exxon, Frito-Lay, and Ben & Jerry's, for example. Open book management has been introduced not only in industry and unionized companies, but also in airlines, hospitals, fund-raising organizations, and government agencies—even in police and fire departments; in short, in any organization whose performance can be measured with financial statements!

It is no wonder that Chris Lee, managing editor of *Training Magazine*, after visiting several open book companies, came away dazzled. Open book management, she wrote admiringly, is "lightning in a bottle."[6]

Self-Directed Work Teams: Lifting the Oppressive Weight of Corporate Bureaucracy

If open book management has the teaching of financials to the entire workforce as its unique feature, the second innovation—self-directed work teams (SDWT)—has as its main thrust the dismantling of company bureaucracy and the liberation of the worker from the chains of drudgery and boredom.

Jack Welch, the former CEO of General Electric, states that the primary cause of stagnant productivity is the deadening weight of corporate bureaucracy—"the cramping artifacts that pile up in the dusty attics of companies: reports, meetings, rituals, approvals, and forests of paper that seem necessary until they are removed."[7]

The SDWT Concept—Opposite of an Assembly Line

An SDWT is a highly trained group of employees (from six to eighteen, on average) fully responsible for turning out a well-defined segment of finished work. Because every member of the team shares equal responsibility, self-directed teams are the conceptual opposite of the assembly line, where each worker has a responsibility for a very narrow function.

Work team members have more resources, a wider range of cross-functional skills, much greater decision-making authority, and better access to the information needed for sound decisions. They plan, set priorities, organize, coordinate with others, measure, solve problems, schedule work, and handle absenteeism, team selection, and evaluation. Each team member receives extensive training in administrative, interpersonal, and technical skills necessary for a self-managed group.

Origins of SWDT

Strange as it may seem, SWDT started with the coal miners and their mentors in South Yorkshire, England in 1949—more than fifty years ago. It then spread to the United States, Sweden, and India. In the last twenty years, it has been embraced by not only industry giants, such as Corning, Xerox, GE, TRW, and others, but also by service industries and not-for-profit institutions.

The Benefits

Self-directed work teams have distinct benefits, both for the company and its workers:

- A productivity increase of 20–40 percent and up to 250 percent

- A reduction in setup time of over 1,000 percent—from one-and-a-half days to one-and-a-half hours

- Flattening the organizational pyramid—transforming supervisors into facilitators

- Paperwork reduction—or even elimination, if not useful to the teams

- Flexibility—with the workflow more suited to focus factories and mass customization

- Quality improvements —with an enthusiasm for problem solving

- Greater commitment to corporate goals

- Improved customer satisfaction and loyalty

- Most important of all, the releasing of the creative juices of people, with a reduction—almost elimination—of alienation

From the Bureaucratic Organization to SDWT

There is a dramatic change, as shown in Table 7-2, from the typical organization to the self-directed team organization.

Table 7-2. The typical bureaucratic vs. the self-directed team organization.

Organizational Level	Bureaucratic Organization	SDWT Organization
Executives	Tactical Decisions	Strategic Decisions
Managers	Control	Coaching, Guiding
Supervisors	Operational Decisions	Facilitators
Operators		
• Job Categories	Many, narrow categories	One or two broad categories
• Authority	By supervisor	Through group decisions
• Output	Minimum work to meet external standards	Exceed self-made standards
Reward System	Tied to individual job, individual performance and seniority	Tied to team performance and individual breadth of skills

Downloading, Not Downsizing

A natural concern of companies contemplating self-directed work teams is that it will lead to downsizing and layoffs. But successful companies use self-directed teams for downloading, not downsizing. Top management can concentrate on strategic planning, downloading operational matters to middle management. Middle managers now have time to coach the teams, champion innovative ideas, concentrate on technology, find resources, and interface between the teams and the larger organization. Supervisors, in turn, no longer have to chase parts and paper, but can concentrate on their natural role of teacher, coach, and guide.

Training—The Engine for Transition to SDWT

Training is an absolute prerequisite to the success of self-directed work teams. It can take two to five years for a team to reach peak effectiveness. Without proper training, the teams can flounder, get frustrated, and suffer "give-up-itis." Training is essential in three areas: technical, administrative, and interpersonal skills.

SDWT Success Stories

A few examples of companies incorporating self-directed work teams will suffice to underline their effectiveness:

- Procter & Gamble gets 30–40 percent higher productivity in its eighteen team-based plants. Until recently, it considered work teams so vital to its success that it deliberately shunned all publicity about them.

- Xerox plants incorporating work teams are at least 30 percent more productive than conventionally organized plants. The same is true for GM.

- Tektronix reports one self-directed work team turns out as many products in three days as it once did with an entire assembly line in fourteen days.

- At General Mills, work teams schedule, operate, and maintain machines so effectively that the night shift operates with zero managers.

- Aid Association for Lutherans (AAL) increased productivity by 20 percent and cut processing time by 75 percent.

- Shenandoah Life processes 50 percent more applications and customer services using work teams with 10 percent fewer people.

The Minicompany: Make People Before You Make Product![9]

If the teaching of financials is the starting point of open book management, and the breakup of bureaucracy that of self-directed work teams, then releasing the wisdom and creativity and sense of ownership of all employees is the hallmark feature of the minicompany. The old-line company transforms from "brick wall" management to a "no wall" management style, from secrecy to transparency.

The Principles of Minicompanies

The principles behind the minicompany concept are simple, but powerful:

- Build people before you build product.

- Provide people with information they need, problem-solving tools, and an educational environment to help them grow—just as children grow under their parents' care.

- Use the collective wisdom people have gained and harness their natural energies once released.

- View every individual in the organization as the "president" of his area of responsibility, providing products or services to satisfy customers (see Chapter 14), using the Next Operation as Customer (NOAC) and the previous operation as supplier. In this way managers see shop-floor people as their customers in the new tradition of the inverted organizational pyramid.

- Extend this concept one step further so that the minicompanies are the "owners" of the little companies within a large company.

- Create total visibility of progress, with scoreboards established and updated by the minicompany "owners" themselves.

- Recognize contributions with tangible rewards.

The Benefits of Running a Minicompany

The overall benefit of the minicompany is that it truly unleashes the human spirit. There are additional benefits, as well:

- People develop a sense of ownership.

- People learn to work as an effective team because of the focus on joint ownership.

- The development of a mission statement and customer-supplier relationship charts will help people focus on clear objectives.

- Barriers between units of organizations are reduced.

- The total organization moves toward goal congruence as each minicompany's plans and progress are shared.

- Because the minicompany framework is the same at all levels, a comprehensive management framework is developed, tying the lowest level of the organization to the highest level.

The Basic Organizational Building Block of a Minicompany

As stated in the principles of a minicompany, each individual in the minicompany can be considered a manager and the team leader (or old supervisor) as the president. The team has internal customers, whose requirements must be met, and suppliers, whose outputs must meet the team's requirements. These suppliers include services provided by the old "white collar" support operations. Managers now are seen as "bankers," shareholders, or even venture capitalists who provide the minicompany with resources—people, equipment, time, and money—to get the job done. Figure 7-3 is a schematic representation of mini-company's organization chart.

Figure 7-3. "Organizational chart" of a minicompany.

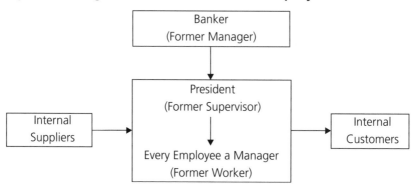

The Wide Application of Minicompanies

As is the case with open book management and self-director work teams, there are a large number of companies at various levels of minicompany implementation. They include Alps, BorgWarner, Robert Bosch, Ford Motor Co., General Motors, McDonald's, Motorola, Toledo Scale, Xerox, and others. Each has shown encouraging results of quality, cost, delivery, safety, and morale improvements. Although the numbers are not as quantified or publicized as with the other two innovations, one thing is clear: With any of these techniques, the genie of the irresistible human spirit is out of the bottle and no amount of backsliding to Taylorism will ever lock it up again!

A Composite of the Best of Open Book Management, SDWT, and Minicompanies

Objectives

- ■ Make people before you make product.

- ■ Dismantle bureaucracy; remove the chains of drudgery, boredom, and fear.

- ■ Ensure that everyone shares directly in the company's success and in the risk of failure.

Organization

- ■ Managers become bankers; the supervisor becomes president of his work responsibility area; the worker becomes a manager.

- Next Operation as Customer (NOAC) reduces organizational barriers.
- Team size should be ten to thirty people.

Tasks

- Plan.
- Set priorities.
- Organize.
- Coordinate with other teams.
- Measure.
- Solve problems.
- Schedule work.
- Handle absenteeism.
- Select team members.
- Evaluate team progress using a scoreboard updated each week.
- Share in financial rewards or losses.

Training

- Technical proficiency in the powerful tools of the twenty-first century (see Chapters 9, 10, and 11)
- Administrative skills (e.g., financial, Kanban, NOAC, job redesign)
- Interpersonal skills (e.g., communication skills, team dynamics, motivation theory and practice, handling interpersonal conflicts)

Implementation

Stage 1— Start-Up. Executive steering committee; prework with managers and employees; teams formed; training begun.

Stage 2—Overcoming Confusion. Efforts to address concerns about job security and managers losing control.

Stage 3—Leader-Centered Teams. Buy-in from support groups; natural leaders emerge within teams; managers gradually pass the baton to the team.

Stage 4—Team Solidarity. Loyalty and protectionism emerges within team, and competition between teams.

Stage 5—Self-Directed Teams. Commitment to team and corporate goals; responsible to internal customer needs; focus on external customers and competition.

The Ten Stages of Empowerment

Table 7-3 is an evolution—in ten stages—of the march from Taylorism to unleashing the human spirit; and the capabilities of workers to rise to their every-increasing potential.

Even in this age of enlightenment, there is still progress yet to be made. Consider the following facts:

- Forty percent of companies are still in stage 1 or 2—bureaucratic, authoritarian, and ruling by fear.

- Another 10 percent of companies have reached stage 3.

- A further 40 percent of companies are in stage 4 or 5, having formed teams, with a focus on problem solving.

- About 8 percent have given their teams the first taste of management—stage 6—although coaching on business financials is an exception, rather than the rule.

- Possibly 1.5 percent of companies have entered stage 7, with a measurable team contribution to the company bottom line.

- Perhaps 0.5 percent have had teams take over noncore operations within their companies—stage 8.

- It is estimated that there are no more than eight to a hundred companies—all told—in stage 9 of true empowerment.

- Only one company—Semco—has possibly reached stage 10.

Table 7-3. Ten stages of empowerment leading to industrial democracy.

Stage	Action	Outcome
1. Bureaucratic	Managers make all decisions; workers a pair of hands.	Passivity
2. Information Sharing	Managers decide, then inform workers.	Conformity
3. Dialogue	Manages seek employee inputs, then decide.	Acceptance
4. Intragroup Problem Solving	Groups within each department meet to solve problems.	Commitment
5. Intergroup Problem Solving	Cross-functional teams solve larger company problems.	Cooperation
6. Start of Self-Direction	Teams improve quality, cost, cycle time; help determine flexible working hours, overtime, and redesign of work areas and business processing; are exposed to financials, business metrics.	Taste of Management
7. Limited Self-Direction	Work with suppliers & customers, limited budget authority. Team contributions to company financials.	Limited Operations Management
8. Self-Direction	Worker committees take over of peripheral areas (e.g., cafeteria, recreation, insurance).	Practice Management
9. Start of Ownership	Teams handle peer evaluation, compensation, hiring and firing of team members, job redesign; start of minicompanies.	Empowerment
10. Ownership	Workers elect leaders, determine promotions, sharing in profits and losses, with bonuses and/or employee stock option plans.	Industrial Democracy

CASE STUDY

SEMCO—A PINNACLE OF INDUSTRIAL DEMOCRACY

There is only one company—Semco,[10] located near São Paulo in Brazil—that can lay claim to having reached stage 10 or total industrial democracy. No other company comes within a mile! Companies from all over the world have made pilgrimages to Semco to learn firsthand about its success. Its president, Ricardo Semler, has captured its spirit in his book Maverick that is a blockbuster. And Semler has been most generous with his time, lecturing in many parts of the globe on unleashing—in fact, not just in theory—the human spirit! Table 7-4 lists the innovations Semco developed for its workers and teams, including:

■ Innovations common to other well-known empowering companies
■ Innovations unique to Semco, making it the capital of industrial democracy

Yet, in terms of financial results, Semco has increased its profits seven times in less than ten years and has a waiting list of job applicants six years long!

CASE STUDY

A BENCHMARK COMPANY IN THE AREA OF ORGANIZATION— SPRINGFIELD REMANUFACTURING COMPANY (SRC)[11]

A U.S. benchmark company and the one that started the open book management revolution in America is the Springfield ReManufacturing Company (SRC) in Springfield, Missouri. Its business is remanufacturing engines and engine components by removing worn-out engines in cars, bulldozers, and eighteen-wheelers and rebuilding them.

Its Shaky Start

SRC was a small department in the huge International Harvester plant in Melrose Park, Illinois. The plant was among the worst in America marred by racial incidents, death threats, burning of effigies, bombings, shootings, and aggravated assaults. Workers and managers were constantly at each other's throats. Things progressed from bad to worse until International Harvester sold the operation to thirty-six of its managers for $9 million. However, they were only able to scrape up $100,000 and had to borrow the rest—a debt-to-equity ratio of 89:1!

Open Book Management to the Rescue

With his back to the wall, Jack Stack, former manager and now CEO of SRC, developed the theory, concepts, and practice of open book management. He cites two preconditions that are essential before open book management can be launched:

1. *Management must have credibility.* It must earn a minimum level of mutual trust and respect. When managers flaunt what they have, when they intimidate, when they treat people badly, they forfeit their power!

2. *Employees should have some fire in their eyes.* They should not be made to feel that they are losers. For people to feel like winners, they must have pride in themselves and in what they do. There is no winning without pride; no ownership without pride.

There are all kinds of techniques to build credibility and light fires in peoples' eyes—listening to the workers and their ideas, encouraging them to dream, creating small wins, and making a big deal out of little victories—and, in the process, having fun!

Rearranging the Financials in Terms Meaningful to Each Employee:

Open book management uses the same two metrics common to all businesses—the balance sheet (which SRC calls the thermometer to know if it's healthy or not) and the income statement (which tells how the company got that way and what you can do about it). But these are not the typical financial statements of the CPA world. The detail is broken down to show how each employee affects the income statement and the balance sheet. Categories where the most money is spent are highlighted. Cost-of-goods-sold is broken down into its basic elements—material, labor, overhead. Every element of the company is quantified—from the percentage of the budget spent on receptionists' notepads to the amount of overhead absorbed each hour that a machinist uses in grinding crankshafts. Sales numbers are posted daily: who's buying, what they're buying, how they're buying. The numbers are broken down not just by customer but by product.

"Skip the Praise, Give Us the Raise!"

The real outcome for the week-by-week knowledge of the financials is SRC's bonus program, nicknamed "Skip the Praise—Give Us The Raise" (shortened to STP-GUTR and pronounced "stop-gooter"). Bonus programs and gain sharing are, by no means, new to industry. Further, SRC's bonus of 13 percent of annual

(continues)

pay is not in the upper tenth percentile of incentives in other companies. There are, however, some unique features that makes STP-GUTR at SRC so cherished by its employees:

■ All employees are in the same boat—from CEO to line operator. The ceiling bonus for managers and professionals is 18 percent of annual pay; for everyone else it is 13 percent. This 5 percent differential is the lowest and most egalitarian among all prevalent incentive systems.

■ The "floor" for opening the bonus gate is a modest profit of 5 percent before taxes or 3.3 percent after-tax profit—one of the lowest in industry. This enables bonuses to be paid even during business down-cycles.

■ As profit margins increase, the bonus percentages are also ratcheted up.

■ There is a tie-in between the profit-on-sales target and the balance sheet goal, to ensure adequate cash flow and liquidity.

■ The payouts are made every quarter as opposed to the usual practice in industry of annual payouts. Annual payouts lose their impact on workers, who might not correlate their individual contributions with the delayed benefits.

■ SRC goes to great lengths to make sure its people understand how the bonus program works. Bad communications is the main reason most bonus systems fail.

■ SRC, with its close tracking of all financials, announces bonus results once a week. It holds meetings, sets up an electronic ticker tape in the cafeteria, and flashes the score at lunch.

■ Finally, SRC believes that the real power of its bonus program lies in its ability to educate its people about business.

Results at SRC in Adopting Open Book Management

The results speak for themselves:

■ At the end of its first year of operation, SRC had a loss of $670,488 on $16 million in sales.

■ Ten years later, SRC had the pretax earnings of $27 million on sales of $83 million.

■ Its stock, worth 10 cents a share at the time of its buyout, was worth $18.36 in ten years, an increase of 18,200 percent!

■ Despite lean year and a recession, it never laid off any of its workers and has never missed a bonus.

Table 7-4. Innovations at Semco to unleash the human spirit.

Common to Other Empowering Companies	Unique to Semco-Revolution in Industrial Democracy
• Uncompromising ethics	• Teams set their own salaries
• Company communications honest—even to media	• Salary incentives/penalties based on company performance
• No corporate debt	• Help in determining profit sharing splits among teams
• "Skunk works" a way of life	
• Autonomous focus factories	• Help in determining plant locations
• No mumbo-jumbo of job titles	• CEO rotational—not permanent
• Only three layers between CEO and workers	• Employees choose their leaders
	• Employees decide on promotions
• Manufacturing cells—not assembly lines	• Growth for the sake of "bigness" is no virtue
• Pay based on a "basket of skills"	• Laid-off workers encouraged/guided to become suppliers
• Visible, transparent scoreboards	
• Self-run cafeterias with sliding-scale rates	• Job openings: first preference for current employees, next for their friends
• No executive dining room	
• No reserved parking	• Worker committees identify surplus managers; challenge expenses; decide on layoffs or lower wages
• Executives share secretaries	
• No office cubicles	
• No office furniture based on rank	• Plant sizes kept to a maximum of 150 people
• No formal dress code	• Hiring/firing of their own team members
• Regular rap sessions	
• Free day-care centers	• Policy manuals to the shredder
• Flextime	• Job descriptions based on what workers want to do
• Computers de-emphasized	
• Reducing dead-end jobs (e.g. clerks)	• Job rotation at manager level
• Encouraging work at home	• Sabbaticals for managers
• Single-page memos	• Worker rating of supervisors
• No time clocks or searches at guard post	• Company health insurance, but employees decide how spent

Self-Assessment/Audit on Employee Empowerment: Implementing Disciplines by Company Type and Months to Complete

I. *Self-Assessment/Audit.* Table 7-5 is a self-assessment/audit to determine a company's business health in the area of employees. It has five key characteristics and sixteen essential disciplines required for implementation, with a maximum of 5 points each, for a total of 80 points.

2. *Implementation Disciplines and Commentary on Time Required for Completion by Company Type.* The history of failures of most companies to inject motivation into their employees indicates the enormity of the task of empowering people. It is, of necessity, a slow process. This is reflected in the extended time required to complete the disciplines in Table 7-7. Even Type A companies that elect to implement either open book management, self-directed work teams, or minicompanies as their empowerment model need time to study and implement it. At the other extreme, Type C companies will find it difficult to even create a climate of empowerment, given its revolutionary concepts, let alone adopt an empowerment model.

Table 7-5. Employees: key characteristics; essential disciplines; audit scores, and time to complete each discipline—by company type (80 points).

Key Characteristics	Essential Disciplines	Rating 1-5 *	Months to Complete, By Company Type		
			A	B	C
1-1 Motivation	1. A survey has been conducted to determine if management and the workers are truly ready for empowerment.		6	9	24
	2. The productive motivation engines of *achievement, recognition, responsibility,* and *advancement* have been				

	diligently pursued in constructing worker jobs.	12	18	36
1-2 Job Redesign	1. The core motivator—*the challenge of the job itself*—has been implemented by combining tasks, forming teams; establishing client relationships, and especially creating vertical job enrichment.	12	24	48
1-3 Creating an Empowerment Climate	1. Line workers attest, through surveys and interviews, that the corrosion of fear has been rooted out.	18	36	–
	2. Beside minimal layoffs, there's a firm job security policy that says worker productivity increases will not result in a loss of their jobs.	6	9	24
	3. Mind-numbing, energy-sapping bureaucratic rules and regulations have been eliminated.	12	18	–
	4. There's pay for performance. Performance, as measured by worker productivity increases, is the sole criteria for merit increases and equitable gain sharing.	12	15	24
	5. Management by Walking Around (MBWA) is institutionalized to listen to people, encourage their ideas, conduct rap sessions, and			

(continues)

Table 7-5. *(Continued.)*

Key Characteristics	Essential Disciplines	Rating 1-5 *	Months to Complete, By Company Type		
			A	**B**	**C**
	cheer and celebrate their success.		12	15	36
	6. Mentoring and counseling by senior management for each worker has been institutional-ized to facilitate quick learning and productivity.		12	18	36
	7. All line workers have learned powerful, but simple *tools* (see Chapters 9, 10, 11) for quality, cost, and cycle time improvement and used them in their work.		18	36	–
1-4 Team Competition	1. The company has institutionalized cross-functional teams to set their own goals to tackle productivity problems, encouraged friendly competition among them, and celebrated winning teams.		15	24	–
1-5 On the Road to Empowerment	1. *Objective.* The company has adopted self-directed work teams (SDWT) to help workers reach their potential and share in the company's success.		12	18	–
	2. *Organization.* Through SDWT managers have been				

transformed into "bankers," supervisors into "presidents," and workers into "managers."	15	18	–
3. *Basics.* All employees have been taught the financials of business.	18	–	–
4. *Training.* All SDWT members have gone through a comprehensive technical, administrative (including financials), and interpersonal training.	18	24	–
5. *Tasks.* All SDWT teams have undertaken reaching out for all operational management tasks previously performed mainly by management (empowerment stages 6, 7, 8, and 9 from Table 7-5).	36	60	–

*The rater grades each discipline on a scale of 1–5, with 1 being the lowest rating and 5 the highest.

CHAPTER 8

From a Customer-Supplier Win-Lose Contest to a Win-Win Partnership for the Entire Supplier Chain

A supplier's main objective for its customer: to create and nurture satisfied, repetitive, and loyal customers who have received added value from the supplier. . . . A customer's main objective for its supplier: to establish a firm partnership with key suppliers, at least at two levels in the supply chain, rendering active, concrete help to them to improve its own cost, lead time, and quality while increasing their profitability. . . .

—KEKI R. BHOTE

The Escalating Importance of Supply Chain Management

There are six factors that underline the ever-increasing importance of supply chain management *vis-à-vis* other disciplines within a company:

1. The enormous leverage for profit improvement

2. The price-material cost squeeze

3. The natural advantages of outsourcing

4. The trend toward suppliers as design partners

5. Gains in supplier quality, cost, and lead-time improvement

6. Unbelievable economic gains in strengthening all links in the supply value chain

129

The Large and Growing Leverage of Supply Management

Direct labor as a percentage of sales accounts for not more than 5 percent (on an average) of the sales dollar, while purchased materials account for at least 50 percent. Supply management has over ten times the leverage of direct labor. Yet where does management allocate its time? Fifty percent to production and a grudging 5 percent to purchased materials! Is it any wonder that industry's weakest link is management? Furthermore, in the factory of tomorrow, direct labor will shrink to 2 percent of the sales dollars and materials will increase to 60 percent, raising supply management's leverage to thirty times direct labor. And, in the "lights out" factory of the near future that's peopleless and paperless, where computers will control computers that run machines, direct labor will evaporate to almost zero while purchased materials will soar to a staggering 70 percent of the sales dollar. What a profit potential!

The Price-Material Cost Squeeze

Another dangerous phenomenon is shown in Figure 8-1. Gone are the days when companies could blissfully raise prices. Customers are not only resistant to higher prices, they also push down prices as their buying options from global competitors increase, as they shop for value, and as customer loyalty can no longer be taken for granted. This price erosion is a minimum of 2 percent to 5 percent a year in stable markets and as much as 25 percent a year in high technology markets. The drastic price erosions in the computer and cellular phone businesses are but two examples of the power of technology to slash prices.

But while the price erosion is a fact of life, the cost of purchased materials from suppliers can continue to escalate because of raw material cost increases, inflation, and other factors. Caught in the middle in this scissors action of customers and suppliers is the squeezed manufacturer. If the trend should continue, the two lines in Figure 8-1 can intersect. Long before that happens, a company will have gone out of business. Supply chain management is the best way to actually reverse the trend. Material costs must decrease at a steeper rate than customer prices.

The Natural Advantages of Outsourcing

The old penchant for vertical integration in companies has been giving way to outsourcing for the last twenty years. Gone are the battles of make-versus-buy decisions, where internal advocates generally used to win this tug-of-war. Today, almost any activity within a company—manufacturing, accounting, management information systems, payroll—is a candidate for outsourcing. The famous Peter F. Drucker concentration decision now extends beyond product. Any activity that is viewed as neither critical nor where the company does not perceive itself to have a core competence can be economically justified to be handed over to partnership suppliers. Witness the rush of electronic companies that are turning over the stuffing, soldering, and testing

Figure 8-1. The scissors effect of customer price erosion and material cost increases.

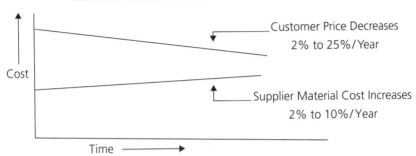

of printed circuit boards—once considered a manufacturing prerogative—to hundreds of contracting suppliers.

The Trend Toward Suppliers as Design Partners

The core competency reasoning now extends to the design function, which can no longer afford to be an expert in all modules of a product design. It should retain those portions of a design that are strategically important and where it has a decided competency and outsource all the others to "black box" partnership suppliers. This decision saves valuable design time, design manpower, design costs, and design quality. This is one of the reasons why the Japanese are more productive in new product launches. Japanese car manufacturers retain engine development as a core competency and outsource almost all other major assemblies to their roster of loyal suppliers. (The supplier share of engineering in Japan is 51 percent as compared with 14 percent in the United States.)

Gains in Supplier Quality, Cost, and Cycle Time Improvement

■ *Quality.* Despite the quality revolution, most suppliers still hide behind acceptable quality levels (AQLs) of one percent defective. World-class companies expect defect levels to be no more than 10 parts per million (ppm) to 50 ppm and their world-class suppliers deliver such levels at reduced cost. Effective supply management is the key.

■ *Lead Time.* Of the various elements that contribute to long manufacturing cycle time—customer order time, factory order time, setup time, build time, ship time, etc.—supplier lead time is the longest and most costly. It is generally five to twenty times as long as manufacturing cycle time. A hard-hitting supply management thrust can reduce supplier lead time by factors of 10:1, even 100:1. This is achieved not only at the supplier's facility, but also by extending supply management to subsuppliers and sub-sub-suppliers.

- **Cost Reductions.** Typically, customer companies attempt supplier cost reductions by pounding the table, changing suppliers, and even by carrying out virtual blackmail, as the notorious Ignatio Lopez, formerly at General Motors, did with his supplier base. The result: a grudging 2 percent to 5 percent cost reduction, with trust and goodwill becoming casualties. There is an amusing story about Lopez when he was at General Motors. His unpopularity with his partnership suppliers had reached fever intensity because of brutal treatment accorded to them. One of his associates told Lopez: "I have good news and bad news." Lopez relied: "Give me the bad news first." The answer: "There is a contract out on your life by your suppliers." "And what is the good news?" asked Lopez. "Why, it's been given to the lowest bidder!" true supply management renders active, concrete help to its partnership suppliers as the best way to help itself. In the process of receiving significant cost reductions year after year (typically 5–15 percent/year), the customer company makes sure that the profits of its partnership suppliers have a corresponding increase.

Unbelievable Economic Gains from Strengthening All Links in the Supply Chain

Supply chain management, for all its rhetoric, has in fact been restricted to the main link—namely, the customer– first-tier supplier interface. Very little has been done to push the frontiers of partnership to upstream supplier links (those second-tier suppliers, let alone third-tier and raw material suppliers) or downstream links (the distributor, dealer, retail chains, servicers).

Upstream Supplier Links

Historically, relations between firms all along a value stream—from raw material suppliers to original equipment manufacturers (OEMs)—are either nonexistent or characterized by the minimum cooperation needed to get the product made. Each company wants to maximize its profits regardless of others in the supply chain. There is little recognition that this is a zero-sum game and even less recognition that "a rising tide lifts all boats"—that the envelope of total profits in the value chain can be much larger for all and for each supplier link if there is mutual trust, full transparency, and full cooperation to:

- Remove or reduce all non–value-added operations along the entire supply chain

- Concentrate at each supply link on reducing cost, defects, and cycle time

- Learn from one another and help one another, on either a one-on-one basis or through a network of supplier associations

Downstream Distributor/ Wholesaler/Franchiser/Dealer/ Servicer Links

Partnerships with distributors and dealers are even rarer and more tenuous than those with first-tier suppliers. They look upon one another with suspicion. Yet distributors and dealers—or retail chains—play a key role because it is almost impossible for a company to keep its finger on the pulse of hundreds and thousands of individual consumers, their requirements, and their loyalty. Furthermore, dealer, retail chain, and service personnel can influence, for better or for worse, sales to consumers with their recommendations.

While the principles, types of help, infrastructure, and development of these downstream links are similar to those for first-tier suppliers, detailed later in this chapter, a few general points need to be stressed:

AVOIDING THE SIREN SONG OF INTERNET BIDDING

There is an absolutely pernicious practice percolating through industry of soliciting bids from a whole host of suppliers through the Internet and selecting the lowest bidder. This can be a virus that can destroy a company in several ways:

- It can sour relations between the company and its close partnership suppliers who, after years of loyal service, find themselves betrayed and left twisting slowing in the wind.

- It trades continuous quality, cost, and cycle time improvement associated with partnership suppliers for the vagaries, disruptions, and deceptions from suppliers of unknown, unproven reputation and trustworthiness.

- It produces short-term gain for a certain, guaranteed long-term loss

- Internet bidding only makes sense where supply partnership is not involved and where there are large numbers of commodity-type suppliers.

- Just as it is important to reduce the customer base (as seen in Chapter 4), it is equally important to reduce the supplier base as well as the distributor/dealer/servicer base. Not all of them are worth keeping. Concentrating on those with true partnership potential conserves a company's limited resources and allows it to service these important constituencies.

Example

Toyota—a model of excellence in manufacturing and lean production—extends its supply management reach to four levels of supplier-subsupplier links. As a result, its raw material inventory turns of 248 is three times the best U.S. figure of 69. But even Toyota has not optimized the cost of its total supply chain. Its manufacturing costs, incurred along its value stream, are as follows:

Supply Chain	Costs
Toyota itself	22 percent
First-tier suppliers	22 percent
Second-tier suppliers	10 percent
Third- and fourth-tier suppliers	3 percent
Raw material suppliers	43 percent[1]

Obviously, even Toyota needs to work with or influence its raw material suppliers more effectively. The principles, type of help, infrastructure, and development of these second- and third-tier suppliers are similar to the ones for first-tier suppliers detailed later in this chapter.

■ Spending time with them is almost as important as spending time with core customers and with customer-contact frontline troops within your company. Listening to them is an attribute of leadership.

■ Supporting them with training, especially technical training, is essential. This training includes seminars, newsletters, videotapes, and field bulletins.

■ Sharing equitably in profits with them ensures profit enhancement for both sides.

World-class companies state that dealer loyalty is a major reason for their success. For example:

■ Caterpillar's dealer organization is placed almost on a par with its customer base by its CEO. In fact, the dealer is the last production step in the complex assembly of its giant products.

- Deere & Company attributes its 98 percent customer retention rate per year to a well-trained dealer network that serves no other company.

- Lexus (see the benchmark case study in Chapter 4) states categorically that its "key to customer loyalty lies in a loyal partnership with our dealers—the single most important element in our success."

Traditional vs. Hyped Six Sigma vs. the "Power of Six Sigma" Approaches to Supply Chain Management

Table 8-1 is a summary of four stages in the evolution of supply chain management:

Stage 1 is representative of a majority of companies that treat their suppliers with suspicion, at best, and like dirt, at worst.

Stage 2 is characteristic of the "hyped Six Sigma" companies, as guided by their consultants and black belt camp followers. They are a long way from Six Sigma.

Stage 3 is the level we reached at Motorola when we developed our original Six Sigma seventeen years ago—a big step toward world-class quality.

Stage 4 is the pinnacle of supply chain management that is reached only by those companies implementing the Power of Ultimate Six Sigma.

Some of the parameters are explained and clarified late in this chapter or in Chapters 9, 10, and 11.

If partnerships are to succeed, the following principles must apply:

Principles of Supply Chain Partnership

- There must be a commitment to partnership by customer and supplier—for a *win-win bond*, rather than the traditional win-lose contest—a zero-sum game.

- Partnership must be based on a foundation of *ethics* and *uncompromising integrity* (discussed in detail in Chapter 5).

- *Mutual trust* must exist—where each side earns the other's trust and strives to live up to the other's trust.

- Agreements are reached with a *handshake*—not hidden behind the fig leaf of legal contracts that spell distrust in capital letters.

Table 8-1. The four stages of supply chain management—a health chart.

Area	Subarea	Stage 1: Traditional Confrontation	Stage 2: Hyped Six Sigma Arms' Length	Stage 3: Motorola Six Sigma Goal Congruence	Stage 4: Power of the Ultimate Six Sigma Win–Win Partnership
Supplier Relationships	Commitment to Partnership	None	Faint	In name, not in substance	Complete
	Trust	Distrust	Suspicion	Limited trust	Full trust
	Help	None	1 or 2 visits/year	Audits	Concrete, active help
	No. of Suppliers	Proliferation	2:1 reduction	2 Suppliers/Pt. No.	Single sourcing
	Power Focus	Customer dictatorship	Customer domination	Shared	Mutual reinforcement
Management	Leadership	Taylorism	Micromanagement	Involvement	Empowerment
	Objective	Reduce costs (C)	Improve quality (Q)	Reduced cycle time (CT)	Improve C, Q, CT
	Focus	Direct labor	Automation	Computer integrated manufacturing	Supply chain management
	Savings to Supplier	Zero	Awarding the business is good enough	10% for contract duration only	Equal sharing, even on future contracts
Organization	Structure	Vertical/departmental	Matrix	Horizontal but centralized	Horizontal, reverse pyramid, and decentralized
	Management Levels	14 to 18	11 to 14	7 to 10	5 maximum

		None	Intradepartmental	Cross-functional	Commodity team—the basic building block
	Teams				
	Purchasing	A traditional department	Supplier quality assurance (SQA) part of purchasing	Sourcing separated from purchasing	Supply management; engineering QA, purchasing, and supplier—one team
Quality	Cost of Poor Quality (COPQ) as % of Sales	Unknown	10% to 20%	5% to 10%	< 2%
	Field Reliability	No responsibility	2% to 5% per year	< 5000 ppm/yr.	<100 ppm/yr.
	Process Capability (Cpk)	Unknown	<1.33	1.33 to 2.0	>2.0
	Quality Tools	Seven tools of QC	Control charts	Shainin/Bhote DOE to solve problems	Shainin/Bhote DOE to prevent problems
	Reliability Tools	None	FMEA (failure mode effects analysis)	HALT/HASS*	MEOST
	Specifications	Pulled out of the air	Worst-case analysis	CAD	Through DOE
Cost	Determination	3 quote syndrome	Electronic bidding	Negotiations (arm twisting)	Cost targeting
	Tools	Learning curves	Group technology	Idea incentives	Total value engineering
	Part No. Reduction	Parts proliferation	Standardization	Product and model numbers reduced	Business concentration
	Incentives	None	10% sharing of savings	50% sharing of savings	Royalties just for ideas

(continues)

Table 8-1. (Continued.)

Area	Subarea	Stage 1: Traditional Confrontation	Stage 2: Hyped Six Sigma Arms' Length	Stage 3: Motorola Six Sigma Goal Congruence	Stage 4: Power of the Ultimate Six Sigma Win-Win Partnership
	Total Productive Maintenance	FOE (factory overall effectiveness): unknown	FOE: < 20%	FOE: < 50%	FOE: > 85%
Cycle Time	System	Large safety stacks	Push system	MRP II	Pull system
	Inventory Turns	3 to 5	10 to15	20 to 30	>60
	Forecasts	Wild oscillations	Oscillations dampened	Smoothing techniques	Not needed
	Change Over Time	2 to 8 hours	1/2 to 1 hour	10 minutes	<3 minutes
	Customer Orders	Unpredictable	Large, infrequent	Small and frequent	Schedule linearity
Results	Main Metric	Price, price, price	Stock-outs	Inventory turns	Total ownership cost: Price + COPQ + Cost of poor delivery
	Supplier Quality	>10,000 ppm	>1000 ppm	<100 ppm	<10 ppm
	Supplier Cost Reduction	>2% per year	>5% per year	>7.5% per year	>15% per year
	Supplier Profit	Not of concern	Allowance for raw material price increases	<2% per year Increase	>5% per year Increase
	Lead Time	10 to 16 weeks	5 to 9 weeks	0.5 to 4 weeks	1 to 3 days

* HALT Highly Accelerated Life Tests
HASS Highly Accelerated Stress Screening
Note: This table applies only to partnership suppliers.

- *Active, concrete help* must be offered on both sides, especially on the part of the company as senior partner, as the best way—no, the only way—to achieve its supply management goals.

- *Supplier cost should be a ceiling*, not a floor. Instead of the old base price, from which the supplier raises costs (which it justifies because of inflation, raw material increases, and union pressures), there is a firm understanding that the supplier will lower prices continuously in return for the customer's concrete help.

- *Supplier profits must be a floor*, not a ceiling. The objective is not to squeeze the supplier dry like a lemon, but to help improve its profits in return for cost, lead time, and quality improvements to the customer.

- An *"open kimono" policy*—where both sides share their strategies, costs, and technology in the spirit of true partnership—is the key to transparency.

- Partnership must be a *long-term marriage*, not a short-term weekend fling

- Supplier must be viewed as an *extension of the customer company*—except for separate finances.

Even though the words *customer* and *supplier* have been used in the above-mentioned context, these principles apply with equal validity to the relationships between:

1. A supplier—as customer—and its subsuppliers along the supply chain

2. A company and its distributors, dealers, and retail chains

Types of Mutual Help

Help is at the very foundation of supply chain management. Yet companies have shied away from rendering it. Why?

- Companies have historically felt that their role is to define the requirements and specifications to the supplier, sign the contract, and pay the price—and from there on, it is the supplier's responsibility to deliver the product. This hands-off syndrome has characterized purchasing for a century.

- Companies believe that helping a supplier is an expenditure of their time and resources, with no return on such investment.

- Companies further believe that helping a supplier may end up helping their competition.

Suppliers, for their part, are also suspicious of such help:

■ They do not want to share proprietary information or to expose their weaknesses.

■ Their help, especially in the design stage, is likely to be benefiting only their customer, leaving them nothing for their helpfulness.

■ Worse, despite their design help to the customer's engineers, the purchasing department can, and often does, place the order with a competitor.

All of these concerns violate the very principles of true partnership. The customer's help to the supplier and vice versa is the best way to improve the bottom line for both. Table 8-2 indicates the specific types of help each partner should render to the other. Most of these are tools that are detailed in Chapters 9, 10, and 11. Unfortunately, many of them are not known to most companies. Even if known, they have no experience in using them. And even if experienced, it takes time to go from novice to expert. As a result, companies remain limited in the help they can render suppliers and in the accruing financial benefits.

Table 8-2. Specific types of help in supplier partnerships.

A. From Customer to Supplier	*B. From Supplier to Customer*
1. *Quality*	1. *Quality*
• Design of Experiments (DOE)	• $c_{pk} \geq 2.0$ on important parameters
• Multiple Environment Over Stress Tests (MEOST)	• Certification through process control
• Cost of poor quality (COPQ)	• Failure mode effects analysis (FMEA)
• Meaningful specifications, classification of characteristics	• Virtual elimination of incoming inspection
• Positrol, Process Certification, Pre-control	• Virtual elimination of line defects
• Poka-Yoke	• Virtual elimination of field failures
2. *Cost*	2. *Cost*
• Cost targeting	• Continuous cost reduction (5% to 15% per year)
• Total value engineering	• Early supplier involvement (ESI)
• Group technology	• Value engineering ideas
• Audits	• Standardization assistance
• Financial incentives/penalties	

A. From Customer to Supplier	**B. From Supplier to Customer**
3. *Cycle Time*	3. *Cycle Time*
• Flowcharting	• "Black box" design help
• Cycle time audits	• Reduced lead times
• Focused factories	• Inventory reduction
• Product vs. process flow	• Lead time reductions in the whole supply chain
• Total productive maintenance (TPM)	
• Pull systems	
• Less necessity for forecasting and master schedules	
4. *General*	4. *General*
• Frequent visits (once per week)	• General
• Training and coaching	• Commitment to terminate or reduce work with customer's competition.
• Larger volumes, longer contracts	
• Drastically reduced competition	• Electronic data interchange (EDI)
• Higher profits and ROI	• Help with next tiers of suppliers
• Long-term partnerships	• Networking with other suppliers in the "family"

Criteria for Selecting Partnership Suppliers

Although several factors need to be weighed in selecting a partnership supplier for a company, a few among them are most important:

■ *Shared Values.* There should be compatibility of values of the supplier with those of the customer. A strong ethical foundation must govern their relationship.

■ *Location, Location, Location.* Preferably the supplier should be in close physical proximity to the customer (see next section).

■ *Supplier Size.* Small is super; big is bad. The chances for reform are much greater with a small supplier than a large, bureaucratic entity that may be muscle-bound and inflexible.

■ *Supplier Attitude.* Select a supplier that is humble and willing to learn. Often, survival (i.e., a threat of extinction) can provide powerful inducement.

Supplier Location

There is a traditional view that the very best supplier should be chosen for a particular commodity, regardless of whether the supplier is in the United States, Europe, Asia, or elsewhere. Others argue that labor costs dictate a country—China, for instance—where cheap labor would be an advantage.

Both these approaches have serious flaws. On the first point, the best suppliers may be separated from the customer company by thousands of miles, breaking a fundamental rule of the customer needing to be able to "kick the tires," as it were. The second point makes even less sense. Cheap labor has shifted in the last twenty years—first to Japan, then Korea, Singapore, Hong Kong, Malaysia, Thailand, and now to China. It is not impossible, in the next twenty years, that labor costs may be the lowest in the United States—if not in wages, in terms of productivity.

There is a firm principle governing supplier location:

■ A company should manufacture its products in the same country or region where it sells.

■ A company should buy its parts or subsystems in the same country or region where it manufactures.

Table 8-3 marshals the very cogent arguments against the much-too-common practice of manufacturing in one country and buying products, supposedly "cheaply," in another. Not only are there hidden cost penalties of unstable governments in many countries, as well as currency fluctuations, but there are also strategic/tactical drawbacks. Worst of all, there are tangible costs associated with long cycle time and poor quality.

The conventional wisdom is that an offshore purchase should cost at least 25 percent less than one onshore. But if the tangible factors alone (listed in Table 8-3) are estimated, an offshore purchase should cost 75 percent less—not 25 percent—than an onshore purchase to break even!

Infrastructure of Supply Chain Management

There are companies that operate their supply management processes without a systematic structure and get by. But a well-crafted infrastructure can ensure better and more sustained results. Its elements include:

Table 8-3. The hidden cost penalties of offshore purchase.

Governmental/Political	Strategic/Tactical	Tangible
• Political instability	• Customer bonds weakened	• Inventory/cycle time increased
• Currency exchange rate fluctuations	• Customer-marketing-engineering links poor	• Poor tooling
• U.S. trade barriers	• Early supplier involvement and value engineering much more difficult	• Quality often a casualty
• Foreign/U.S. government regulations		• Extra source inspection costs
• Public Law 98-39	• Visits/tech help/training to suppliers ruled out	• Freight costs higher
• EPA restrictions	• Longer product cycles	• U.S. tariffs
• Product liability exposure	• Design changes more difficult	• Customs delays
• Patent infringements		• Brokerage fees
• Foreign content laws	• Longer lead times	• Port entry fees
• Foreign tax structure	• Schedules must be frozen	• Labor cost escalations
• Foreign work rules		• Cash flow problems
• Standards differences (e.g., EIA vs. JIS)	• Perils of long-range forecasting	• Cost of frozen cash
	• Danger of forward integration	• Premature payments with no guarantee of good, usable products
	• Technology transfer drain	
	• Travel/communica-tion costs increased	
	• Cultural/language barriers	

---

1. Steering Committee

2. Supplier and Distributor Councils

3. Commodity Teams and Distributor/Dealer Teams

Steering Committee

With the CEO of a company (or the division manager in a business) as the chairman, the steering committee consists of members of his senior staff. Their responsibilities include:

- Drafting a vision/mission statement and committing the company to the entire chain of supply management

- Communicating the importance of supply chain management to the whole organization

- Establishing goals for supply management: quality, cost, lead-time, reduction of the supply/distributor/dealer base, and reduction of the part number base

- Selecting commodities for prioritization

- Selecting commodity teams

- Monitoring partnership progress and acting as the "supreme court" to resolve conflicts internally, with suppliers or with distributors/dealers

- Provide recognition and rewards to commodity teams and to outstanding partnership suppliers, distributors, and dealers

Supplier/Distributor/Dealer/Servicer Councils and Conferences

The objective of these company-supplier and company-distributor/dealer councils are to:

- Advance partnership for mutual economic benefit

- Provide a forum for policy, expectations, plans, and consultations

- Resolve conflicts and evaluate recommendations

- Measure partnership progress

The structure of the councils consists of an equal number of company and supplier representatives (and distributor/dealer senior management). They meet two to four times a year and plan an annual conference for state of the company messages, technological developments and other issues. The most productive aspect of these council meetings is the ability to air mutual concerns and frustrations and seeing them quickly and effectively resolved. No company can afford to do without them.

The Commodity Team

This is the workhorse of supply chain management. No company can achieve breakthrough results without it. Its main purpose is advancing supplier development, along technical and business lines, so that a supplier can grow into becoming a viable partner of the company. (The formulation of the downstream company-distributor/dealer teams and their main objective, which is the development of the distributor/dealer network as a viable partner, is the same as that of the commodity team.)

The team consists of a team leader, along with members drawn from the old department structures of engineering, purchasing, quality, and the partnership supplier as a core group. It is reinforced, as needed, by specialists in the technology of the commodity, tooling, and other disciplines. It should be a full-time activity. Companies can evaluate full-time commodity team effectiveness by estimating team costs (A) of payroll and travel, for example, and projecting potential savings (B) in terms of cost, quality, and cycle time improvements. A formula that any reasonable management will not refuse is to show that $1/2$ B ≥ 2A—in short, a 4:1 return on investment (ROI). This is because traditionally costs are underestimated and savings are overestimated. Our experience has shown that $1/3$ B ≥ 3A—that is, a 9:1 ROI.

Just as in the case of a concurrent engineering team, a part-time team spells part-time, mediocre results. To be most effective, the team should be at the plants of the partnership suppliers most of the time. Having team members sitting chained to their desks because of headcount and travel freezes is the surest way for the supply chain to atrophy. Commodity teams are part of the order fulfillment process in a horizontal process-centered organization (see Figure 6-2) as opposed to a vertical departmentalized organization.

The commodity team's initial responsibilities include:

1. Establishing goals and timetables for the commodity: quality, cost, cycle time, maximum number of partnership suppliers (typically two or three), and reduced part numbers

2. Reviewing the technology of the commodity for growth, obsolescence, or breakthroughs

3. Designing guidelines for engineers that would be helpful to partnership suppliers

4. Running Design of Experiments (DOE) studies with design teams to translate product specifications into component specs

5. Promoting the outsourcing of the entire "black box" design to capable partnership suppliers

6. Benchmarking best-in-class companies for superior supplier chain practices

7. Benchmarking new suppliers, including transplant suppliers

8. Training commodity team members in a number of supplier development techniques, especially quality, cost, and cycle time improvement

9. Thinning out the supplier base down to a finalist list

10. Selecting partnership suppliers (typically two) based on actual visits and detailed audits

Partnership Supplier Development

It is often assumed that the partnership supplier is more a master of the component's or product's technology than is the customer company. So what need is there to help the supplier's development? In many ways, the supplier is far less knowledgeable about all nontechnological disciplines, including cost, quality, cycle time, and management. Table 8-4 is a list of development techniques where coaching becomes essential. Of course, the commodity teams must become professional in their own companies in these techniques before they can presume to help the supplier. Otherwise, they could be accused of the Ford slogan coined by skeptical suppliers: "Do as I say, don't do as I do"—a preacher command rather than a practitioner's helpfulness. The list is a veritable miniversion of the Ultimate Six Sigma contents of this book. To be effective, the commodity team should visit the partnership supplier once a week and follow up on assignments and "to do's" of the previous week. The process continues until the supplier's development no longer requires nursing and there is a momentum for business excellence, as determined by the customer.

(text continues on page 149)

Table 8-4. Supplier development: issues to address, by area.

Area	Development Techniques
Leadership/ Management	• Encourage a shift from management to leadership. • Encourage supplier's leaders to free the creative genie in every employee. • Encourage driving out fear among the employees. • Encourage leaders to walk the talk. • Conduct comprehensive supplier training/workshops.
Organization	• Encourage horizontal cross-functional teams, rather than a vertical department organization. • Encourage the reduction in the number of layers of management. • Encourage the reduction of paperwork, e-mail, policy manuals, and endless meetings to reduce bureaucracy.

Employees	• Encourage job redesign to tap the fountain of inner motivation in all employees.
	• Encourage employee study of financial statements and the formation of self-directed minicompanies.
Quality/Cycle Time/Cost	• Conduct detailed quality and cycle time audits.
	• Review audit weaknesses and work with supplier to overcome them.
	• Conduct a plant tour to pluck the "low lying fruit" in quality, cost, and cycle time.
	• Draw joint plans and timetable for longer-range improvements.
	• Gather, analyze, and reduce the cost of poor quality (COPQ).
	• Flowchart the supplier cycle time—from purchase order to customer delivery.
	• Eliminate or drastically reduce all non-value-added steps.
	• Encourage forming focus factories and manufacturing cells.
	• Encourage plant rearrangement from process flow to product flow.
	• Institute total productive maintenance (TPM) and measure overall equipment effectiveness (OEE) progress.
	• Introduce "pull" system and lesson dependence on forecasts and master schedules.
	• Drastically reduce setup time/changeover time.
	• Institutionalize Shainin/Bhote DOE, MEOST, Total VE, and NOAC with demonstration projects.
Design	• Encourage formation of concurrent engineering team.
	• Encourage design for manufacturing (DFM) principles and practices.
	• Act as liaison between customer's design team and supplier technical personnel to make early supplier involvement (ESI) a way of life.

(continues)

Table 8-4. (Continued.)

Area	Development Techniques
Second- and Third-Tier Suppliers	• Encourage partnership relationships with second- and third-tier suppliers. • Strengthen the purchasing power of suppliers by banding them together for joint purchases. • Encourage helping these subsuppliers with the same type of development help being rendered by the company. • Institutionalize commodity teams.
Manufacturing	• Introduce the disciplines of Process Certification, Positrol, and Precontrol. • Equip operators with Poka-Yoke sensors to prevent operator-controllable errors. • Encourage monitoring effectiveness of analyzing quality defects. • Introduce "field escape" control. • Ensure that the accuracy of measuring instruments: product accuracy is 5:1.
Field	• Ensure adequacy of packaging and transportation. • Encourage professional failure analysis capability. • Ensure completeness of manuals, installation instructions.
Support Services	• Encourage the concept, implementation, and measurement of the Next Operation as Customer (NOAC). • Encourage making the internal customer the scorekeeper and primary evaluator of the internal supplier. • Encourage out-of-the-box thinking to revolutionize business processes.
Results	• Establish metrics in all areas. • Set up a "customer effectiveness index" to monitor customer feedback.

Supplier/Distributor Evaluation of the Company as Partner

Most of this chapter has been about how to evaluate, measure, and improve upstream supplier performance or downstream distributor/dealer performance. But it is equally important to know how well the partnership is working from the supplier/distributor perspective. Progressive companies like to be in the position of being perceived by the partnership supplier or distributor as their best customer. Table 8-5 is a typical scorecard by which suppliers or distributors rate their customer company *vis-à-vis* their best customer. Feedback of this nature can have a sobering effect on a customer company's ego.

CASE STUDY

BENCHMARK COMPANY IN THE AREA OF SUPPLY CHAIN MANAGEMENT[2]—TOYOTA

Toyota Motor Corp. has been recognized not only as the most effective car company in the world, but also as the preeminent manufacturing company anywhere on the globe (see Chapter 13). What is not generally recognized is the fact that it is also a giant in the area of supply chain management; that it has been in that leadership role since shortly after World War II; and that it has completely revolutionized relationships between a company and its partnership suppliers.

As early as 1949, Toyota made a dramatic departure from vertical integration to create three famous companies as partnership suppliers—Nippondenso, Aisin Seiki, and Toyota Gosei. Each was also given major design responsibilities.

By the late 1950s, Toyota reduced its own added value to the average vehicle from 75 percent down to 25 percent. Even 50 percent of its final assembly was farmed out to partnership suppliers.

Toyota's supply base is only 190 as compared with over 2,000 at GM and over 1,500 at Ford. It manages this base with a supply management staff of 185, compared with nearly 4,000 at GM and more than 2,000 at Ford.

Toyota pioneered the concept of continuous cost reductions from its suppliers when the common practice was to accept constantly increasing costs in an era of rampant inflation.

When the "oil shock" of the Arab embargo hit Japan in 1973, it extended the concept to its second-tier suppliers, not by squeezing them, but by teaching them its world-famous Toyota Production System (TPS) to go from batch production and the "push" system to single-piece flow and the "pull" system.

Toyota has further extended supply chain management to third-tier suppliers.

(continues)

(But it has yet to capitalize on the last extension to its fourth-tier raw material suppliers that still control more than 40 percent of its manufacturing costs.)

Other supply chain management innovations pioneered by Toyota include:

1. *Establishing Mutual Help Groups.* These help groups were established among forty-two of the car maker's largest and most important suppliers, divided into six groups of seven suppliers and requested, with Toyota's help, to conduct one major improvement activity each month. These suppliers were then persuaded to set up similar networks with their second-tier suppliers with the objective of lean production as a way of life. The result: A continuous cost reduction on every part, every year, from every supplier. The suppliers were delighted because of the extra profits they could realize with their other customers.

2. *Early Supplier Involvement.* ESI became an integral part of Toyota's new product development with its hard-driving shusa—or team leader (see Chapter 12).

3. *Cost Targeting.* This practice obsoleted the three-bid syndrome and put the customer company in the driver's seat for determining the price.

Self-Assessment/Audit on Supply Chain Management: Implementing Disciplines by Company Type and Months to Complete

1. *Self-Assessment/Audit.* Table 8-6 is a self-assessment/audit to determine a company's business health in the area of supply chain management. It has four key characteristics with sixteen disciplines required for practical implementation, each with a maximum of 5 points, for a total of 80 points.

2. *Implementation Disciplines and Commentary on Time Required for Completion by Company Type.* Supply chain management marshals disciplines that go beyond a company's direct influence and control Hence, companies—especially Type C companies—that do not really trust their suppliers are reluctant to build bridges with partnership suppliers. Type A companies, on the other hand, recognize the gold mine of supply chain management and can implement almost all the disciplines within one year.

Table 8-5. Supplier/distributor evaluation of the customer company.

Item	Company Rating *					Best Customer Rating				
	1	2	3	4	5	1	2	3	4	5
1. Effectiveness of overall partnership										
2. Equitable sharing of profit increases										
3. Increases in business volume										
4. Longer-term agreements										
5. Ethics, trust—in action, not words										
6. Transparency—sharing of costs, strategy, technology										
7. Concrete development help— in quality, cost, cycle time, leadership										
8. Development help to second-, third-tier suppliers and dealers and servicers										
9. Training: seminars, workshops, demonstration projects										
10. Early supplier/distributor involvement										
11. Granting "black box" design responsibility to supplier										
12. Clear, meaningful, mutually determined specifications										
13. Financial incentives for quality, delivery, performance										
14. Royalties for ideas, even without an order										
15. Receptivity to suggestions										
16. Forecast accuracy, dependability										
17. Schedule sharing										
18. Electronic data interchange										
19. Volume variable pricing										
20. Networking initiatives										

* Rating: 1 ≥ lowest; 5 ≥ highest

Table 8-6. Supply chain management: key characteristics, essential disciplines, audit scores, and time to complete each discipline—by company type (80 points).

Key Characteristics	Essential Disciplines	Rating 1-5 *	Months to Complete, By Company Type		
			A	B	C
1-1 Company Policies	1. As many of the company's activities that are peripheral in importance have been outsourced; but all core competencies have been retained within the company.		6	12	18
	2. Piece-part procurement from many sources has been replaced with black-box procurement from suppliers[1] at the design stage.		9	12	24
	3. The supply chain base has been greatly reduced to concentrate on a win-win partnership with a few key supply chain members.		6	9	18
1-2 Partnership Supplier Selection	1. Procurement has been from the same geographic region where manufacturing is located (and manufacturing is from the same geographic region where sales are located).		12	18	—
	2. Suppliers have been chosen based on ethics, integrity, trust, and values aligned to those of the company.		12	18	—
	3. Suppliers that are small, humble, willing to learn, and nearby have				

	been chosen in preference to large, bureaucratic, distant ones.	9	15	—
	4. Current, but deficient, suppliers have been chosen for partnership and improvement with coaching, rather than selecting suppliers thousands of miles away.	12	18	—
1-3 Supply Chain Infrastructure	1. A top management steering committee is in existence to oversee and monitor progress.	6	—	—
	2. Commodity teams have been in place to render active help to suppliers.	9	15	—
	3. Supplier/distributor councils have been in place to build productive relationships with suppliers.	12	18	—
	4. Networking and benchmarking among suppliers/distributors has been promoted.	12	—	—
	5. Tangible help has been extended two levels down to suppliers of current supplies.	18	—	—
1-4 Supplier Development	1. Active, concrete, and continuous help has been rendered to suppliers, especially in quality, cost, and cycle time.	9	15	—
	2. Commodity teams have trained and coached suppliers in all needed disciplines, with a preamble that the commodity team members have themselves.	12	18	—

(continues)

Table 8-6. (Continued.)

Key Characteristics	Essential Disciplines	Rating 1-5 *	Months to Complete, By Company Type		
			A	B	C
	been made professional in such disciplines.		12	18	—
	3. Periodic feedback from suppliers on their perceptions of partnership effectiveness has been institutionalized.		12	18	—
	4. The company has extended its influence and development of suppliers beyond its first-tier suppliers to at least its second- and third-tier suppliers.				

* The rater grades each discipline on a scale of 1< > 5, with 1 being the lowest rating and 5 being the highest

1. In this table, the term supplier is limited to partnership suppliers.

Part Three

The Power of Ultimate Six Sigma
The High Octane Engines of Thrust

CHAPTER 9

Quality: From Wheel-Spinning to World Class

There is only one definition of quality that counts. Quality is
what the customer says it is. . . .   —W. EDWARDS DEMING

The Disappointing Returns on the Investment in Quality

No discipline, in recent times, has received more attention than quality; and yet no discipline has produced less bottom-line results, relative to the effort, as has quality. Chapter 1 detailed the fads, potions, and nostrums of the quality movement in the last fifty years. It also showed the ineffectiveness of most quality systems and quality tools that were forced down the throats of a reluctant industry.

By contrast, this chapter deals with powerful tools that can resurrect quality to its rightful place in the pantheon of business disciplines. It is useful, however, to first survey the progression of quality from the dismal levels that continue to be practiced among many companies to higher levels approaching and finally reaching world-class quality, with Power of Six Sigma as its pinnacle.

The Four Stages of Quality—Assessing a Company's Quality Health

Table 9-1 is a matrix of four stages of quality that I had developed in ten areas—namely, the company's customers, leadership, organization, employees, tools, supply

(text continues on page 162)

157

Table 9-1. The four stages of quality (a company's quality health chart).

Area	Subarea	Stage 1 Awareness (3 Sigma)	Stage 2 Exploration (4 Sigma)	Stage 3 Commitment (5 Sigma)	Stage 4 World Class (6 Sigma)
Customer	Company Objective	Profit	Shareholder value	Customer value	Stakeholder value
	Loyalty/Retention	No concern	Defections ignored	Measured, but no action	Chief customer officer (CCO) and SWAT team
	Customer Base	Indiscriminate	Larger, the better	Fixation on market share	Core customers
	Role of Quality Professional	No contact with customer	Concentration only on defects	Auditing	Customer's advocate in company
Leadership	% of Full Worker Creativity Released	None	Start	10%	50%
	Improvement Goal	None	10:1 in 10 years	10:1 in 5 years	10:1 in 2 years
	Responsibility for Quality	No focal point	Quality function—responsibility but no authority	Quality function—"the cop"	All functions—quality, the coach
	Quality Perspective	A necessary evil	High quality, low cost, an oxymoron	An economic imperative	A superordinate value
Organization	Structure	Vertical management	Departmental organization chart	Matrix management	Cross-functional team
	Rules and Regulations	Overbearing, burdensome	Bureaucratic	Moderate	Few—only if it serves customer

	16	12	8	Maximum of 5
Levels Between CEO and Worker (large company)				
Role of Quality in Organization	Cop	Full responsibility, no authority	Auditor	Coach, teacher
Employees				
Climate	Fear, alienation	Suspicion	Participatory	Freedom
Job Security	None	Layoff churn	Mainly line workers laid off	Managers laid off first, before worker
Pay Raises	Minimal	Small, *pro forma*	Narrow differentials	No raises, but large bonuses for performance
Promotions	Minimal	Unclear guidelines	Based on performance	Based on growth potential and entrepreneurship
Empowerment	Stage 1, 2	Stage 3	Stage 4,5	Stages 6, 7, 8, 9
Supply Chain Management				
Relationships	Adversarial	Suspicion	Limited trust	Full partnership
Outsourcing	Vertical integration	Make vs. buy	Only piece parts outsourced	Only core competencies retained in-house
Help to Suppliers	None	Rare visits	Audits	Concrete, continuous help
Supplier Development	None	None	None	Full coaching—with commodity teams

(continues)

Table 9-1. (Continued.)

Area	Subarea	Stage 1 Awareness (3 Sigma)	Stage 2 Exploration (4 Sigma)	Stage 3 Commitment (5 Sigma)	Stage 4 World Class (6 Sigma)
Tools	Problem Solving	Sorting, brute force	Seven tools of quality control (QC)	DMAIC (design, measure, analyze, improve, control)	DOE (Shainin/Bhote)
	Reliability	Limited to customer complaints	Military life tests	FMEA (failure mode effects analysis)	MEOST (Multiple Environment Over Stress Tests)
	Support Services	No metrics	Flow charting	DMAIC	NOAC (Next Operation as Customer)
	Customer Requirements	Voice of the engineer	Market research	QFD (quality function deployment)	Mass customization
Design	Structure	Design in isolation	Engineering/ manufacturing team	Concurrent engineering (CE)	CE + ESI (early supplier involvement)
	Objective	Toss over the wall	Design for lowest product cost	Design for quality	Design for customer "wow"
	Product Liability	No preventive action	Minimal documentation	Minimum documentation	Product liability analysis (PLA)
	Robustness	No action	No action	Taguchi, orthogonal array	Variables Search
	Derating	No policy	10%	30%	>50%
Manufacturing	Yield Improvement	Brute-force inspection	SPC	DMAIC	Process characterization/

	Murphy's Law	ISO-9000	QS-9000	Positrol and Process Certification
Process Error Control	Murphy's Law	Control charts	Precontrol	Poka-Yoke
Operator Error Control	Brute-force inspection			
Total Productive Maintenance (TPM)	Fix when broke	Corrective maintenance	Preventive maintenance	Factory overall effectiveness (FOE) >85%
Services				
Internal Customer	"The enemy"	No attention	Next Operation as Customer (NOAC)	NOAC with incentives/penalties
Structure	None	Ad hoc	Intradepartment teams	Business process reengineering
Improvement Techniques	None	Pareto, C&E diagrams, control charts	Brainstorming, force field analysis	Total value engineering, process redesign, out-of-the-box thinking
Results				
Cost of Poor Quality: % of Sales	>25%	15%	10%	< 2%
Field Reliability % Failure/Year	>15%	3–5%	1%	< 500 ppm
Outgoing Quality Defect %	>3%	1%	5,000 ppm	< 100 ppm
Total Defects/Unit (TDPU)	>10	1	0.1	0.01
C_{PK} (critical parameters)	—	< 1.0	1.33	>2.0

chain management, design, manufacturing, services, and results. Each area has three to five subareas. I developed the matrix as a template to measure the quality health of any company and have used it to assess more than a hundred companies. The most important use of the matrix is highlighting the pockets of weakness and prioritizing urgent action by the company's senior management.

Stage 1—called the stage of awareness—can be likened, in quality health terms, to being "terminally ill," or in sigma terms, as a poor 3-Sigma company in the dark ages of quality. Unfortunately, around 70 percent of companies are still in stage 1.

Stage 2—called the stage of exploration—is the equivalent of being "hospitalized" in quality health terms. Signifying a modest 4-Sigma company, stage 2 is characteristic of companies that have embraced total quality management (TQM) yet have not profited from TQM. About 20 percent of companies have reached stage 2.

Stage 3—called the stage of commitment—is representative of a company in good quality health but in need of frequent checkups. It can aspire to a 5-Sigma level. Charitably, "hyped" Six Sigma companies begin to enter stage 3—spanning about 9 percent of the population.

Stage 4—called the world-class stage—is associated with a company in robust quality health that's truly a Six Sigma company, not in name alone, but in fact. Only a handful of companies have that distinction.

Powerful Quality/Reliability Tools to Solve/Prevent Chronic Quality Problems

There are five blockbuster tools that can achieve at least an order or two of magnitude improvements in quality in any corporation. I originated and used all of them at Motorola to achieve the 10:1, 100:1, and almost 1000:1 quality improvement in the company. None of these tools are used or even known by the hyped Six Sigma companies or their black belt practitioners:

1. Design of Experiments (DOE)—Shainin/Bhote (not classical or Taguchi)—for 100:1 and 1000:1 quality improvements.

2. Multiple Environment Over Stress Tests (MEOST)—for 10:1 and 100:1 reduction of field failures.

3. Poka-Yoke—for eliminating operator-controllable errors.

4. Cost of Poor Quality (COPQ)—for reducing COPQ costs from 10 percent to 20 percent of sales to less than 2 percent of sales, thereby doubling or even tripling a

company's profits. (At Motorola, we reduced COPQ costs by $9 billion over a period of ten years!)

5. Mass Customization—for capturing the "voice of the customer." Although quality function deployment (QFD), with its House of Quality matrix, became popular in the 1980s and 1990s, it has fallen out of favor for several reasons:

- QFD requires a large group of customers with similar needs. The trend, with mass customization, is going the other way.

- The way QFD gathers customer requirements can be flawed.

- The amassing of more than forty customer requirements—a common QFD mistake—can be unwieldy.

- Most QFD studies stop at the first cascade—translating the "what" of the customer into the "how" of engineering specifications. The remaining cascades—parts, processes, and tests—should also be deployed.

Design of Experiments (DOE): Shainin/Bhote Not Classical or Taguchi—Problem-Solving Tool Par Excellence

Starting in the 1930s, the late Dorian Shainin—who was more effective than Dr. W. Edwards Deming and Dr. Joseph M. Juran put together in problem solving—introduced a series of DOE techniques that are simple, easy to understand and implement, cost-effective, and above all, statistically powerful. As a disciple of Shainin for the last forty years, I enhanced and honed his techniques at Motorola, especially since 1982, when our chairman, Bob Galvin, challenged us to achieve a 1000:1 quality improvement in ten years. Without our DOE, Motorola would not have achieved the spectacular results that accorded it worldwide fame. The record is captured in my two landmark books.[1] The first, published in 1991, has been translated into four European languages, and more than 100,000 copies have been sold. The second edition, published in 2000, is even more comprehensive—with additional techniques, case studies, and workshop exercises—and it has received even further worldwide acclaim.

Weaknesses of Classical/Taguchi DOE and Strengths of Shainin/Bhote DOE

Although all three approaches to DOE—classical, Taguchi, and Shainin/Bhote are superior to all other problem-solving techniques, the classical and Taguchi methods

Table 9-2. Classical/Taguchi DOE weaknesses and Shainin/Bhote DOE strengths.

Characteristic	Classical/ Taguchi Weaknesses	Shainin/Bhote Strengths
Philosophy	Causal factors determined by guesses, opinions, hunches, and theories.	Causal factors determined by "talking to the parts. The parts are smarter than the engineers."
Statistical Power	Weak: All second-order and higher-order interactions confounded with main effects.	Excellent separation and quantification of main and interaction effects.
Versatility	Poor: Only 1 or 2 techniques	Excellent: 12 techniques
Comprehension/ Implementation	Difficult for engineers to even understand, much less use.	Easy, even for direct labor to understand and implement.
Training Time	1 to 3 weeks	2 days (1 day instruction and 1 day of hands-on practice)
Cost	High: Up to 5-10 trials per problem, because of wrong guesses.	Low: Clue-generation tools reduce number of trials to 1 to 2.
Results	Modest: 2:1 to 3:1 improvement at best.	High: 5:1 to >100:1 improvement. Average: over 10:1.
Worker Involvement	Black belts only: 1 out of every 100 workers.	Move to convert a whole factory into black belt performers!
Climate	Passivity among most employees.	Joy in the workplace. DOE success begets more success.

Figure 9-1. Contributions of DOE to business excellence: a spider chart.

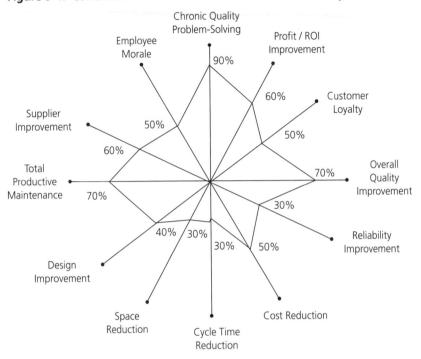

The total length of each spoke in the spider chart represents a maximum of 100 percent benefit. The contribution of a particular technique (in this case DOE) is shown as a percentage of overall benefit.

have fundamental, philosophical, statistical, cost, and effectiveness weaknesses that have rendered their appeal an illusionary mirage. Table 9-2 lists the weaknesses of classical/Taguchi DOE versus the Shainin/Bhote DOE strengths in a number of important characteristics.

With this brief background on the three approaches to DOE, the remainder of this section focuses on the Shainin/Bhote DOE. Figure 9-1 graphically portrays the very significant contributions of DOE to business excellence in the form of a "spider chart."

DOE aids so profoundly in so many areas—problem solving; profit/return on investment; customer loyalty/retention; overall quality breakthrough; reliability; cost reduction; cycle time reduction; space reduction; robust design; total productive maintenance (TPM), supplier chain optimization; and employee morale—that no company can afford to do without it.

Figure 9-2. Problem-solving/variation reduction block diagram.

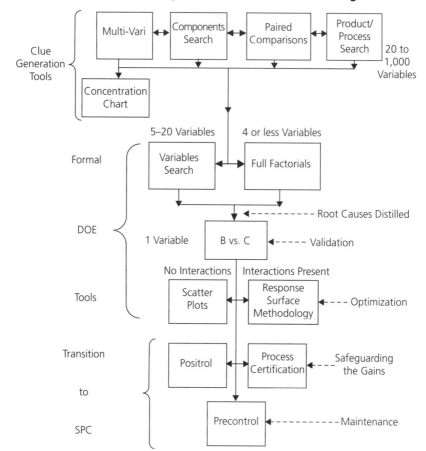

Method of Achieving Success

The versatility of the twelve Shainin/Bhote DOE techniques are shown in block diagram form in Figure 9-2.

In all my consultations, I have had 98 percent success in marshaling one or more of these tools. (The only problems that are difficult to solve are when a full 100 percent of the product is bad, indicating a poor design. But even in such cases, many of these designs have been corrected using our Rolls-Royce technique—Variables Search.)

Problem-Solving Tools: "Talking to the Parts"

One of the brilliant features of the Shainin/Bhote DOE is the ability to generate clues in problem solving by "talking to the parts" as compared with relying on the guesses, hunches, theories, and opinions of engineers, which form the basis of the poorer classical DOE and the Taguchi DOE (see again Table 9-2).

There are four simple but powerful clue generation tools—all of which talk to the parts. A brief summary of each technique, with a simple case study example, reveals its power. The reader is directed to my earlier book, *World Class Quality—Using Design of Experiments to Make It Happen,*[2] for a much more detailed treatment of each technique, including case studies and workshop examples.

Multi-Vari[3]

Objective	To reduce a large number of unmanageable variables to a smaller family of related variables containing the root cause (known as Red X). The major families are time-to-time; unit-to-unit; and within unit, with subfamilies in each.
Where Applicable	In process-oriented manufacturing. Multi-Vari gives a quick snapshot of product variations going through the process, without massive historical data that is of very little value.
Sample Size	Minimum nine to fifteen units, or until 80 percent of the historic variation is captured.
Methodology	Take periodic product samples of three to five units at a time drawn from the process and plot the variations in time-to-time, unit-to-unit, and within unit families. The Red X is always in the family with the largest variation.

Components Search[4]

Objective	To home in on the Red X from among hundreds of components in a product.
Where Applicable	In assembly-oriented manufacturing, where the units are capable of disassembly and reassembly.
Sample Size	Two units—one very good, the other very bad, with as wide a separation between the two.
Methodology	Swap a suspected part or subassembly from the good unit to the bad and vice versa. If the good unit remains good, the part or subassembly is not the problem. If the good unit becomes completely bad and the bad unit completely good, the part or subassembly is the Red X. If the good unit becomes partially bad and the bad unit becomes partially good, the part or subassembly is important along with another untried part (indicative of an interaction effect).

CASE STUDY

USING MULTI-VARI

A printed circuit board with 1,000 solder connections was running at a defect rate of 1,500 parts per million (ppm) for several months at Motorola's Melbourne plant in Australia. A Multi-Vari study was run: 1) at three times—9 A.M., 9:30 A.M., and 10 A.M.; 2) with five panels, each with five boards for each of the three times; and 3) the locations of the solder defects were noted on each of the seventy-five boards.

The Multi-Vari results indicated that there was little variation in the three time trials; little variation from panel to panel; and little variation from board to board. The Red X family was within each board. A concentration chart of the exact location of these solder defects indicated 1) an accumulation of pinhole rejects in the top-middle area of the board and 2) two I.F. (intermediate frequency) cans displayed poor solder. The remaining 980 connections had perfect solder.

The manufacturing team working with me eliminated the pinhole defects by removing the slight tilt of the panel fixtures as they progressed through the wave-solder machine. That reduced the defect rate to around 500 ppm—a 3:1 improvement in half a day. We then tackled the I.F. can solder problem by changing the ratio of the hole size in the board to the lead diameter in the I.F. cans. That took one day of trial and error, but we got the defect rate down to zero ppm—not bad for one-and-a-half-day's work!

Paired Comparisons[5]

Objective	To determine, among many quality characteristics or parameters common to both good and bad units, which of them are important in explaining the difference between good and bad units and which parameters are unimportant.
Where Applicable	In assembly-oriented manufacturing, where the units cannot be disassembled and reassembled without damaging or destroying them.
Sample Size	Six or eight good units and six or eight bad units, with as large a difference between them as possible.
Methodology	Select six or eight of the best and six or eight of the worst units. List as many parameters as possible that might explain the difference (e.g., electrical, mechanical, chemical, metallurgical, and

---

CASE STUDY

USING COMPONENTS SEARCH

A tape deck being supplied from Motorola's Seguin plant in Texas to General Motors was experiencing an azimuth (i.e., stereo sound unbalance) problem for over two months. A team of direct-labor people decided to tackle the problem. They selected one tape deck that had a low unbalance of 2 db, and another at an unacceptable unbalance of 5 db. Figure 9-3 shows a simple Components Search experiment. When the team swapped the diaphragm from the good unit to the bad and vice versa, the good unit stayed good, the bad stayed bad. Therefore, the diaphragm was not the problem. The same happened when the capstan and flywheel were swapped, and also with the pressure rollers. But when the head arm and lever assembly were swapped, a complete reversal of good and bad took place. It was the culprit Red X.

Figure 9-3. Components Search: tape deck azimuth example.

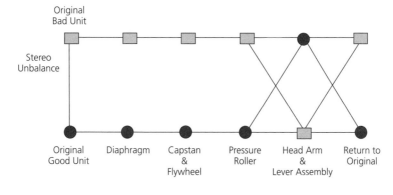

---

cosmetic). Measure each parameter. Rank each parameter on all sixteen units from the smallest reading to the largest, or vice versa. (This rank test, called the Tukey test, is one of the most powerful tools in DOE work.)* Divide this ranking into three zones. The top zone (called the top end count) should have read-

---

*The Tukey test is named after the renowned John Tukey of Princeton University, who also gave expression to two terms widely used today in the Internet age—"digital" and "binary."

CASE STUDY

USING PAIRED COMPARISONS

In an investigation of the optical accuracy of a contact lens, six of the best lenses and six of the worst lenses were selected. Five lens parameters were measured on each of the twelve lenses; they were cylinder (i.e., the curvature in the front side of the lens), cylinder BP side (i.e., the curvature in the back side of the lens), ultra-violet absorbence, polarizer, and mold fabrication. Table 9-3 shows only two of these parameters arranged in ascending rank.

Table 9-3: Paired Comparison ranking and Tukey test.

	UV Absorbence %		*Cylinder (Curvature: mm)*
↑	7.4 B	↑	0.016 G
Top	7.8 B		0.018 G
End	8.7 B		0.020 G
Count	8.8 B	Top	0.026 G
X	8.9 G	End	0.030 G
	9.1 G	Count	0.030 G
Overlap	9.3 B	X	0.048 B
	9.8 B	Bottom	0.051 B
	9.9 G	End	0.051 B
	10.9 G	Count	0.053 B
Bottom	11.1 B	↓	0.055 B
End Count	11.2 G		0.056 B

B = Bad lens; G = Good lens

Parameter	Top End Count	Bottom End Count	Total End Count	Confidence
UV Absorbence	4	1	5	Not enough confidence: <90%
Cylinder	6	6	12	>90% (actually 99.6%)

The results show that UV absorbence, with less than 90 percent confidence, is not important as a parameter in explaining the difference between good and bad lenses; whereas the cylinder is very important—a huge 99.6 percent confidence—in explaining the difference between good and bad lenses.

ings only from the good units (or vice versa). The bottom zone should have readings opposite to the top zone—that is, from bad units if the top zone has only good units (or vice versa). The middle zone (called overlap) contains both good and bad units. Add the numbers in the top and bottom zones. This is the total end count. Only if the total end count is six or more, is there 90 percent or higher confidence that the particular parameter is important in explaining the difference between good and bad units.

Product/Process Search[6]

Objective   To determine, among many process parameters, which are important and which are unimportant in explaining the difference between good and bad product produced by the process.

Where Applicable   For all processes and machines in process-oriented or assembly-oriented manufacturing.

Sample Size   Six or eight good units (product) and six or eight bad units (product), with as large a difference as possible.

Methodology   Allow a sufficient number of units (product) to go through the process. Measure each of the important process parameters (actual readings, not settings) that are associated with each product as it goes through the process. At the end of the process, select six or eight of the best units (product) and six or eight of the worst units—with as large a difference between the good and

the bad as possible. Then rank each process parameter associated with the twelve or sixteen products in ascending or descending order of magnitude. Apply the Tukey test.

As in Paired Comparisons, if the total end count is six or more,
that parameter is important in the process and should be carefully
monitored. If the total end count is less than six, that process
parameter is not important and its tolerance can be opened up
and its cost reduced.

Variables Search[7]

The Variables Search can be used to solve chronic quality problems in production, following the generation of clues from prior Multi-Vari, Components Search, Paired
Comparisons, or Product/Process Search experiments. But its greatest use is at the
design stage of a product or process, *to prevent problems going into production in the first*

CASE STUDY

USING PRODUCT/PROCESS SEARCH

In a plastic injection molding machine that was producing up to a 40 percent
defect rate for short shots in a toy product, eight process parameters were considered important. A Product/Process Search was conducted and the eight best
and eight worst products were ranked in terms of each process parameter and
their total end counts determined, as shown in Table 9-4.

Table 9-4. Product/Process Search.

Parameter	Total End Count	Confidence	Important
Mold Temperature	4	< 90%	No
Material Temperature	8	> 90%	Yes
Pressure	2	< 90%	No
Back Pressure	8	> 90%	Yes
Injection Speed	6	90%	Yes
Screw Speed	2	< 90%	No
Mold Vents	2	< 90%	No
Injection Time	2	< 90%	No

place. Because of its vital importance, the Variables Search technique is explained in greater depth, along with a case study to demonstrate its effectiveness.

Variables Search Objectives

1. To separate the important variables from the unimportant ones

2. To tightly control the important variables with a $^c p_K$ of 2.0 or more

3. To open up the tolerances of the unimportant variables to reduce costs

The detailed procedure, outlined in my book *World Class Quality, Second Edition,* is ideal if there are five or more variables to investigate.

Test of Significance. Rules 1 and 2 should both pass. Rule 1: The three best levels should *all* outrank the three marginal levels. Rule 2: The $\overline{d}$ ratio should be a minimum of 1.25, where D is the difference between the medians of the three B levels and the three M levels and $\overline{d}$ the average of the ranges seen within the three B and the three M levels.

> ### A COMMENTARY ON THE DOE CLUE-GENERATION TECHNIQUE
>
> At a first exposure to these clue-generation techniques, engineers tend to dismiss them as too simple. After all, they say, the parts did not go to college! And the higher they are on the technical ladder, the more skeptical they are. But, as often happens, manufacturing engineers, manufacturing technicians, and manufacturing line operators reach for these techniques as a drowning man reaches for a floating log. They've been stuck with problems they haven't been able to solve, and they've gotten little real help from cloud nine engineers. And these clue-generation techniques have solved problem after problem for them. One of the distinct pleasures in the DOE business is to see how line operators solve problems with these tools, to see their eyes light up with joy at their accomplishments. And all that the engineering leaders can say is, "There go my people, I must follow them, for I am their leader!"

5. If the $D/\overline{d}$ ratio is greater than 1.25, stage 1 is successful. It means that the right variables have been captured.

6. If the $D/\overline{d}$ ratio is less than 1.25, one of the following possibilities exists:

B vs. C Validation[8]

C stands for a current product, B for a better or improved product. The purpose of a B vs. C test is to validate or verify that the improvement is effective and permanent. Often, designers think that they have achieved a product improvement, only to discover a week or two later that the improvement has vanished. They find themselves thrown back to square one. To avoid these premature judgments, it is necessary to go back to the old design to see if the problem has reappeared, then return to the new design to see if the improvement is reconfirmed. This back-and-forth process must be repeated twice. It is the equivalent of turning a light switch "on" and turning it "off."

Then the three "B" readings and the three "C" readings must be arranged in descending rank order. Only if the three Bs outrank the three Cs can there be a 95 percent confidence that the B product is significantly better than the C product. A mixed rank order would indicate that a significant improvement could not be validated. (Note: The sequence of testing three Bs and three Cs must be randomized.)

The B vs. C test is also very useful in determining a reliability improvement very quickly. Usually, a design change for reliability takes months of exposure in the field to verify. No one can afford that length of time. And so half-baked improvements are prematurely made and only much later does anyone discover that the design change was ineffective.

Product Optimization[9]

Based on forty years of experience in working with engineers, I can bluntly state that as a rule, 90 percent of engineering specifications are wrong. How, then, can realistic specifications and realistic tolerances be established by the design team? One simple, graphical, and effective way is with Scatter Plots. Scatter Plots can be used if there are negligible interaction effects between two or more input variables. If the interactions are suspected to be significant, a DOE technique called Response Surface Methodology (RSM) 50 is used. (For a detailed treatment of Scatter Plots and RSM, the reader can review Chapters 16 and 17 in my book *World Class Quality—Using Design of Experiments to Make It Happen,* Second Edition.)

Positrol[10]

One of the weaknesses of industry is that engineers try to control a process by checking the product it produces. That is too late. An analogy would be to steer a boat by looking at its wake! Once important process variables have been identified through Variables Search and optimized through Scatter Plots and Response Surface Methodology, with realistic specifications and realistic tolerances, the purpose of Positrol is to freeze the process gains by continuously monitoring the process so that its important variables or parameters—the "what"—never exceed their carefully crafted tolerances.

This "freezing the gains" is done by a regiment in which each parameter is monitored with:

a *who*   either an operator, maintenance person, or automatic controls

a *how*   an accurate instrumentation

a *where*   at the most critical point in the process

a *when*   the frequency of monitoring—say, either once a day, once an hour, or continuously

Positrol is a discipline that 95 percent of industry doesn't even know, much less follow. Yet it is vital if the gains through careful DOE studies are not to be frittered away by well-meaning but "diddle artist" technicians. I have seen so many good DOE studies set back because process technicians take the law into their own hands. They must be persuaded to believe that positrol is not a spy system on their behavior but a police system on the behavior of the process!

Process Certification[11]

If St. Patrick is the patron saint of Ireland, St. Murphy is, undoubtedly, the patron saint of industry. In fact, the humorous but very real foundation of Process Certification is Murphy's Law, which states: "If something can go wrong, it will." Murphy's Law is omnipresent in industry. The task of Process Certification is to round up these little Murphies and incarcerate them.

There are a number of peripherals that can contribute to poor quality. They can be divided into five broad categories:

- Management/Supervision Inadequacies
- Violation of Good Manufacturing Practices
- Plant/Equipment Inattention
- Environmental Neglect
- Human Shortcomings

Some misguided companies believe that the discipline of ISO-9000 documentation can cure these ills. But ISO-9000 standards are so contractually determined that if the contract allows scrap, ISO-9000 will do it consistently! Process Certification goes way, way beyond ISO-9000 or QS-9000 or any other quality standard. Its purpose is to so reduce these uncontrollable factors that their collective noise is much less than the purity of the signal required for a DOE study. In other words, it ensures a good signal-to-noise ratio and gives DOE a chance to really succeed. It is one of the best ways to make a process robust. As such, Process Certification should both precede as well as follow a DOE study.

Unfortunately, as in the case of positrol, more than 90 percent of companies do not understand Process Certification. Yet its methodology is simple:

- Process Certification is best conducted by an interdisciplinary team.

- The team prepares a list of quality peripherals (based on Murphy's Law— where every procedure, every process, every practice, every housekeeping measure, every environmental control, every test equipment is suspect!).

- The team then audits the process to highlight potential quality problems and performs a "process scrub" before certification is granted for the process to start manufacturing the product.

- Periodically, the process is recertified so that the old bad practices do not sneak back in and new ones are not introduced.

Multiple Environment Over Stress Tests (MEOST):[12] The Drive for Zero Field Failures

Background

Reliability is much more important than quality. It has two dimensions that quality does not have—time and stress. In addition, it is more directly related to the customer's requirements. To quote one of Motorola's vice presidents: "Regardless of specifications, the product must work—in the hands of the customer!" Yet the traditional tools to achieve reliability—such as reliability prediction studies, failure mode effects analysis (FMEA), fault tree analysis (FTA), and brute-force mass testing—are woefully inadequate. They are, for the most part, paper studies and based on guesses, hunches, and opinions.

Traditional reliability tests have been patterned after the military approach— throw money at the problem! The convoluted logic says that since you do not have the time to test one unit for 10,000 hours (to calculate mean time between failures, or MTBF), why not test 10,000 units for one hour! In the 1970s, accelerated life tests (ALTs) gained some currency, but they only conduct one environment or stress test at a time and completely miss the interaction effects between two or more stresses that combine to produce failures. In the 1980s, two improvements were made—HALT (highly accelerated life tests) and HASS (highly accelerated stress screening). HALT is used in prototype development. Although it does combine stresses, it takes these to product destruction limits, creating artificial failures and wasting time correcting each artificial failure. HASS is used in production but is expensive since 100 percent of the product is stressed. Furthermore, 10–20 percent of its useful life is wasted in such 100 percent tests.

Multiple Environment Over Stress Tests (MEOST) was first introduced in the days of the Apollo missions at NASA in the 1960s, when every piece of space hardware had failed, with the exception of the lunar module, which took the two astronauts up to the moon and back safely. The lunar module had been tested with MEOST. Had it failed, we would have had the moon over populated by two people!

MEOST Principles

1. We cannot permit the customer in the field ascertaining product reliability. It is too late, too expensive (in terms of potential customer defections), and a fundamental abdication of a company's responsibility. By the same token, we cannot wait for six months to a year to determine if product changes to correct field problems are effective. That is only one step better than rolling the dice at Las Vegas.

2. The objective of MEOST is to *eliminate failures,* not to measure unreliability.

3. Only through failures, forced in the prototype stage of a product, can the weak links of design be smoked out.

4. Failures can be smoked out in the laboratory, prior to production and way before the product reaches the field, by:

■ Combining environments/stresses that simultaneously impinge upon the product in the hands of the customer

■ Going beyond design stress to a *maximum practical over stress*

■ Accelerating the rate of stress increase

5. By combining stresses, applying a maximum practical over stress, and accelerating the rate of stress increase, failures can be forced out in two or three days—or even hours-instead of weeks, months, and years

6. All parts have built-in stresses, but weak parts have induced stresses two and three times the stresses in strong parts

7. These weak parts can be forced out in a very short time, leaving the strong parts intact.

8. MEOST testing must be able to reproduce the same failures—the same failure modes and the same failure mechanisms—as failures in the field on the same product or similar product. That is the litmus test of MEOST's effectiveness.

It is beyond the scope of this book to go through a detailed MEOST roadmap. The reader is referred to my latest book, being published by the Society of Automotive Engineers, on *MEOST, A Breakthrough Technique for Reliability.*

Poka-Yoke:[13] Prevention of Operator-Controlled Errors

Background

Generally, management lays most of the blame for quality defects on the line operator, even though it is well known that 85 percent and more of quality problems are caused by management, while 15 percent or less are caused by direct labor. Even assuming that a residue of quality defects is caused by direct labor, there is little merit in threatening or punishing them. Human beings do make mistakes. Poka-Yoke is a 1961 invention of the versatile Shigeo Shingo of Japan. It provides sensors—electrical, mechanical, or visual—that warn a line operator that a mistake has been made or, preferably, is about to be made and thus can be prevented from becoming a permanent defect. It is widely used in Japan in place of much less effective control charts; however, its introduction into the United States is barely fifteen years old and its use limited to just a handful of progressive companies.

Method of Achieving Success

A simple example can illustrate the principle of Poka-Yoke. A line operator, inserting a microprocessor with twenty leads (ten on each side) into a printed circuit board, can, by mistake, reverse its orientation. In that event, the electronic circuit would not work. Asking the operator to be more careful, or catching the mistake at an inspection station several positions down the assembly line, is too ineffective and too late. Instead, a simple design change of adding a dummy leg to the microprocessor—with ten leads on one side and eleven on the other, and ten holes in the associated printed circuit on one side and eleven on the other—is a Poka-Yoke sensor. If the operator attempted to put the part in backwards, he would be unable to physically insert the part into the printed circuit board. Such prevention is better than later correction down the line.

Most Poka-Yoke sensors are simple fixtures, often designed by the line operators themselves. This not only improves the quality of the product, it also offers a challenge to the line operators and generates job excitement when they succeed.

The Cost of Poor Quality (COPQ)

Dr. Joseph Juran, one of the quality gurus of the world, stressed that for the quality movement to be credible, it must convert quality from the language of defect levels to the management language of money. COPQ is less a quality tool than it is a measurement tool. Yet it is so very important that it must be the opening canon on the war on quality defects.

Armand V. Feigenbaum of General Electric introduced the concept of the cost of quality more than years ago in his landmark book, *Total Quality Control*. It has four categories: external failure costs; internal failure costs; appraisal costs; and preventive costs. Of these, only the last is desirable. The other three are undesirable and constitute the cost of poor quality. The most easily gathered elements of COPQ are shown in Table 9-5.

Table 9-5. Easily gathered elements of COPQ.

External Failure Costs	Internal Failure Costs	Appraisal Costs
Warranty	Scrap	Incoming inspection
Product recalls	Analyzing	In-process inspection
Liability lawsuits	Repair/rework	Outgoing checks
	Inventory carrying costs	All testing

For a company that has not begun the quality revolution, this cost of poor quality ranges from 10–20 percent of the sales dollar. That is pure waste. And when it is realized that the average profit on sales for a company is only 5 percent, the COPQ loss is *two to four times* the profit. Here is one of industry's greatest moneymaking machines, next only to reducing customer defections. A 50 percent reduction in COPQ can increase profit 100 percent! Yet the accounting system is blissfully ignorant of its profit potential, just as it is ignorant of customer defection reduction; of the cumulative impact of one truly dissatisfied customer over a lifetime; of ABC-based allocations for overhead costs; and of the impact of inventory, which it views as an asset instead of a liability.

I have made a parallel study of the cost of poor quality for a company that has not addressed the profit potential of quality. That figure per employee per day is $100 to $200. (One enterprising company dramatized this cost to its employees by smashing a brand-new Mercedes car in the parking lot. That is how much, the company said, it cost for poor quality each day!) If COPQ can be cut to one-third, from $150 a day to $50 a day, the total savings, for the United States as a whole, could be $500 billion per year (assuming twenty million people in manufacturing alone and 250 working days a year). Even if 50 percent of these savings is passed on to customers, the positive impact on tax receipts to the U.S. treasury would be $75 billion.

The COPQ elements in Table 9-8 are just the tip of the iceberg of COPQ costs. Figure 9-4 depicts the hidden cost of poor quality—those far more insidious elements below the water line that accounting is largely incapable of even defining, much less measuring. It is estimated that if these hidden COPQ costs were capable of being measured, the true and total quality loss to a company could be as high as 50 percent of the sales dollar!

Figure 9-4. The hidden costs of poor quality.

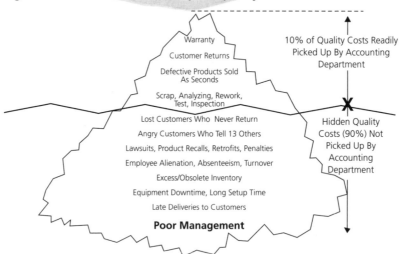

Warranty

Customer Returns

Defective Products Sold
As Seconds

Scrap, Analyzing, Rework,
Test, Inspection

Lost Customers Who Never Return

Angry Customers Who Tell 13 Others

Lawsuits, Product Recalls, Retrofits, Penalties

Employee Alienation, Absenteeism, Turnover

Excess/Obsolete Inventory

Equipment Downtime, Long Setup Time

Late Deliveries to Customers

Poor Management

10% of Quality Costs Readily
Picked Up By Accounting
Department

Hidden Quality
Costs (90%) Not
Picked Up By
Accounting
Department

Warranty Costs vs. Lifetime Costs of a Defecting Customer

Most companies are unaware of the multiplier effect in sale losses caused by a defecting customer. Worse, their nineteenth-century accounting departments do not know how to even begin estimating that loss. Typically warranty costs run between 0.5 percent and 2.0 percent of the sales dollar. CEOs are not phased by these apparently small percentages, even though they are just the tip of the iceberg that can sink their companies.

What is the real cost of a customer who is so frustrated with a company's products that he will never, ever buy from that company again? The automotive industry has estimated that cost to be more than just the cost of one car sale—say, $30,000—but as much as $500,000 to $1.5 million! How? Let's assume that:

- The customer, during his adult life, would buy ten cars.

- He will tell twenty other people of his extremely poor experience with Car Company A.

- Three of those people will be influenced not to buy that company's cars.

The loss, therefore, is not $30,000 but $300,000 x 3 = $900,000. Add to this figure the loss to Car Company A of out-of-warranty service, out-of-warranty parts, and financing costs—say, another $20,000 in four years. The total: $920,000.

Mass Customization

The mass customization movement, which started more than ten years ago, recognizes that each customer is unique and has highly individualized requirements. Each customer today wants *exactly what he wants, where he wants it, when he wants it, at prices he wants.*

Mass customization conducts a dialogue with each core customer, binding producer and consumer together. "It is a switch from measuring market share to measuring a customer's lifetime value."[14] This is made even easier by the Internet, which allows the "democratization of goods and services."[15] The challenge for a company, then, is to produce a quantity of one as economically as a much larger volume, with the help of information technology (IT), computer-integrated manufacturing (CIM), flexible manufacturing systems (FMS), and just-in-time (JIT) practices. Companies embracing mass customization now number in the hundreds. Among the prominent ones are Dell Computer, Levi Strauss & Co., Mattel, Paris Miki, Express Custom Tailors, Hewlett-Packard, Motorola, and The Ritz Carton Hotel Company.

The Role of the Quality Professional

In companies, where quality consciousness is practiced in the traditional manner, the quality function has become bloated and arrogant. Quality assurance departments suffer from the same bureaucratic creep as other staff operations. It is no wonder that quality professionals are, for the most part, obsolete and ineffective.

Example
When I first go into a company for consultation work and address their management and workers, I ask for a show of hands of who is responsible for quality in the company. If only a few hands are raised I know the company is in trouble. If a forest of hands pop up, I sense that the company is well positioned for a quality takeoff.

Quality should be everyone's responsibility. The quality assurance (QA) group should be small—no, tiny—but very professional. One rule of thumb is one quality professional for a minimum of 1,000 employees. (At Motorola, as its senior corporate consultant for quality and productivity improvement, with more than fifty plants worldwide, I was a staff of one. Yet I had more influence, greater acceptance, and out-standing success than I had with a staff of a hundred as group director for quality and value assurance in its automotive and industrial electronics group. I was no longer looked upon as a cop. I was welcomed as a coach.)

The role of the quality professionals must radically change—from doing to guid-ing, from boss to coach, from cop to consultant. You don't need large quality staffs. They are counterproductive. But you must be highly knowledgeable—in leadership vision; in customer sensitivity; in employee motivation; in supplier partnerships; in new product launches; in manufacturing skills; in white-collar reengineering; and above all, in the newer and powerful techniques of quality, cost, and cycle time improvement.

CASE STUDY

A BENCHMARK COMPANY IN THE AREA OF QUALITY—MOTOROLA

Motorola is the company that put quality on the world map with its launch of the Six Sigma process. Hundreds and thousands of companies all over the globe have tried to copy its success. But Motorola, despite some business reverses, remains a lone benchmark in the quality arena.

On Customers. Eighteen years ago, Motorola changed its objective from profit to total customer satisfaction. It created senior managers as customer czars in each sector. It made the quality function the customer's advocate in the com-pany. And it initiated a policy that each senior executive had to visit ten of his most important customers to determine what they *wanted,* instead of what it thought they *needed.*

On Leadership. The brilliant leadership of Bob Galvin, our Motorola Chairman, has been covered in Chapter 5 on leadership. Suffice it to say that he designed a template for leadership that no leader has been able to emulate—including Jack Welch of General Electric fame, whose ethics are a blot on his career.

On Organization. Motorola was one of the earlier American companies to delayer its organization, from sixteen levels to seven and, in some plants with more than 4,000 people, down to four layers of management. It has committed over 5 percent of its payroll to training, with 40 percent spent on quality. Every employee receives a minimum of forty hours of training each year, some as many as 120 hours.

On Employees. Motorola experimented with gain sharing for more than thirty years. Its teams tackle their own projects for improvement and generally receive incentives that average 15 percent of their salaries—some as high as 40 percent. Its famous Total Customer Satisfaction (TCS) Competition spans over 6,000 teams and nets savings of $2 to 3 billion per year to the company.

On Supply Chain Management. The company benchmarked Xerox and has now become a benchmark in its own right, with a yearly cost reduction averaging 7 percent in material for partnership suppliers, a defect level largely under 100 parts per million (ppm), and lead times less than one week. That translates to more than $1 billion in savings each year.

On Quality /Reliability Results. Motorola's 10:1, 100:1, and 1000:1 quality improvement is well known. The tools to achieve those levels are documented in this chapter. As a result, our customers receive defect levels below 30 ppm and experience failure rates in the field below 100 ppm per year—some even below 10 ppm per year.

On Cycle Time. Having been one of the earliest companies to experience the tie-in between quality and cycle time, Motorola instituted a 10:1 improvement in cycle time every five years. It has exceeded those goals in manufacturing and in several business processes.

On Design. Motorola introduced the concepts of the contract book, the lessons learned log, early supplier involvement, the 25 percent maximum redesign rule, and the use of Design of Experiments (DOE) for product robustness and Multiple Environment Over Stress Testing (MEOST) for a breakthrough in reliability. A highlight was the response to an OEM customer requirement that our product should travel a minimum of 200,000 miles on their engine. With MEOST, we so improved our engine control module that we went for seven years without a single field failure! Some of our modules, in the meantime, had logged more than 500,000 miles.

On Manufacturing. Motorola registered phenomenal success in quality problem solving using DOE and, above all, extending it to line workers, who could then solve their own problems with little or no help from engineers. It discarded the use of control charts and put precontrol in place, instead—which is simpler, easier, and statistically more powerful than control charts. Quality levels were monitored in all Motorola plants worldwide with the popular 5-up charts depicting cost of poor quality, field failure rates, outgoing quality, total defects per unit (TDPU), and c_{pk} on critical parameters.

On Services. We developed the discipline of the Next Operation as Customer (NOAC) that tied all business processes in all white-collar areas to an evaluation by the internal customer of the internal supplier's effectiveness. In all 50,000 people were trained in NOAC methodology, with flowcharting used as a principal tool and cycle time reduction the most tangible benefit.

Self-Assessment/Audit on Quality: Implementing Disciplines by Company Type and Months to Complete

1. *Audit.* Table 9-10 is a self-assessment/audit by which a company can measure its quality health. It has nine key characteristics and sixteen essential disciplines, with 5 points each, for practical implementation. The total score is 80 points.

2. *Implementation Disciplines.* The disciplines have been carefully selected as being the most important, the most practical, and the most conducive to quick results.

3. *Timetable by Company Type.* As explained in Chapter 3, the timetable to implement each discipline varies by company type.

Type A companies (generally stage 2 to 3) are the most receptive to the disciplines and the most eager to reach world-class status. They also have a reasonable level of quality expertise.

Type B companies (generally in stage 2) have less resources, less knowledge, and are, of necessity, slower implementers.

Type C companies (generally in stage 1) are the most resistant to change. Their attachment, managerially and culturally, to the *status quo* makes them laggards in implementation. They are also the furthest behind in recognizing the importance and need for quality.

Table 9-6. Quality audit and scores: key characteristics, essential disciplines, and timetable to complete—by company type (80 points).

Key Characteristics	Essential Disciplines	Rating 1-5 *	Months to Complete, By Company Type		
			A	B	C
1-1 Customers	1. The quality function has been involved in quantifying customer defections and their impact on profit.		6	12	—

	2. The quality function has acted as the customer's advocate in the company and a member of its SWAT team.	3	6	18
1-2 Leadership	1. Quality is among the few superordinate and unchanging values of the corporation.	3	6	12
1-3 Organi-zation	1. Quality responsibility has been firmly established for all employees, not just relegated to the quality function.	6	12	18
	2. The quality function is kept small in number and high in professionalism, so as to guide line functions to excellence.	12	18	36
1-4 Employees	1. The quality function has rendered concrete help in implementing problem-solving techniques to line operators and in bringing joy to the workplace.	18	36	—
	2. The quality function has actively helped in the transition of empowerment from stages 1-5 to 6-9 (explained in Chapter 7).	24	48	—
1-5 Supply Chain Management	1. As a member of the commodity team, the quality member has rendered continuous help to partnership suppliers in quality, cost, and cycle time.	12	18	36
1-6 Design	1. The quality function has demonstrated success in			

(continues)

Table 9-6. (Continued.)

Key Characteristics	Essential Disciplines	Rating 1-5 *	Months to Complete, By Company Type		
			A	B	C
	implementing DOE in design to make products robust.		15	30	48
	2. The quality function has demonstrated success in implementing MEOST to achieve breakthrough reliability.		18	36	60
	3. The quality function has institutionalized the disciplines of derating and product liability analysis (PLA) in design.		15	24	36
1-7 Manufacturing	1. The quality function has institutionalized the disciplines of Positrol, Process Certification, Precontrol, and Poka-Yoke in manufacturing.		9	15	36
1-8 Services	1. The quality function has championed and led the discipline of NOAC to improve the quality, cost, and cycle time of business processes.		15	24	48
	2. The quality function has facilitated the use of "out of the box" thinking to achieve breakthroughs in business process productivity and cycle time.				

| 1-9 Results | 1. The quality function has analyzed and reduced the cost of poor quality (COPQ) by a factor of 5:1 in three years. | | 36 | 48 | — |
| | 2. The quality function has reduced field failure rates by 10:1 in three years. | | 36 | 48 | — |

* The rater grades the company on each discipline on a scale of 1–5, with 1 being the least effective and 5 being the most effective.

CHAPTER 10

From Cost Reduction "with Mirrors" to a Robust Bottom Line

A man was searching frantically for a lost gold coin, when his friend pointed out: "But why are you searching in this room, when earlier you said that you had lost it in another?" The man replied: "Because the light is better here!"

—UNKNOWN AUTHOR

Management Searches in the Wrong Places for the Gold Coin of Cost Reduction

The opening quote is so typical of management's futile search for the cost reduction. It thrashes around in the wrong places. The usual knee-jerk actions are:

- A freeze on hiring

- A clampdown on all travel

- An order that all pencil requisitions be approved by seven vice presidents

- Deep, indiscriminate layoffs

Eye Openers for Blind Management

The Power of Ultimate Six Sigma offers scores of techniques for cost reduction and profit improvement that are far, far more effective than traditional management cost-cutting practices and—at the same time—boost employee morale. These disciplines

189

and techniques are discussed throughout this book. The most prominent of these cost reduction techniques are:

- Increased Customer Retention (Chapter 4)

- Reduced Customer Base (Chapter 4)

- Reduced Cost of Poor Quality (Chapter 9)

- Improved Factory Overall Efficiency (Chapter 13)

- Supplier Cost Reduction (Chapter 8)

- Increased Inventory Turns (Chapter 11)

- Reduced Design Cycle Time (Chapter 12)

- Reduced Cycle Time in Business Processes (Chapter 14)

- Employee Empowerment (Chapter 7)

- Total Customer Satisfaction Team Competitions (Chapter 7)

Collectively, the profit increase of these ten techniques alone can double, triple, and quadruple corporate profits. This chapter explores other powerful disciplines of which most companies are blissfully ignorant. But before detailing them, assessing a company's cost reduction is in order.

The Four Stages of Cost Reduction—Assessing a Company's Cost Health Chart

Similar to the four stages of quality, described in Chapter 9, I have developed the four stages of cost reduction in a company, ranging from a primitive stage to an enlightenment stage.

Stage 1—the "Scrooge" stage—is a company that is terminally ill in cost reduction "health" terms, or at a 3-Sigma level. It is myopic and obsessed with the greed of short-term profit. About 60 percent of companies are mired in stage 1.

Stage 2—the "frugal" stage—is a company that is in the cost reduction hospital, or at a 4-Sigma level. It is conventional in its outlook and takes few risks. Since the "hyped" Six Sigma companies pay scant attention to cost (even as compared with their modest quality achievement), they are mostly in stage 2, along with over 30 percent of the total number of companies.

Stage 3—called the "conservation/progressive" stage—is a company that is in good cost reduction health but needs frequent checkups. Its heart is progressive, but its head is conservative. It can and does aspire to a 5-Sigma level. About 5 percent of the companies are in stage 3.

Stage 4—called the "enlightened state"—is the Ultimate Six Sigma. These very few companies are in robust health and have advanced to Six Sigma levels.

Table 10-1 is a matrix of these four stages of cost reduction in ten areas—corporate purpose, leadership, organization, employees, supply chain management, tools, design, manufacturing, services, and results. Each area has two to seven subareas. The table is self-explanatory, and many of its elements are further detailed in the appropriate chapters in this book. It can also be used as a template to audit a company's cost reduction health. It has proved beneficial in exploring a company's cost strengths and cost weaknesses, enabling a concentration on overcoming the latter and moving the company to a higher stage in each area.

Powerful Cost Reduction Tools to Make a Company's Profits Sparkle

There are seventeen important cost reduction disciplines that can fuel the engine of profit. Of these, ten are of a more general nature; they were listed at the outset of this chapter and are described in the referenced chapters. The other seven are more specific tools that need some elaboration. They are:

1. Total Value Engineering

2. SBU, Product, Model, and Part Number Reduction

3. Group Technology

4. Early Supplier Involvement

5. Cost Targeting

6. Challenging Specifications

7. Financial Incentives/Penalties with Customers and Suppliers

Total Value Engineering: Maximizing Customer Loyalty at Minimum Cost

Value engineering (VE) differs from plain cost reduction. The latter retains the original design of the product or part but attempts to make it cheaper, with only slight

(text continues on page 195)

Table 10-1. The four stages of cost reduction: a company's cost health chart.

Area	Subarea	Stage 1 "Scrooge" (3 Sigma)	Stage 2 Frugal (4 Sigma)	Stage 3 Conservative/ Progressive (5 Sigma)	Stage 4 Enlightened (6 Sigma)
Corporate Purpose	Objective	Short-term profit	Shareholder value	Return on investment	Customer loyalty/retention
	Focus	Cost squeeze	High-volume growth	High market share	Optimum costs for entire supply chain
Leadership	Style	Theory X	Micromanagement	Participative	Freedom—growth for all employees
	Profit Improvement Goal	"Make money while you can"	5%	10%–15%	>50%
	Value Added/ Employee/Year	$30,000	$70,000–$100,000	$150,000–$300,000	>$600,000
Organization	Hiring	Off the street, indiscriminate	Selection by skill	Selection by holistic education	Selection based on team player and entrepreneurship criteria
	Performance Appraisal	Infrequent to none	By boss	By internal customer	360-degree evaluation
	Pay Raises	Minimal raises	Token—mainly cost-of-living	Small raises, low differentials	No raises—but large bonuses for performance
	Training	None	For professionals only	Up to 1.5% of payroll	Minimum 5% of payroll
Employees	Downsizing Strategy	Frequent and deep	Direct labor— main target	Staff cuts before direct labor	Kept to a minimum— managers let go first

	Suggestions	Untapped	Tokenism—0.1/ employee/year	1/employee/year	>10/employee/year

	Suggestions	Untapped	Tokenism—0.1/employee/year	1/employee/year	>10/employee/year
	Teams	No worker involvement	Intradepartment teams	Cross-functional teams	Companywide team competitions
	Gain Sharing as % of Worker Salary	0%	5%	10%	>50%
Supply Chain Management	Trust	No trust	Suspicion	Shallow trust	Full trust
	Strategy	Squeeze supplier for cost reduction	Electronic bidding	Nominal partnerships	Continual cost reduction and profit increase for supplier
	Outsourcing	Vertical integration	Piece parts only	"Black box" outsourcing	Only core competencies retained in-house
	Financial Incentives	None	None	None	For reliability, delivery
Tools	Value Engineering	Cost reduction only	Value analysis	Value engineering	Total value engineering
	Customer/Supplier/Distributor Base Reduction	Proliferation	Status quo	Supplier base reduced	Customer/supplier/distributor based reduced 50% to 80%
	Specifications Challenge	Specs "God given"	None	Sensitivity analysis	Scatter Plots: customer perceptions vs. parameter
	SBU, Product, Model, and Part Number Reduction	Proliferation	No action to reduce	Part number reduction only	10% to 50% reduction of entire base
	Group Technology	Unknown	Unknown	Preferred parts	30% to 80% savings in key areas
	Cost Targeting	3-bid syndrome	Negotiations	Electronic bidding	Customer company sets price

(continues)

Table 10-1. (Continued.)

Area	Subarea	Stage 1 "Scrooge" (3 Sigma)	Stage 2 Frugal (4 Sigma)	Stage 3 Conservative/ Progressive (5 Sigma)	Stage 4 Enlightened (6 Sigma)
	Incentives/Penalties —Suppliers and Customers	None	None	Penalties only	± 10% to 15%
Design	Design Objective % Redesign of Current Product	Lowest cost 100%	Ease of manufacture 75%	Minimum variation 50%	Customer "WOW" Maximum 25%
	Benchmarking/ Reverse Engineering	None	Benchmarking	Reverse engineering	Benchmarking and reverse engineering Cost targeting
	Price Determination (Suppliers)	3 quote bidding	Negotiation— arm twisting	Electronic bidding	
Manufacturing	Concentration	Direct labor	Offshore manufacturing	Automation	Only core competencies retained
	Inventory	Large safety stocks	Forecast cushion	Master schedules	Pull systems
Services	Next Operation as Customer (NOAC)	None	None	Concept only	Full NOAC
	Process Redesign	None	None	None	Reduction in all staff departments
Results	Profit Tie-In with Customer Retention	0%	0%	0%	35% to 85% profit increase
	Cost of Poor Quality (COPQ)	15% to 25%	10% to 15%	5% to 10%	2%
	Bill of Materials Reduction	2% to 5% (increase)	0%	2%	5% to 15%
	Customer, Supplier, Distributor Base Reduction	2% to 5% (increase)	0%	5%	40% to 60%

modifications. Value engineering, by contrast, concentrates on the function of the product or part and provides that function in very different ways to improve quality while reducing cost.

Invented by Larry Miles of General Electric[1] in the 1940s, VE was quickly championed by the Defense Department of the United States to eliminate "gold plating" (i.e., unnecessary specifications that add costs but little value). Unfortunately, outside of the defense industry, VE did not catch fire. Instead, the Japanese have embraced it with the vigor of Sinbad the sailor and use it to milk every yen of cost out of a product.

Total value engineering[2] was developed by me as an enlargement of traditional value engineering. The latter concentrates on cost reduction while not deteriorating quality and reliability. Total value engineering goes beyond VE not only to enhance quality and reliability, but—more important—*to maximize customer retention and loyalty while reducing costs*. It aims for customer "wow." Table 10-2 differentiates traditional value engineering and total value engineering in ten distinct areas.

SBU, Product, Model, and Part Number Reduction

Part number proliferation is a design and manufacturing disease. Every engineer wants his own part number to meet the exact requirements of design. Every line manager in manufacturing wants his own unique part number on a common part so that other lines would not raid his hoarded stock. The result is part number pollution! One defense contractor, with a base of 30,000 parts, had ballooned the total to over 300,000 part numbers!

The starting point for reduction is not at the part level but at the strategic business unit (SBU) level. Figure 10-1 is the well-known Boston Consulting Group (BCG) portfolio analysis that separates SBUs into four categories on the basis of their relative competency versus their industrial attractiveness.

1. Dog SBUs, with low competency and low industry attractiveness, should be divested.

2. Cash cow SBUs, with high competency but low industry attractiveness, should be "harvested" (i.e., milked for cash, with minimal resources poured into them, to feed the question mark and star SBUs).

3. Question mark SBUs, with low competency but high industry attractiveness, should be "nurtured" with cash inflows to move them into the star category.

4. Star SBUs, with high competency and high industry attractiveness should be a major focus for the company.

Table 10-2. Traditional value engineering vs. total value engineering.

Area	Traditional VE	Total VE
Objective	Reduces cost without sacrificing quality	Enhances all elements of customer satisfaction
Scope	Generally confined to product	Covers product; services; administration; organization; people
Customers	Addresses specifications only	Determines customer requirements, measures his satisfaction and excitement, turns it into customer "wow"
Design	Improves design cost only	Improves design quality, cost, cycle time, manufacturability, serviceability, and diagnostics
Suppliers	Improves material cost only	Improves supplier quality, cost, cycle time; reduces supplier base; creates partnership with suppliers
Manu-facturing	Improves production cost only	Improves production cost, quality, cost, cycle time, and total productive maintenance
Field	Negligible involvement	Improves reliability, diagnostics and serviceability
Support Services	Negligible involvement	Improves quality, cost, cycle time in white-collar operations
Management	Negligible involvement	Improves motivation, job excitement; facilitates gain sharing
Organization	Cross-functional teams	Cross-functional teams and flat pyramid

Example

The methodology of total value engineering is best illustrated by a case study. The project was the design of a flexible dust cover for an outdoor, portable metal carrying case containing electronic checkout equipment. The case and its equipment were to be carried and operated at a missile site. The case was 18" x 14" x 10" and contained thirty-seven pounds of instrumentation.

Provisions were to be made for storing the dust cover in the lid of the carrying case when the equipment was in operation. The material for the dust cover was specified as "Mil-Grey" (military gray) in color and qualified under the environmental requirements mandated for all ground support equipment.

The defense contractor set about designing the flexible dust cover for an estimated cost of $124 per unit. This cost included the product meeting all the environmental requirements imposed by the Defense Department. A total value engineering team then reexamined the problem by asking a series of simple questions:

Question 1	What is the function of the dust cover?
Answer	To protect the metal carrying case during transportation and storage. On the other hand, the metal carrying case protected the dust cover during operation at the missile site!
Question 2	What was the "gold plating" in the military specifications?
Answer	Why do we need the "Mil-Grey" color? Why do we need environmental requirements, when in actual operations the metal case is protecting the dust cover, not the other way around?
Question 3	What else will provide the function of protecting the metal case?
Answer	A paper bag, a laundry bag, a plastic zip-lock bag, even no bag.

The final total value engineering solution: Provide a rubber-seal gasket on the lid of the metal carrying case to protect it against dust and rain. Cost $1.10—more than a 100:1 savings!

Figure 10-1. BCG portfolio on value of business units in a corporation competency focus.

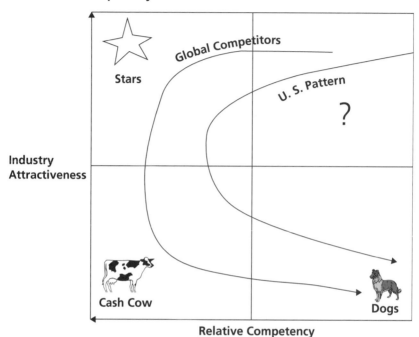

The unprofitable dog SBUs should be divested first. As the great Peter F. Drucker stresses, a company must make a concentration decision and shed its unprofitable businesses from time to time. This could reduce a large volume of part numbers in one stroke. As an example, a medium-size company, in deciding to exit its consumer business, reduced its total part number base from 64,000 to 37,000.

Next in line should be the reduction of unprofitable product lines that are also relatively unimportant to customers. A third step should be to reduce the vast array of model numbers within a product line. Only then can a systematic attack on part number reduction be attempted through standardization or group technology.

Group Technology (GT)[3]

The principle of group technology is that parts that are similar in shape, tolerance, size, and other design characteristics can be consolidated into fewer parts, and that parts using similar manufacturing processes can be grouped together in smaller, dedicated processes called group technology cells. GT's main use is in parts design and design retrieval coding.

Before the use of computers, a seven-digit part number could not describe a part, other than its broad category. With computers, a code of twenty to thirty digits could be assigned and completely characterize the part for shape, dimensions, tolerances, chemistry, surface finish, manufacturing processes, supplier, and price.

Group technology is the needed medicine for an astonishing parts proliferation malady. At General Dynamics,[4] a virtually identical nut and coupling unit had been designed on five separate occasions by five different design engineers and draftsmen. To compound the irony, the parts were purchased from five different suppliers at prices ranging form 22 cents to $7.50 each!

Proponents of the GT methodology claim huge cost savings in new part design, drawings, industrial engineering time, floor space, material stocks, throughput time, and inventories.

A *Harvard Business Review* article on GT goes even further. It states that the cost of introducing a new part into a company ranges from $1,300 to $12,000, including expenses for design; planning and control; procurement; inspection; storing; tools and fixtures. Reducing no more than 500 part numbers would save a company from $650,000 up to $6 million.

Early Supplier Involvement (ESI)

ESI represents a symbolic continental divide between the archaic, old-line procurement practices of soliciting three bids and the newfangled mass-bidding approach through the Internet and modern supply management principles involving the preselection of a partnership supplier. Several benefits accrue both to the company and the partnership supplier through ESI, including: value engineering ideas; shorter design cycle time, better specifications, and supplies technology gains; and improved quality, cost, and cycle time.

The most important benefit of ESI is that it permits parallel development of a design in an iterative interaction with the partnership supplier rather than the "series" handover of the design to the supplier, with the design cast in concrete and incapable of any significant improvement.

Concept Phase

■ Two or three of partnership suppliers capable of producing the product are chosen.

Feasibility Phase

■ ESI is started with all of the selected suppliers to generate a maximum number of ideas for quality, cost, and cycle time improvement.

Prototype Phase

- Selected ideas are incorporated into the design.

- Financial incentives are awarded to each supplier in proportion to the projected savings contributed by each of them.

Cost Targeting

For decades, supplier costs were determined by soliciting bids from three suppliers and either selecting the lowest cost supplier or whipsawing them into negotiated cost reductions.

Cost targeting, introduced twenty-odd years ago, is based on working with just one supplier—the best—who has been preselected as the partnership supplier. The part or product cost, however, is not determined by the supplier, but by the customer's design team, based on a computerized determination of the expected material cost and the estimated labor and overhead costs. This information is then given to the supplier, as a target, to meet or to beat *vis-à-vis* competition. Then, using ESI and value engineering, a mutual agreement is reached to lower even the targeted cost as well as how to attain the reduction.

Challenging Specifications: "Ninety Percent of Them Are Wrong"

In translating customer requirements into engineering specifications, techniques such as quality function deployment (QFD) are supposed to be employed. Yet specifications are still pulled out of the air. Euphemistically, the practice is called "atmospheric analysis." Why are specifications so vague and arbitrary? There are several reasons:

- Specifications are lifted from older designs and drawings.

- Engineering relies on boilerplate requirements or supplier-published specifications.

- There's reliance on the computer for determining tolerances. This can only be done, though, if the formula governing the relationship between the output (i.e., the dependent variable) and the independent variables is known, which is rarely the case in complex designs.

- Worst-case analysis is performed. Because of the very low probability of such occurrences, there is an appreciable addition to cost, with no value added.

- Statistical tolerancing—a formula approach—is inaccurate in actual practice.

- Engineering conservatism (otherwise known as "cover your hide") is a prevailing attitude. Engineers know that tight specifications and tight tolerances may be costly, but loose specifications and tolerances, resulting in product defects/failures, may cost them their jobs.

- Reliability is not a specification. If it is, it is not accurately predicted and tested in laboratory checks.

- Field environments/stresses are not measured, combined, or simulated in laboratory.

- Ergonomics are not considered sufficiently. Engineers do not take into account the customer's lack of familiarity with the product or the misuses to which it could be subjected.

- Product safety is not pursued aggressively and product liability prevention is not practiced enough as a design discipline.

- Built-in diagnostics are not yet a design culture.

- Correlation studies, which chart levels of customer preference versus levels of one or more product parameters, aren't conducted. (For an example of this point, see the case study on edge defects in contact lenses.)

CASE STUDY

EDGE DEFECTS IN CONTACT LENSES

A manufacturer of contact lenses was convinced that edge defects—scratches, chips, and inclusions—around the periphery of the lens were objectionable to customers and had to be rooted out with four to five repeated inspections using high-powered microscopes.

The company had spent millions of dollars with this brute-force approach and yet was losing market share to its competitor. In a reverse engineering study, it found, to its amazement, that the competitor's contact lenses had far more edge defects than its own. This initiated a correlation study comparing various levels of customer acceptance versus levels of edge defects. The study revealed little correlation. The edge defects were of minor concern to the lens wearers because they were only on the periphery of the lens, could not be seen with the naked eye, and did not affect vision. The superiority of the competitor's product lay in 1) its closer adherence to the exact lens prescription (high c_{pk}), which meant it produced better vision for the customer, and 2) its greater wearing comfort.

(continues)

> The company rapidly changed its concentration from edge defects to pre-scription accuracy (achieving ^cp_Ks of 2.5 and higher) and to wearing comfort. In the process, it saved millions of dollars and restored its share within eighteen months.

A Comprehensive Specifications Checklist

The design team has to tackle several issues at the concept stage, then revisit them at the prototype stage of design, to ensure that the various priorities of customer requirements are adequately translated into engineering specifications.

Financial Incentives/Penalties with Suppliers and Customers

In recent years, the principle of incentive contracting, which originated with the Department of Defense, has gradually been extended to the commercial industry. It operates on the theory of the carrot and the stick. There's a financial carrot (i.e., an incentive) for a supplier for better than agreed-on quality, reliability, delivery, or performance, and a financial stick (i.e., a penalty) for worse than agreed-on levels of those parameters. Both incentives and penalties are, usually, in the range of ±5 percent to ±10 percent.

The principle is attractive. The practice is another matter. Suppliers are reluctant to accept financial penalties, especially for reliability targets not reached, and customers are reluctant to extend financial incentives to suppliers if agreed-on targets are not met. The next example, taken from my personal experience, illustrates the roadblocks to incentive contracting.

Early Supplier Involvement Financial Incentives

A problem that arises in early supplier involvement (ESI) is the selection of just one partnership supplier, when two or three suppliers are all worthy of partnership. The others feel, under such circumstances, that having partnership status is meaningless. And yet only one supplier can get the order. Dividing a limited pie would not be economical.

An imaginative solution is to bring in, say, all three partnership suppliers for ESI discussions and encourage them to present value engineering ideas. Each accepted idea would be incorporated into the design. Each supplier would receive a value engineering royalty payment or incentive award representing a fraction (usually 40–50 percent) of the savings for the first year of the contract, regardless of whether that supplier got the contract. The suppliers who did not win the contract would still earn a clear profit, with no investment other than the exercise of their brainpower. It is a win-win-win-win situation for all!

Example

Several years ago, Ford Motor Company approached Motorola with a proposal to establish a penalty if we did not meet a specified reliability target for our engine control system in Ford vehicles. The general manager and I went to Ford's glass house in Dearborn. We agreed readily to the financial penalty (we were confident of our reliability achievements), provided Ford would also offer us a financial incentive for exceeding the reliability target. "No way," was Ford's response. We picked up our offer and walked away from the table.

Fast-forward a dozen years later. Ford accepted Motorola's proposal for both a reliability penalty as well as an incentive. We met the target and received a partial payment of $100,000 from Ford. (The project manager quickly cashed the check before Ford's management changed its mind!)

A Focal Point for Cost Reduction in an Organization

While the quality function has been departmentalized in almost all companies in the form, generally, of quality assurance (QA), the cost function within a company has been diffused organizationally. This is both good and bad. It is good because cost is everybody's responsibility, just as quality is everybody's responsibility. It is bad in the sense that there is no focal point for cost as there is for quality.

A few enlightened companies have provided a focal point for cost—calling it value engineering (VE). It is wider in scope than cost reduction because it ensures that quality/reliability is not sacrificed at the altar of cost reduction. Total value engineering (TVE) is even wider in scope than traditional value engineering because it ensures that customer "wow" and customer retention are paramount, even if costs should increase incrementally.

The role of the total value engineering or VE function is to act as a coach, consultant, and teacher to the line departments and support services. The main engine of TVE (or VE) is the formation of cross-functional teams to tackle reach-out projects selected by top management or a steering committee. The results are measured in savings from quality, cost, or cycle time improvements; greater customer delight and retention; or other tangible parameters. Training for VE, with its definite discipline, is a prerequisite. A distinct by-product of the VE team project is the enthusiasm generated among the team members. In my many experiences in directing and coaching these teams, I've fulfilled the leader's role (as urged by Dr. Deming) by encouraging the "creation of joy in the workplace."

CASE STUDY

A BENCHMARK COMPANY IN THE AREA OF COST—
U.S. DEFENSE DEPARTMENT

Given the publicity of cost overruns and outrageous prices for garden-variety items and military hardware, the Department of Defense (DOD) of the United States may be held up for ridicule as a benchmark for cost reduction. Yet two factors commend its consideration as a benchmark: 1) its championing the cause of value engineering and its promotion of the technique with crusading zeal (with substantial benefits to the United States) and 2) recent efforts by the Clinton and Bush administrations for a major drive on cost reduction. In this book, I shall concentrate on the heroic efforts by DOD to institutionalize value engineering, not only among its defense contractors but also in the commercial sector.

Value engineering wouldn't have seen the light of industrial day had not DOD become its foremost crusader. Early on, Secretary of Defense Robert McNamara—himself one of "the Whiz Kids" who had earlier developed quantitative analysis techniques for Ford Motor—introduced incentive clauses for defense contractors to develop and submit VE ideas for cost reduction and quality improvement. Savings from approved ideas would be shared on an equitable basis (usually 50-50) between DOD and the contractor. Even if the contractor did not win a bid, his ideas would still receive a value engineering royalty (approximately 10 percent of the first year savings).

With this financial stimulus, VE floodgates opened to the DOD agencies. As manager of value engineering in Motorola's Military Division, I submitted many value engineering change proposals (VECPs) and we received several million dollars in incentives and royalties. DOD conducted seminars, tutorials, and conferences on VE for industry. It created a focal point for value engineering and cost reduction within each defense contractor company. It researched imaginative VE and cost reduction techniques that were far in advance of commercial industry.

But, then, sad to say, the VE movement began to fade in the United States. The Society for American Value Engineers (SAVE) went into eclipse while its companion organization—the American Society for Quality (ASQ)—grew from strength to strength. With changes in administration, management, and priorities, DOD de-emphasized VE. Today, the value engineering movement is alive and well, not in America, but in Japan, where every yen is scrubbed for VE ideas and cost reductions. We need a clarion call for value engineering's resurrection.

Self-Assessment/Audit on Cost Health: Implementing Disciplines by Company Type and Months to Complete

Table 10-3 is a self-assessment/audit by which a company can gauge its cost health. It has six key characteristics and sixteen essential disciplines, with 5 points each, for a total score of 80 points.

    1. *Implementation Disciplines.* The disciplines have been carefully selected as being the most important, practical, and the most conducive to quick results.

    2. *Timetable to Complete by Company Type.* As explained in Chapter 3, the implementation timetable for each discipline varies by company type:

    Type A companies have some background in cost reduction, along with the desire to excel.

    Type B companies are limited by experience and resources.

    Type C companies' success is father to their potential failure (i.e., their success may make it difficult for them to accept some of the disciplines for improvement, much less implement them).

Table 10-3. Cost: audit and scores, key characteristics, essential disciplines, and timetable to complete—by company type (80 points).

Key Characteristics	Essential Disciplines	Rating 1-5*	Months to Complete, By Company Type		
			A	B	C
1-1 Customers	1. The company has added value to the customer, as perceived by the customer.		12	15	24
1-2 Leadership	1. The customer, supplier, and distributor bases have been reduced by at least 30% to 70% to focus on core constituencies.		12	12	48

(continues)

Table 10-3. (Continued.)

Key Characteristics	Essential Disciplines	Rating 1-5*	Months to Complete, By Company Type		
			A	B	C
1-3 Supply Chain Management	1. There have been reduced optimized costs along the entire supply chain, from first-, second-, and third-tier suppliers through distributors and customers.				
	2. The company retains only core competencies in-house and outsources all other peripheral activities.		18	24	–
	3. Purchased material costs have been reduced by a minimum of 5% per year.		12	18	48
	4. Inventory turns have been increased to a minimum of 50 per year.		24	36	–
1-4 Tools	1. SBUs, products, models, and part numbers have been reduced to create focus and reduce costs.		12	18	36
	2. Financial incentives/penalties have been made operative for suppliers and customers.		36	–	–
	3. Total value engineering (VE) has been created as a focal point and VE teams have generated substantial savings to improve quality, cost, cycle time, and customer retention.		18	36	–
	4. Total productive management (TPM) has been implemented				

	to improve effectiveness of key manufacturing processes.		12	18	–
	5. Group technology has been implemented to improve manufacturing productivity and to reduce part number proliferation.		18	36	–
	6. Early supplier involvement (ESI) has been implemented to reduce costs, improve quality, and reduce design cycle time.		9	12	24
	7. Cost targeting has replaced 3-quote bidding and electronic bidding, so that the company determines product/part cost, not the supplier.		12	24	–
1-5 Design	1. Specifications challenges happen —that is, every engineering specification is challenged, with a correlation between a customer's real requirements and a given parameter.		12	18	–
1-6 Manufacturing	1. Team competition between cross-functional teams is promoted to maximize savings to the company.		9	18	36
	2. Suggestions/ideas for improvement are promoted among all workers, fairly evaluated, and quickly implemented to generate savings.		3	6	12

*The rater grades the company on each discipline on a scale of 1–5, with 1 being the least effective and 5 being the most effective.

CHAPTER 11

Cycle Time: From a Black Hole to the Best Metric of Effectiveness

Cycle Time = ∫ Quality, Cost, Delivery, Effectiveness

—KEKI R. BHOTE

Cycle Time, the Integrator

A funny thing happened on the way to our achieving quality excellence at Motorola. Almost by serendipity, we discovered that as we improved quality, we improved cycle time as well. We came to the conclusion that quality and cycle time were two sides of the same coin. We went further. By measuring cycle time, we could obtain a good correlation with quality. Then, by extending the study, we found an even further correlation with the measure of process effectiveness. (Delivery, of course, is a direct consequence of cycle time.) Hence, the slogan (presented as a calculus formula) that cycle time is the integrator of quality, cost, delivery, and effectiveness.

Cycle time, therefore, can be the single metric to assess improvements in quality, cost, delivery, and effectiveness. This is especially a vital metric in areas such as services and white-collar operations, where cost is difficult to quantify and quality is subjective. In fact, speed—a synonym for cycle time—is rapidly becoming a top objective at the highest levels of a corporation and as a key strategy in design.

(text continues on page 213)

209

Table 11-1. The four stages of cycle time reduction: a company's cycle time health chart.

Area	Subarea	Stage 1 Snail (3 Sigma)	Stage 2 Tortoise (4 Sigma)	Stage 3 Jack Rabbit (5 Sigma)	Stage 4 Panther (6 Sigma)
Customer	Delivery (days beyond required date)	>14	7 to 13	2 to 6	On-time
	New Model Introduction (months)	>24	19 to 24	13 to 18	6 to 12
	New Model Introduction (months behind competition)	6 to 12	3 to 6	−3 to +3	−3 to −6
Leadership	Improvement Goal				
	• Manufacturing	None	2:1 in 5 years	5:1 in 5 years	10: 1 in 5 years
	• Business Processes	None	1:5 in 5 years	3:1 in 5 years	10: 1 in 5 years
	• Design	None	None	2:1 in 5 years	4: 1 in 5 years
Organization	Hiring: Days Required	—	>90	60	<30
	Performance Appraisal	—	Once a year	Once every six months	Continuous, nonthreatening
	Sales Forecast Accuracy	> ± 50%	> ± 30%	± 10%	No need with JIT
Supply Chain Management	Lead Times	> 16 weeks	6 to 10 weeks	1 to 3 weeks	< 2 days
	Partial Build Authorizations	None	None	None	Prepayment for supplier raw materials (90% lower lead time)
	Forecasts to Suppliers	Unpredictable	±20% of actual order	±10% of actual order	Pull system—forecasts not needed
	Blanket Orders and Volume Variable Printing	—	—	Start of concept	Swings of ±10%

Design				
Development Sequence	Haphazard	Ad hoc	Series development	Parallel development
Speed of Capturing Customer Needs	Determined by engineering	Determined by management	QFD	Mass customization
Determining Specifications	"Atmospheric analysis"	Boiler plate	Historic, conventional	Scatter Plots: customer desires vs. engineering parameter
Early Supplier Involvement (ESI)	None	When specifications are frozen	Pilot run stage	Feasibility and prototype stage
Cost of Human Inventory	4-year payback	3-year payback	2-year payback	<1-year payback
Tools in Manufacturing				
Systems	"Just in case"	"Push" system	MRPII	Kanban
Total Productive Maintenance (TPM)	Factory overall effectiveness (FOE): unknown	FOE: 20%	FOE: 50%	FOE: > 85%
Lot Sizes	Large—long production runs	Large	Medium	Small
Setup Time	4 to 8 hours	1 to 3 hours	20 to 40 minutes	< 3 minutes
Factory Segmentation	None—all products for all customers	None	Large volume and small volume lines	Focused factories
Product Travel	Long—spider trails	Process flow	Process flow	Product flow (U-shaped)
Worker Flexibility	None—union straitjacket	None— single skills	Several job classifications	Multiskilled, few job classifications

(continues)

Table 11-1. (Continued.)

Area	Subarea	Stage 1 Snail (3 Sigma)	Stage 2 Tortoise (4 Sigma)	Stage 3 Jack Rabbit (5 Sigma)	Stage 4 Panther (6 Sigma)
	Customer Demand Flow and Supplier Order Flow	Large, infrequent orders	Large, infrequent orders	Supplier holds the inventory	Small orders, frequently scheduled
Services	Process Mapping	None	Non-value-added steps retained	30% reduction in non-value-added time	Process overhauled with out-of-the-box thinking
	Improvement Tools	None	Seven tools of QC	DMAIC	Process redesign out-of-the-box VE
	Metrics for Improvement	No measurement tools	Improvement estimates—fuzzy	Improvement subjective	Cycle time—the integrator
Results	Design Time Reduction (from historic)	None	10%	25%	> 75%
	Cycle Time (from customer order to shipping)	12 to 16 weeks	6 to 10 weeks	1 to 2 weeks	< 4 hours
	Cycle Time (reductions from historic)	None	10%	30%	> 80%

The Four Stages of Cycle Time—Assessing a Company's Cycle Time Health

Table 11-1 is a matrix of the four stages of cycle time that's similar to the ones I developed for quality and for cost reduction. It measures the cycle time health of a company, in each of four stages, in the areas of customers, leadership, organization, supply chain management, design, tools/manufacturing, services, and results.

Stage 1—the "snail stage"—is characteristic of companies that are not even aware of the meaning and power of cycle time. They are "terminally ill" in my health chart and can be considered at a level of 3-Sigma. About 80 percent of companies are stuck in stage 1.

Stage 2—the "tortoise stage"—is characteristic of companies in the cycle time hospital, or those at a 4-Sigma level. They have been exposed to cycle time disciplines but have not taken the actual plunge. Among them are the "hyped" Six Sigma companies that focus on quality but achieve no spectacular results in either quality or cycle time. About 15 percent of companies have reached stage 2.

Stage 3—called the "jack rabbit stage"—is characteristic of companies that are off to a fast start, but run out of gas soon. They are in good health, but need an oxygen boost from time to time. They can graduate to a 5-Sigma level with persistence. They may comprise about 4 percent of the population.

Stage 4—the "panther stage" (named after the fastest in the animal kingdom)— is characteristic of companies in robust cycle time health and operating at a Six Sigma level. Only a very small number of companies have reached this pinnacle.

Powerful Cycle Time Tools to Speed a Company to the Bottom Line

There are important cycle time tools that can be incorporated in every area of a company. However, they are particularly applicable in three areas:

- Design

- Manufacturing

- Services (namely, white-collar operations, which are detailed in Chapter 14)

Design Cycle Time Tools

Among the design cycle time tools described in this chapter are:

1. Outsourcing All Except Core Competencies

2. "Black Box" vs. Piece-Part Procurement

3. Early Supplier Involvement (ESI)

4. Mass Customization

5. Parallel Development

6. Daily Team Interchanges

7. Part Number Reduction, Preferred Parts, and Parts Qualification

8. Design of Experiments (DOE)

9. Multiple Environment Over Stress Tests (MOEST)

Outsourcing All Except Core Competencies

It is now well established that companies should retain, for in-house design, only those subassemblies or subsystems where a core competency exists. All other parts of a design where a company does not have a core competency or where they are peripheral in importance should be siphoned off to partnership suppliers who have developed cost-effective design and manufacturing capabilities of their own. This results in huge savings in design time, design manpower, design costs and—if the partnership is managed well—product quality as well. Witness the large number of suppliers, such as Flextronics and Solectron, that have practically taken over the fabrication, stuffing, soldering, and testing of printed circuit boards from the electronic industry giants.

"Black Box" vs. Piece-Part Procurement

The same advantage of saving management, design, and procurement time accrues when a company can order the whole assembly associated with the piece parts from a partnership supplier, instead of ordering scores and hundreds of piece parts from many suppliers. Now there is only one part number to worry about instead of many, many part numbers with their numerous suppliers, individual transactions, individual scheduling, and individual tracking.

Early Supplier Involvement (ESI)

The subject of ESI has been covered in-depth in Chapter 10 on cost reduction. However, ESI also has a great impact on reducing valuable design cycle time. By selecting a key supplier as a design partner, the designer need only provide the broadest requirements and an outline drawing. The partnership supplier can, then, develop the design in detail and save the company's designers hundreds of man-hours of working on their design benches.

Mass Customization

Mass customization was discussed as a quality improvement tool in Chapter 9. It can also serve as a tool for cycle time improvement. Mass customization not only captures an individual customer's actual requirements accurately, but also speedily. There is no need to predict customer requirements in the aggregate, as happens in quality function deployment, and find later that there are large deviations of such requirements from customer to customer. This saves a considerable amount of time in the continual reworking of designs.

Parallel Development

Older design cycles were characterized by "series" practices—one activity wouldn't start until the previous one was finished. This added considerably to cycle time. It also added to higher cost and poorer quality as various steps in the design cycle had to be abandoned and a fresh start made all over again. Parallel development allows different portions of the design to move forward simultaneously and to significantly reduce design cycle time.

Daily Team Interchanges

A potential problem with parallel development is that it can lead to confusion, with the left hand not knowing what the right hand is doing. This problem can be eliminated by daily interchanges between the different teams. The interchanges are facilitated by audio/videoconferencing and e-mail exchanges, where product, process, material, and die designs are exchanged between the teams.

Part Number Reduction, Preferred Parts and Parts Qualification

Part number reduction through strategic business unit (SBU), product, and model reductions and the application of group technology has been covered in Chapter 10 on cost reduction. For each of these measures, there is a reflected cycle time reduction as well.

The use of preferred parts not only helps with reliability but eliminates the need to go through lengthy parts qualifications. And if the latter is necessary, it need not be undertaken separately by a components' engineering group, but in parallel with the partnership supplier, at the supplier's facility.

Design of Experiments (DOE)

As described in Chapter 9, DOE not only achieves outstanding quality and cost improvements, but cycle time reductions as well. Initially, when engineers are exposed to DOE, they may object to the time it takes to conduct these experiments. The counterarguments are powerful, though. For example:

- DOE does not take more than a couple of days.

- Running the experiment can be done by technicians

- The greatest time savings is not having to redesign because of unsolved quality problems. (It is amazing how designers do not have time for good designs the first time, but have all the time in the world to redo designs three and four times!)

Multiple Environment Over Stress Tests (MEOST)

The tremendous advantage of MEOST is that it can predict failures months before they would otherwise occur in the field and need to be corrected. It reduces the number of units on test from hundreds in conventional reliability testing to ten or less. Above all, it reduces reliability test time in the laboratory from hundreds of hours and days to twenty-four hours (for the most part). No self-respecting company can afford to do without MEOST.

Removing Non-Value-Added Operations—A General Approach to Cycle Time Reduction

In any industrial process, whether it is manufacturing or white-collar work, there are many non-value-added operations. Figure 11-1 is an example of typical non-value-added operations in production, each of which lengthens the cycle time from start to finish. Cycle time management is therefore a war on waste. The elements of waste include poor quality, machine breakdowns, poor space utilization, long setup time, long transport time, and the killer—waiting time.

Similarly, in the total manufacturing cycle time loop (labeled B in Figure 11-4), receiving, incoming inspection, and the stockroom are at the front end of production and finished goods at the back end. Ninety percent of these support operations as well as 90 percent of the production operations (from A) are a waste. Therefore the total manufacturing cycle time can be reduced by 90 percent.

The in-plant cycle time loop (labeled C in Figure 11-4) consists of planning, forecasting, scheduling, and purchasing—ahead of the manufacturing cycle. In an ideal

Figure 11-1. Non-value-added operations in production.

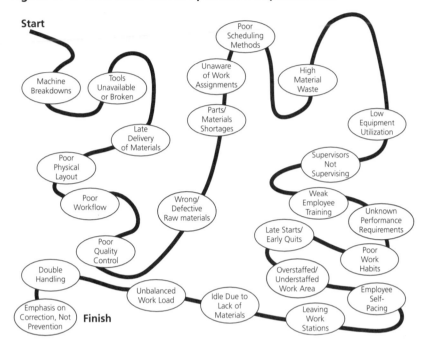

just-in-time (JIT) plant, these preliminary activities can be eliminated or significantly reduced in time. As an example, with a pull system, small lots, and focused factories, forecasting is no longer necessary. Consider also the typical waste in the purchase cycle. Purchase order releases, acknowledgments, expediting, counting, inspecting, sorting, scrap, rework, repackaging, and invoices add almost no value. The other functions can all be reduced to achieve a total in-plant cycle time reduction of 90 percent.

The last repetitive cycle time loop (labeled D) is from the time the customer's order is booked to the time it is shipped to the customer. The longest single element in this loop is supplier lead time, which can also be reduced by 90 percent and more.

Finally, there are similar cycle time loops in all support services and white-collar work, of which the new product introduction cycle time is the most important. The first cycle time element is the customer/marketing/sales/engineering interface. The second and largest element is design cycle time, which is so important that it can make or break a company.

A Blueprint for Drastic Cycle Time Reduction in Manufacturing

Several major characteristics of cycle time management must be present for a significant breakthrough in cycle time reduction. Figure 11-2 links these elements together.

The Focused Factory

As opposed to the behemoth factories of yesterday that produced a wide variety of products, the focused factory is a plant within a plant that manufactures only a family of closely related products and is managed by a dedicated, semiautonomous, interdisciplinary team.

To ensure the transition from the all-purpose plant to the focused factory, the product designs should be scrubbed for best manufacturability, part number reduction, component standardization, modularization to accommodate mass customization, a simplified bill of material structure, and simplified routing.

Unified Teams

In the old, unfocused factory, line support operations reported to bosses who were detached from manufacturing except at the very top rung—the plant manager. Departments such as manufacturing engineering, industrial engineering, process engineering, plant quality, plant purchasing, and maintenance protected their own fiefdoms. Teamwork was difficult at best.

In the focused factory, these departmental walls come tumbling down. The one focal point is a business manager or product manager to whom all support functions report, with the only exception being a few specialists who serve as internal consultants covering several focused factories. In the ideal focused factory, this not only includes all manufacturing support functions but others such as purchasing, engineering, and sales as well.

Product Flow vs. Process Flow

Conventional thinking was premised on common processes being located in one area, generating "process islands" scattered throughout a plant. Backtracking and crossovers were common. As a result, the enemies of cycle time reduction—transport time and waiting time—escalated. In one factory, a part actually traveled nine miles within a plant area of 30,000 square feet before shipment. As one wag noted, "It went round and round the plant until it developed enough kinetic energy to go out the door!"

Structured flow paths, by contrast, make for a smooth product flow that minimizes transport and waiting time. Preferably, the product flow is a U-shaped design that allows maximum operator flexibility and control. Although this creates some

Figure 11-2. Manufacturing cycle time optimization.

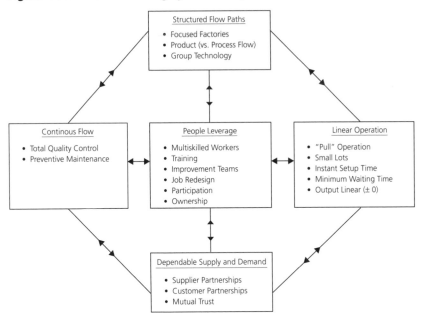

duplication of processes, the advantages of substantially improved inventory turns and other cycle time benefits greatly outweigh the increased capital equipment costs. Furthermore, even these capital costs can be minimized by the use of smaller, simpler, and more flexible processes and equipment. The old order believed that people and equipment must be kept busy at all times, no mater how much excess inventory they produced. The new order believes that permitting workers and equipment to stand idle is not a crime, but that having idle material is a sin.

A simple way to assess product flow is to measure travel distances for all products and then to establish plans for their systematic reduction. Another method is to determine product flows between plants. There have been horror stories of products fabricated in the United States, assembled in Korea, tested in Hong Kong, quality audited in the United States again, and distributed abroad again—all in the name of chasing direct labor or getting around tariff barriers and other intergovernmental regulations. The damage caused by these practices to cycle time and return on investment is almost too painful to measure. In one company, there was actually a case of a part that crossed the oceans seven times during the total manufacturing cycle! Any departure from a single plant, even a feeder plant, for product movement should be considered only as a last resort.

The ideal focused factory layout is line-of-sight manufacturing, where the production status can be visually ascertained by all at a glance. Production rates, quality levels, maintenance charts, and so forth should be posted for all to see. Storage racks, the handmaiden of work-in-process inventory, should be banished.

Multiskilled Workers

In a focused factory, cycle time training is given to all people in order to maximize understanding, commitment, and enthusiastic involvement in cycle time management. Through cross training, the number of job classifications are drastically reduced. A worker's flexibility and problem-solving ability now become the criteria for pay grade elevation and eventual promotion. In one of Motorola's divisions, the pay grades in one of its focused factories are based on the total number of machines and processes that an operator is certified to handle. Its focused factory, located in a high-wage area in the United States, has not only successfully challenged Japanese competition; it has knocked out several of its Japanese competitors.

Continuous Flow

Continuous flow as an attribute of cycle time management represents quality at its best. The object is to ensure that poor designs, unstable processes, defective materials, and marginal workmanship are not just corrected but prevented so that there can be a continuous, uninterrupted, and one-way flow of product with zero defects, 100 percent yield, minimal variation within specification limits, and no inspection and test. This, of course, is an ideal, but the techniques of Design of Experiments, Poka-Yoke, and total productive maintenance (TPM) offer an excellent blueprint for the eventual attainment of this ideal.

Total Productive Maintenance: Maximizing Equipment/Process Productivity[1]

TPM can be rated among the top-five techniques for profit improvement. The old industrial philosophy on plant equipment and maintenance was: "If it ain't broke, don't fix it!" This shortsightedness led to the perpetuation of quality/yield problems, cost overruns, and production stoppages. The first major reform was preventive maintenance, introduced in the United States in the 1950s. Nippondenso, a first-tier supplier to Toyota Motor Corp., went further to develop total productive maintenance in 1969. Today, the TPM Prize in Japan is coveted almost as much as the Deming Prize, with an OEE level (defined below) of 85 percent as a minimum required to even apply for the prize. Kodak's Tennessee Eastman was the first U.S. company to begin TPM in 1987. With 110 TPM teams, it has registered an 800 percent return on its investment. Unfortunately, most U.S. companies are not even aware of TPM, and the few that do use it average a dismal OEE level below 50 percent!

Overall Equipment Effectiveness: A Definition
The metric for TPM is called overall equipment effectiveness (OEE) or factory overall effectiveness (FOE). It is the product of three percentages:

1. Yield as a percentage

2. Uptime (the reciprocal of downtime) as a percentage

3. Machine efficiency as a percentage, where:

$$\text{Machine efficiency} = \frac{\text{Theoretical runtime}}{\text{Actual runtime} + \text{Setup time}}$$

For a machine/process to achieve an OEE of 85 percent as a minimum, each of these three percentages must be over 95 percent.

Method of Achieving Success
TPM plays an especially important role in reducing cycle time, increasing throughput, and reducing costs up to 4 percent to 9 percent of sales. To achieve success with TPM:

1. Train line operators and maintenance technicians in simple pre-DOE techniques, such as Pareto charts, cause-and-effect diagrams, CEDAC, and "the five whys."

2. Train line operators and maintenance technicians in Process Certification.

3. Train line operators and maintenance technicians in the clue-generation techniques of DOE (as covered in Chapter 9).

4. Form line operator/maintenance teams to improve yields and reduce machine downtime.

5. Reduce setup/changeover times by factors of 50:1 and more with techniques such as flowcharting, videotaping, and intensive practice runs (as done by pit crews in auto racing).

6. Give line operators responsibility for all routine preventive maintenance, such as cleaning, lubrication, record-keeping, tool storage/retrieval, Positrol, and Precontrol.

7. Utilize predictive maintenance with diagnostics and alarm signals to monitor key processes such as temperature, vibration, noise, and lubrication.

Pull vs. Push System

The fame of the Japanese *Kanban* system has heightened interest in the "pull" system of product control as opposed to the old "push" system. In the latter, operators pile up product at a workstation in adherence to a master schedule or to keep machines and people busy, regardless of the pileup of inventory or the lack of need for product further down the line. In the pull system the last workstation in the line paces the entire line, with each previous workstation producing only the exact amount needed by the next station.

In the push system, problems are hidden. The cushion of large work-in-process (WIP) inventories allows for a leisurely approach to problem solving. The best feature of the pull system is that it heightens the visibility of any problem. If there is a quality or delivery or other problem that shuts down a given workstation, the previous workstation, sensing that product is not needed at the next station, also shuts down. The ripple effect is fast, and soon the entire production line is down. There is nothing more visible than a whole line shut down. This accentuates the urgency of immediately solving the problem at the offending workstation. Workers, technicians, and engineers swarm over the station like bees to rapidly restore it to health so that the whole line can start up again.

Small Lot Sizes

A central feature of the pull system is that lot sizes are drastically reduced. In batch production, which is prevalent in most companies, large runs are the norm. If a process produces a 1,000-part run, with 10 at the exact same time, 990 parts do nothing but wait and twiddle their thumbs. If the lot size is reduced to 10, waiting time is reduced to zero. This is the crucial difference between batch production and short cycle manufacturing using continuous flows.

Setup Time Reduction

Small lots, however, require significant reductions in setup time in order to facilitate a line changeover rapidly from one model to the next. It has been demonstrated that setup time can be reduced by factors of 60 to 1 and more, given the use of ingenious industrial engineering methods fueled by workers' ideas.[2] One such ingenious method is to videotape the changeover process to pinpoint where time and motion are wasted.

Another technique is readying the workplace so that all tools and materials will be instantly available and there will be no need for even first piece-part quality evaluations through external audits. A classic example would be changing a tire in record-breaking time. The operation takes the average motorist at least twenty minutes. At the Indy 500, taking as much as fifteen seconds to change four tires could mean losing the race. Granted that the manpower and expense involved in effecting such a rapid changeover, though necessary to car racing, is impractical in most industrial situations. Yet the sport's masterful organization of material and labor, honed to a fine science through practice and drill, can provide many useful tips to manufacturing. Another example is provided by Toyota. In the early 1970s, it took three hours to make a die change in its large stamping machines. Hearing that Volkswagen had perfected a method to make the change in one-and-a-half hours, Toyota engineers went to study VW's techniques, installed these techniques at Toyota, and went on to shave another half-hour off setup time. Proudly they announced to their general manager that they had beaten VW. The manager said: "Good. My congratulations to your team. Now change the dies in three minutes!" As unattainable as the new goal seemed, the Toyota engineers—by the late 1970s—achieved this industrial equivalent of the four-minute mile by proceeding to shave setup time down to one-and-a-half minutes.

Linear Output

The benefits of a pull system are limited if the total quantity required by master schedules is allowed to vary from day to day. Such schedules should have nearly constant rates—known as "fidelity" or "linearity"—over short periods of time, with quantities being ramped up or down slowly. There can be model mixes within this linearity, but the total output of the mix should be held to an ideal ± 0 deviation from the constant rate.

Material Control

The old "just in case" system was characterized by incomplete picks, partial builds, expediting, parts chasing, inventory auditing, and an antediluvian cost accounting system—a bloated superstructure built on the vanishing foundations of a direct labor base.

In cycle time management, with a steady and dependable stream of just-in-time parts from suppliers, incomplete picks and partial builds are no longer necessary. Neither are parts chasing and expediting by supervisors, who can now divert the 90 percent of time previously spent on these useless activities to helping and coaching their people. The burdensome chores of physical inventory audits conducted once a month now disappear. The line-of-sight layout, the pull system, and small lot sizes facilitate easy counting, at no extra cost, directly by the operators themselves on a daily and even an hourly basis. Cost accounting, too, is beginning to enter the twenty-first century—directly from the nineteenth—with cycle time rather than direct labor as the base for overhead cost allocations.

Dependable Supply and Demand

It is only when a company has put its own house in order by slashing its work-in-process inventory that it has a right to approach its suppliers and customers as partners in cycle time reduction. With the aid of these techniques, suppliers can be encouraged, especially within the framework of partnership, to deliver a linear output of their products in smaller, frequent lots.

Customers may also become converts to cycle time management when a company can deliver their order with shorter and shorter lead times. They can then begin, with greater confidence, to order smaller quantities more frequently. In time, customers can also be persuaded to give longer-term contracts, blanket orders, and more stable forecasts—in short, to be partnership customers.

Role of the Cycle Time Professional

The discipline of quality has a focal point in the quality assurance function. The discipline of cost reduction sometimes has a focal point in the value engineering function. Generally, though, there is no focal point in the cycle time reduction function. There should be one, however, whose role should be to coach, guide, inspire, and lead all line operations in their drive to reduce cycle time. Otherwise, these efforts would get diffused and spasmodic.

CASE STUDY

A BENCHMARK COMPANY IN THE AREA OF CYCLE TIME REDUCTION—TOYOTA

Toyota is rated, by universal acclaim, as the best managed company in the world. Although it can lay claim to be the benchmark in several fields, it is so dominant in the field of cycle time that it has spawned a new language of speed—Kanban, pull systems; stockless production, zero inventories, just-in-time (JIT) and lean manufacturing.

Although it was old Henry Ford who started the cycle time revolution by converting iron ore into finished cars in forty-eight hours (Ford hasn't been able to replicate the recipe since!), the real impetus came from Taiichi Ohno, the brilliant executive who launched the world-famous Toyota production system. That system has revolutionized the way companies deal with customers, employees, suppliers, designs, and manufacturing, with cycle time as the driver. Here are a few highlights.

■ *Optimization of the Entire Supply Chain.* Toyota's attention span goes beyond its own manufacturing and its first-tier suppliers. It influences and helps suppliers *four levels down* to not only reduce costs and defect levels at each tier but, more important, to reduce cycle time. And profits are shared, instead of the suppliers being squeezed dry.

■ *Supplier Share of Engineering.* It is over 50 percent at Toyota, as compared with half that percentage in the West. This is an important factor that explains why the development time for a new car at Toyota is 25 percent less than in the West.

■ *Black Box Designs.* Toyota considers its core competency to be in the design of engines. The rest it gives to its partnership suppliers—Nippondenso, Aisin Seiki, Toyoda Gosei, for example. And instead of ordering piece parts from these suppliers, it orders entire systems from them, saving itself the headaches of designing, ordering, checking, and assembling hundreds of parts in each system or assembly. Nippondenso is Toyota's single supplier for all of its electrical and electronic assemblies.

■ *Process Development vs. Product Development.* Toyota's development of manufacturing processes leads its product development by one to two years, whereas in the West, the order is reversed, with process development lagging product development by six months to a year. As a result, manufacturing in the West is never able to launch a new product into production without painful delays.

■ *Kanban: Pull vs. Push Systems.* With the introduction of its renowned Kanban or pull system, Toyota obsoleted the whole, cumbersome paraphernalia of MRPII and its handmaidens, the master schedule and forecasting. With the final station as the gatekeeper, work-in-process inventories and cycle times shrank by factors of more than 10:1.

■ *Setup/Changeover Time Reductions.* The key to low inventories is small lots, and the key to small lots is vastly reduced setup/changeover time. Under the tutelage of Shigeo Shingo, Ohno's equally renowned associate, the SMED (Single Minute Exchange of Dies) system is a fantastic technique that can achieve changeover times in minutes instead of hours, and even in seconds instead of minutes.

■ *Poka-Yoke.* Discussed in Chapter 9, this is another Shigeo Shingo creation that prevents operator-controllable errors right at the fabrication/assembly stage without the need for inspection and without the need for control charts. Since it is part of the assembly task, this 100 percent check is automatic, less costly, and less time-consuming than cumbersome control charts.

Self-Assessment/Audit on Cycle Time: Implementing Disciplines by Company Type and Months to Complete

1. *Audit.* Table 11-2 is a self-assessment by which a company can measure its cycle time health. It has six key characteristics and sixteen essential disciplines, with 5 points each, for practical implementation. The total score is 80 points.

2. *Implementation Disciplines.* The disciplines have been carefully selected as being the most important, practical, and conducive of quick implementation.

3. *Timetable to Complete by Company Type.* As explained in Chapter 3, the timetable for implementing each discipline varies by company type:

> *Type A* companies have the greatest receptivity and desire to reduce cycle time, as well as some degree of familiarity with the subject.
>
> *Type B* companies, with less resources and less knowledge of the benefits of cycle time reduction, may want to do a pilot run in a product niche first before extending it to the whole corporation.
>
> *Type C* companies, with their bureaucracy, may not be convinced about the need for cycle time reduction. They might want to benchmark companies with a proven cycle time record before embracing the discipline.

Table 11-2. Cycle time: audit and scores, key characteristics, essential disciplines, and timetable to complete—by company type (80 points).

Key Characteristics	Essential Disciplines	Rating 1-5 *	Months to Complete, By Company Type		
			A	B	C
1-1 Supply Chain Management	1. The company has influenced and helped its suppliers three levels down to optimize costs and cycle time all down the supply chain.		36	60	—

	2. The company has retained only those activities that are its core competencies and farmed out the rest to partnership suppliers, preferably as "black boxes" rather than piece parts.	24	36	60
1-2 Design	1. The discipline of early supplier involvement (ESI) has been institutionalized to shorten design cycle time and reduce costs.	12	18	36
	2. The practice of parallel rather than series development has been routinized to reduce design cycle time.	6	9	12
	3. The cost-time profile of human inventory in design has been created to measure the reduction in payback time.	12	24	—
1-3 Manufacturing	1. Focus factories with dedicated customers, dedicated teams, and dedicated equipment have been created to reduce cycle time and improve manufacturing effectiveness.	9	15	36
	2. The plant layout has been converted from a process flow to a product flow to reduce transport time and waiting time.	9	18	36
	3. Total productive maintenance (TPM) has been institutionalized to reduce downtime and improve quality and efficiency of processes.	9	15	—

(continues)

Table 11-2. (Continued.)

Key Characteristics	Essential Disciplines	Rating 1-5 *	Months to Complete, By Company Type		
			A	B	C
	4. Kanban and pull systems have replaced MRPII and master schedules to reduce waiting time and inventories.		12	18	—
	5. Setup /changeover times have been drastically reduced using SMED principles and facilitating small lots.		12	18	36
	6. Level-loading has been used in scheduling to achieve a near-constant rate of production		9	12	36
1-4 Employees	1. Line workers have been converted into multiskilled operators capable of handling several jobs instead of one.		9	15	24
1-5 Customers/ Suppliers	1. Customers and suppliers have been encouraged to order/ship smaller quantities, more frequently.		6	9	15
1-6 Support Services	1. Every process has implemented the practice of Next Operation as Customer (NOAC)— see Chapter 14.		12	15	24
	2. All business processes have been flowcharted to identify and reduce all non-value-added operations.		15	24	48

	3. Out-of-the-box thinking and value engineering have been used to drastically change and improve business processes.			15	24	48

* The rater grades the company on each discipline on a scale of 1–5, with 1 being the least effective and 5 being the most effective.

Part Four

The Power of Ultimate Six Sigma
Applications in Major Line Functions

Design: From Historic Levels to Designs in Half the Time, with Half the Defects, Half the Costs, and Half the Manpower

Product life cycles today are shorter than design cycle times of yesterday. In this environment, the company with the shortest design cycle time will have the greatest competitive advantage. One of the most important factors in reducing this design cycle time is first-time quality success.

—JIM SWARTZ, MANAGER OF BENCHMARKING, DELCO ELECTRONICS

Poor Quality: The *Bête Noire* of Design

The corrosive influence of poor design quality is universal. Eighty percent of quality problems are, unwittingly but nevertheless, actually designed into the product. As a consequence:

- Customers see design problems not on just a few units, but often across the board.

- Reliability in design is more a quantitative false hope, given the engineer's inability to accurately predict, accurately test, and accurately estimate field failure rates at the time of product launch.

- Suppliers get blamed, even though more than 50 percent of poor specifications are the engineer's fault.

- Manufacturing is in the unenviable position of catching engineering's half-baked product tossed over the wall, with the time bomb ticking, and muddling through to shipment.

■ Service receives the storm of complaints that, ironically, it warned about earlier in the design cycle.

■ Line workers become the scapegoats, as engineering conveniently blames them for having "lost their pride of workmanship."

■ Hovering over all these effects caused by poor engineering is the ever-present danger of product liability suits. Prosecution lawyers wax ecstatic whenever they discover a design flaw that affects not just one but 100 percent of the units in the field.

Tough Design Costs: A Vicious Downward Spiral

It is well known that 70–75 percent of product costs are a function of the design. The large number of defects uncovered in the design cycle adds to these costs, making it difficult for the company to be competitive. Because of this competition, pressure is applied on the engineers to cut corners and reduce costs. The result is a further sacrifice of quality and reliability, producing, in turn, more costs, more delays, and more frustration—a veritable downward spiral.

Long Design Cycle Time: Giving the Keys to Your Competition

It is now a well-accepted axiom that the better the quality, the shorter is the cycle time, and the shorter the cycle time, the better the quality. Design cycle times have been reduced in recent years, but they are still far too long, allowing nimble competitors to steal a march. Design cycle time today is the name of the game. A company that can design and launch a product into the marketplace much quicker than its competition will be the Charles Lindbergh of design flights to the marketplace. (Ever hear of the number-two flier to cross the Atlantic?)

Stunted Innovations

Finally, because designers are not given free rein to exercise their creative juices by an impatient management, many innovations remain unborn. The dollar amount of sales from new products as a percentage of total sales remains low; the frequency of a stream of new products, introduced to keep competition off balance, is also dismally low; and "skunk work" projects dry up in the withering heat of management opposition.

The Ultimate Six Sigma Objective in Design

The main objective of a far-reaching engineering/development/R&D effort is to attain customer "wow" designs in half the time, with half the costs, half the defects, and half the manpower of older designs. This requires a revolution in:

- Organization of the Engineering Function

- Management Reinforcement

- Capturing the Voice of the Customer

- Breakthrough Quality/Reliability Technologies

- Steeper Cost Reduction Techniques

- Accelerated Cycle Time Reductions

- Releasing the Natural, but Currently Bottled-Up, Creativity of the Engineer

Organization of New Product Introduction (NPI)

Concurrent Engineering—A Team Effort

In the last fifteen years and more, companies have abandoned the traditional engineering role as a self-contained, isolated, departmental function. They have also, to a lesser extent, departed from matrix management, with its solid and dotted lines, which results in two bosses—a functional boss and a project boss—fighting for control.

They have embraced the principle of a team approach—concurrent engineering (also called simultaneous engineering). The first step is to team manufacturing with engineering at the start of design to overcome design weaknesses when the product reaches production. The second step is to expand the team concept by adding the disciplines of quality, purchasing, service, and finance at the start of design. A program manager or project manager leads the team.

Unfortunately, the fine intent of concurrent engineering has been diluted in practice. The main reason is the turf warfare between functional managers who loan their members to the project team and the program manager. Both demand allegiance to themselves and the team members are caught in the middle. Successful companies have solved this dilemma by granting full and unequivocal authority to the program manager once the team is formed and running. He becomes the undisputed czar of the project—from inception till it is launched in the field. In Japan, he is the *shusa*—a veritable shogun—invested with great power, including the placement of team members after product launch is completed.

Another dilution is the part-time use of most of the team members. Part-time use ends up with part-time results. There are so many activities and duties in a product launch that a resourceful program manager can and should keep all team members busy with full-time, meaningful work. Even if it is outside their specialized disciplines, team members are adept at multiple skills and the design project moves forward in harmony and speed.

Milestone Chart and Sign-Off Authority

Once the project team is formed, an agreement—sometimes called the *contract book*—is drawn up between top management and the team on their respective financing and capital equipment necessary to support the projects. The team, in turn, agrees to meet the quality, cost and design cycle time goals on the project. The contract book prevents finger-pointing and excuses on derailed projects that can happen because a prior agreement had not been made clear.

Table 12-1, the milestone chart for new product introduction, provides a detailed roadmap for the major steps and sequences as the design progresses. It shows:

- The team member with prime responsibility (P) for each step and those team members with contributing responsibility (C) for that step.

- Sign-off authority (S) at critical stages of the design's progress, which enables top management to either approve continuation of the project or scrub it.

- Sign-off authority (S) for the program manager during three vital design reviews and at the start of production, to modify the scope or direction of the project.

- The major tools that should be used at each step of the design. This is most important because without the proper tools and disciplines, the design is likely to be weak, delayed, costly, and unresponsive to the customer's true needs.

Management Guidelines

There are several important management guidelines that should govern a design and that could be incorporated into the contract book. They include:

- Maximum 25 Percent Redesign Rule

- A Stream of New Products Rapidly and Frequently Introduced

- Supply Management Directives

- Parts Philosophy

- Lessons Learned Log

- Reverse Engineering

The Maximum 25 Percent Redesign Rule

The maximum 25 percent rule means that a minimum of 75 percent of the new design should be common to the previous design (by volume) unless there is a major

(text continues on page 240)

Table 12-1. New product introduction: milestones and responsibilities chart.

No.	Milestone	Sr Mgmt	Program Mgr	Design Lead	Mfg	Quality	Sales/Mktg	Service	Sourcing	Finance	Major Tools
A.	**Organization**										
1.	Program Team Kick-Off	S	P	C	C	C	C	C	C	C	Concurrent Engineering
B.	**Mgmt. Guidelines**										
2.	Max. 25% Redesign	S	P	P		C	C			C	Contract Book
3.	Stream of Rapid New Products	S	P	P		C	C			C	Lessons Learned Log
C.	**Voice of Customer**										
4.	Elements of Customer "WOW"		P	P	C	C	C	C	C	C	"Bhote's Law"
5.	Customer Specifications		P	P	C	C	C	C	C	C	QFD, Mass Customization
D.	**Design Quality/Reliability**										
1.	Feasibility Study										CAD; Software Architecture
2.	Preliminary Design		P	P		C	C	C	C	C	Derating, FMEA, FTA, PLA
3.	First Design Review	S	P	P	C	C	C	C	C	C	Checklist

(continues)

Table 12-1. (Continued.)

No.	Milestone	Sr Mgmt	Prgm Mgr	Design Ldr	Mfg Ldr	Quality	Sales/Mktg	Service	Sourcing	Finance	Major Tools
4.	Prototype Design	C	C	P	C	C	C	C	C	C	DOE, MEOST, Metrology
5.	Quality Systems Audit	C	C	C	C	P	C	C	C	C	The Ultimate Six Sigma Assessment
6.	Second Design Review	S	S	P	C	C	C	C	C	C	Checklist
7.	Pilot Run	C	C	P	C	C		C	C		B vs. C; Positrol; Process Certification; Precontrol
8.	Design for Manufacturability			P	P	C		C		C	Boothroyd-Dewhurst Scoring
E.	**Design Cost Reduction**										
9.	Total Value Engineering	C	C	P	C	C		C	C	C	V.E. Job Plan, "Fast" Diagram
10.	Part Number Reduction			P	C	C	C	C	C	C	SBU, Product, Model Reduction
11.	Early Supplier Involvement	C	C	P		C		C	P	C	Cost Targeting, Financial Incentives
12.	Patent Study	C	C	P						C	
F.	**Design Cycle Time Reduction**										
13.	Outsourcing	C	C	P	C	C		C	P	C	"Black-box" Supplier Design
14.	"Human Inventory"	C	C	C				C	C	P	Integration of Cost-Time Curve
15.	Third Design Review	S	S	P	C	C	C	C	C	C	Checklist

G.	Product Launch									
16.	Customer/Field Tests		C	P	C	P		C		DOE at Customer Site
17.	Management Review	S	P	C	C	C	C	C	C	Authorization for Full Production
18.	Production Run	S	C	P	C	C	C	C		Mini-MEOST, TDPU, COPQ
19.	Management Audit	P	P	C	C	C	C	C	C	Lessons Learned
20.	Initial Customer Feedback		P	C	C	P	P	C	C	Survey Instrument

Responsibility Codes:

S = Sign-Off Authority

P = Prime Responsiblity

C = Contributing Responsibility

new platform—which may occur only once in a few years. In the West, there is a tendency for a 100 percent new design, based on the engineers' ego and their desire to have their names etched into the product in perpetuity. The result is a delay in design cycle time by a factor of ten as compared to the 25 percent rule.

A Stream of New Products Rapidly and Frequently Introduced

Even more important than the attendant cycle time reduction, the 25 percent rule allows a company to introduce a new product every few months—say, every three months as opposed to once a year or once in eighteen months. This constant stream of new products introducing new features and innovations then moves a company four to six generations ahead of competition, leaving the latter in the dust. The classical example is Nike, Inc., a company that constantly introduces small changes so frequently that it has surged ahead of its competitors in every measure of business performance.

Supply Management Directives

Early in the design cycle, management must stipulate to the team a few key practices in its dealings with suppliers. They may include:

- Selecting key suppliers based on ethics, trust, and mutual help, to promote a win-win partnership

- Outsourcing not just piece parts, but higher-level assemblies and "black box" designs, where these are not core competencies of the company

- Encouraging (even mandating) the team's enthusiastic acceptance of early supplier involvement in the prototype stage of design as one of the best ways to reduce costs and improve quality

- Using cost targeting, where the company prescribes the price paid to the supplier rather than the reverse (the old three-quote syndrome), based on computer-aided estimates of material and labor costs

- Outlawing the totally destructive practice of sending out bids on the Internet on key parts with previously established partnership suppliers

Parts Philosophy

To ensure high standards of field reliability:

- Ninety percent of the parts must have a proven track record of reliability. There is a need for using state-of-the-art new parts, but such experimentation should be kept to a minimum.

- There should be an ironclad directive to the team that all critical parts must have a built-in factor of safety or derating. Derating is explained fully later in this chapter.

Lessons Learned Log

There is a predilection in many companies to sweep design mistakes under the rug. The objective of the lessons learned log—either a paper or computer trail—is not to embarrass the design team or punish it, but to ensure that the sad lessons of historical errors are not condemned to repeat themselves, either for the next product or the next generation of engineers.

Reverse Engineering

Known earlier as competitive analysis, reverse engineering should be standard practice in any progressive company's design cycle. The competitor's product is stripped down and evaluated, part by part, for its design, reliability, materials, and cost (through cost targeting).

Reverse engineering is also supported by quality function deployment and benchmarking studies to compare the customer's perception of the design *vis-à-vis* the company's best competitors.

Designing for the "Voice of the Customer"

Chapter 4 highlighted the several elements that combine to result in customer "wow," both for products (Figure 4-3) and services (Figure 4-4). While no single element of customer "wow" is necessarily more important than any other, for all customers, at all times, in all places, Bhote's Law states that it is that element of customer "wow" missing from a company's product or service (provided it is truly important to the customer) that requires maximum top management attention.

The Elements of Customer "Wow"

The design team should ascertain, at the very start—the concept stage—the core customers' priorities associated with these elements of "wow." This is done with mass customization (Chapter 9) and with quality function deployment (QFD). QFD, however, tends to concentrate on technical performance only, at the expense of other elements that the customer may deem more important. The Japanese have shifted their customer attention from *atarimar hinshitsu*—"taken for granted" quality—to *miryo kuteki hinshitsu*—quality that fascinates, bewitches, and delights. The design team should therefore research features that core customer have not expected but that, when introduced, would thrill them.

Specifications: Ninety Percent of Them Are Wrong

In translating customer requirements into engineering specifications, techniques such as QFD are supposed to be employed. Yet specifications are still pulled out of the air. Euphemistically, the practice is called "atmospheric analysis." Why are specifications so vague and arbitrary? There are several reasons that were detailed in Chapter 10. As a result, either product costs are needlessly excessive or the product quality/reliability is endangered. The contact lens case study, described in Chapter 10, showed how the company lost millions of dollars with specifications that its customers considered unimportant. It reestablished realistic specifications and went on to save millions of new dollars.

A Comprehensive Specifications Checklist

Answers to the questions in Table 12-2 should be tackled by the design team at the concept stage and revisited at the prototype stage of design to ensure that the various priorities of customer requirements are adequately translated into engineering specifications.

Design Quality/Reliability

Quality and reliability should be addressed in each stage of design, namely during:

1. Product Feasibility Study

2. Preliminary Design

3. Prototype Design

4. Engineering Pilot Run

5. Production Pilot Run

6. Production

7. Field Rollout

Product Feasibility Study (Concept Stage)

An invaluable starting point is to consult the "lessons learned" log from previous designs. The lessons learned log is a quick way for new engineers to avoid design pitfalls and shorten their learning time.

Computer-Aided Designs (CAD)

There are a number of software programs, ranging from Monte Carlo simulation, E-chip, MiniTab, and other modeling techniques, that can be used at the product feasibility stage. Given the fascination with the computer, these methods are becoming

Table 12-2. A specifications checklist.

Customer Element	Checklist of Associated Requirements/Specifications
Quality	• Are acceptance/rejection criteria established, and are they based on customer expectations, not the company's?
	• Are target COPQ, yields/cycle time, TDPU established?
	• Are the Shainin/Bhote DOE requirements to prevent quality problems in production sufficiently well known and practiced?
Reliability	• Are targets (percent failure rate/year, MTBF, etc.) "reach out" to meet future reliability expectations, such as:
	—Sharp reductions in the gap between failure rates of complex vs. simple products?
	—Component failure rates below 1 ppm/year?
	—Use of incentive/penalty clauses for exceeding/not achieving reliability targets?
	• Are maximum field environments/stresses measured?
	• Are adequate test chambers in place to combine and accelerate stresses rapidly, to reliably predict and prevent failure rates, using MEOST?
	• Is there a firm derating (factor of safety) protocol in place and followed?
Maintainability	• Are targets for mean time to diagnose (MTTD) and mean time to repair (MTTR) established?
Diagnostics	• Are MTTD targets helped by built-in diagnostics and MTTR targets by modular designs?
Uniformity	• Are target values and minimum $C_{pk}s$ determined for key parameters?
Dependability	• Are warranty targets/times being extended toward lifetime warranties?
Availability	• Is there a targeted uptime as a percent of the total product use time?

(continues)

Table 12-2. (Continued.)

Customer Element	Checklist of Associated Requirements/Specifications
Technical Performance	• Are target performance parameters established with the customer as the "supreme court," and are they correlated with customer expectations?
	• How do target performance parameters compare with competition?
Safety place	• Is a formal, written product liability prevention process in place?
Ergonomics	• Is user-friendliness tested with employee/focus groups, and how does it compare with competition?
Future Expectations	• Are future expectations continually solicited from customers through mass customization?
Service Before Sales	• Are sales/service parameters formulated to measure the effectiveness of service to the customer?
Services After Sales	• Are there targets for repair service accuracy and timeliness?
	• Is there a systematic and continuous follow-up of customers after sale?
Price/Cost	• Have targeted prices, targeted costs, and targeted product life been determined?
	• Have price elasticities been determined?
	• Have incremental specifications vs. incremental costs been tested with key customers?
Delivery	• Is there a targeted design cycle time that is at least half (or less) of a previous design of comparable complexity?
	• Is the design inventory, made up of design manpower, expressed in terms of a negative cash flow equivalent of months of sales?
Delight Features	• Are there a targeted number of delight features, unexpected by the customer, to generate customer "wow"?

ever more popular. Worst-case analysis, fail/safe conditions, and self-test software architecture can all be examined.

However, an important prerequisite for CAD is a proven mathematical formula, or equation, that governs the relationship between a number of independent variables and their dependent variable. Sometimes, such formulas can be developed based on experience—a sort of rearview mirror approach. Often, though, the computer cannot be programmed for unknown interaction effects and can lead to poor designs. One inviolate rule is captured in President Reagan's pithy advice about the Russians: "Trust but verify!" Computer simulations must be verified at the prototype stage with actual hardware using powerful Design of Experiment tools.

Software Architecture
A review of the software architecture is also necessary at this product feasibility stage.

Reliability Block Diagram and Budgeting
The targeted reliability of the product as whole must be subdivided into targets for each module and each subassembly comprising the total design. This task is given the pompous name of reliability budgeting. Often, incompatibilities between the total reliability target and the feasibility of achieving a reliability target for a particular module show up at this early stage of design.

Preliminary Design (Breadboard Stage)
The elements of quality/reliability in preliminary design include:

- Thermal Plots

- Derating and Structural Analysis

- Reliability Prediction Studies

- Failure Mode Effects Analysis (FMEA)

- Fault Tree Analysis (FTA)

- Product Liability Analysis (PLA)

Thermal Plots
In many products, especially in electronics, heat is the enemy of reliability. A useful discipline, therefore, is to scan the preliminary product with infrared scanners to detect hot spots in the design that are likely to accelerate failure rates and can be corrected *a priori*. Failure to conduct thermal plots is one of the reasons for early field failures.

Derating and Structural Analysis

When civil engineers design a bridge or building, they design it to bear a load three to six times greater than the load expected in actual use. In other words, they design in a factor for safety of three to six. Yet this discipline is seldom carried over into other branches of engineering, especially in electronics engineering, since engineers are reluctant to use even a minimum 20 percent safety margin—or derating—because of fear of added material costs in the design.

CASE STUDY

THE 1-AMP DISASTER

The history of reliability disasters is replete with such design myopia. A multinational company used a 1-amp diode in a diode trio subassembly that formed part of an alternator in a passenger car. The failure rates, low in early production, soon escalated into a major calamity, costing the company millions of dollars. The engineers had been reluctant to derate the diode because a higher-rated part would cost a nickel more! Finally, the threat of the total loss of the alternator business forced them to design a 3-amp diode (i.e., a derating of 67 percent or a factor of safety of three). The result: On 800,000 new alternators with the larger diode, the total failure was one—a failure rate of 1.25 parts per million (ppm), as compared to the previous failure rate of 15 percent or 150,000 ppm.

In the world of electronics, for instance, every important part should have a minimum derating of 40–60 percent in terms of voltage, current, power, and temperature. The parts should be able to "loaf" with the much-reduced stresses imposed on them. In mechanical products, the factor of safety should be 2:1.

Reliability Prediction Studies

The United States, Britain, France, and Germany issue cookbook reliability studies, with failure rates on each part, based on applications. Most of them are almost worthless. The U.S. Defense Department uses a reliability study called Mil-Handbook 217E. Like its international counterparts, the predicted failure rates miss the actual field failure rates by 2:1 or even 10:1. They are either too low or too high, but invariably they are wrong. Computer programs for reliability, such as CB Predictor, are gaining currency, but they are no better than the cookbook approaches. The best practice is for a company to generate its own library of field failures based on the "school of hard knocks"—that is, the actual field history, with superimposed stresses.

Failure Mode Effects Analysis (FMEA)

Although this thirty-year-old discipline is much touted as a major reliability tool, it is a relatively weak technique, not worth the hours and hours spent on constructing it. Its objectives are good:

■ To identify the weak links of design

■ To predict the top failure modes and their effects on customers; prioritize and quantify the risks of using such parts; and reduce the risk through redesign, or redundancy, or tests, or supplier changes

The weaknesses of FMEA, however, overshadow its strengths. It is only a paper study that attempts to quantify the engineer's opinions and concerns. It is an almost opaque crystal ball in predicting true field failures.

A failure mode effects analysis is recommended only as a preliminary study. Not much time should be wasted in its development.

Fault Tree Analysis (FTA)

This is a mirror image of an FMEA. Whereas an FMEA starts with potential causes of failure and determines their effect on the customer, an FTA starts with failures that could be observed by customers and traces their root causes in an attempt to prevent such root causes before the fact. Fault tree analysis is somewhat more useful as a preliminary tool for product liability analysis (discussed next).

Product Liability Analysis (PLA)

Many people think of the United States not as a nation of laws but a nation of lawyers! Product liability lawsuits have become a bonanza for unscrupulous lawyers pressing for huge settlements in punitive damage. To protect against a plethora of frivolous lawsuits, companies must document their actions to prevent failures that can cause personal injuries. A PLA, which is derivative of an FTA, can provide courts with evidence that preventive measures have been designed into the product.

Prototype Design Stage

Shainin/Bhote Design of Experiments

There are numerous simple but statistically powerful and cost-effective Design of Experiments (DOE) tools that make up the Shainin/Bhote methodology. Chapter 9 gives a thorough introduction to these techniques.

Multiple Environment Over Stress Tests (MEOST)

Chapter 9 has amply described the need, objectives, and benefits of MEOST, along with its principles and its powerful methodology. MEOST is the tool, *par excellence,* for reliability just as DOE is the tool, *par excellence* for quality and problem solving/prevention. Yet, of all the tools described in Chapter 9, MEOST is almost totally foreign to industry, with only one percent of leading companies even aware of it and 0.05 percent using it. For the average company, MEOST is a totally unknown black hole.

MEOST is most effective at the prototype stage of design, where potential failures that take months to occur in the field can be replicated in design, typically in less than twenty-four hours with extremely small prototype samples of three of less. It should be repeated in the pilot run stage to make sure that engineering changes and tooling have not adversely affected reliability. It should also be repeated in production before shipment to the customer, to ensure that production workmanship/processes and suppliers have not degraded the design intent.

My experience with MEOST has resulted in product field failure rates of 4 ppm to 10 ppm/year; and in one product line with hostile environments, we achieved zero failures in over seven years of field use, with each engine traveling over 500,000 miles.

c_{p_K} of 2.0 or More on All Important Parameters

Following a Variables Search, where all the important parameters of a product have been defined, their target values (i.e., design centers) should be aimed for in design and their c_{p_K}s should be specified at 2.0 or higher. This also applies to the important parameters for suppliers and should be part of their specifications and drawings.

Instrument Accuracy

There is an inviolate rule in the quality discipline that the accuracy of the instrument measuring the product should be at least five times the accuracy of the product. Instrument accuracy is made of the variations within instrument (V_{WI}), instrument-to-instrument (V_{I-I}), and operator-to-operator (V_{O-O}), as expressed by the formula:

Total Instrument Variation (V_{IT}) = $\sqrt{V_{WI}^2 + V_{I-I}^2 + V_{O-O}^2}$

Product Variation (V_P) = Specification Width

This means that V_P / V_{IT} should be equal to or greater than 5:1.

Many a problem in design and in production goes unsolved because this 5:1 minimum instrument accuracy rule is not heeded.

Modular Designs

Modular designs should also be a "must" for the design team. This facilitates diagnostics in the field, ease of service, and above all, the postponement of options in mass customization as far down the assembly line as possible.

Quality Systems Audit

It is at the prototype stage that any existing quality system audit that may be in place should be reexamined and updated for effectiveness. The self-assessment/audit contained at the end of each chapter of this book goes well beyond just quality. Nevertheless, it is useful in covering weaknesses in all areas, starting with design. Under no circumstances should weak quality systems, such as the Malcolm Baldrige National Quality Award or the European Quality Award, or the even weaker ISO-9000 and QS-9000, be given a second thought!

Failure Analysis Capability

A major weakness in many companies is the inability to conduct comprehensive failure analysis on products and components. Dependence on suppliers is risky, both in terms of time and accuracy. Dependence on outside failure analysis laboratories is, at the least, expensive. There is no substitute for a professional failure analysis staff within the company, along with costly but necessary failure analysis equipment such as scanning electron microscopes (SEMs) and spectral analysis, to get to the root cause (Red X) of a problem. This is especially true today, as more and more products use a larger share of electronics, such as integrated circuits and microprocessors. (It is estimated that more than 50 percent of a passenger car will be composed of its electronic content by dollars in a few years.)

Pilot Run Stage

B vs. C Validation Tests

Chapter 9 has explained B vs. C as an integral part of Design of Experiments (DOE). This test validates that a design improvement is effective and permanent, at a high confidence (95 percent) level and at low cost—three Bs and three Cs.

Design for Manufacturability (DFM)

There are ten basic rules for achieving ease of manufacturing at the design stage:

1. Minimize the number of parts.

2. Minimize assembly surfaces.

3. Design for Z-axis assembly.

4. Minimize part variation (through DOE).

5. Design parts for multiuse and ease of fabrication.

6. Maximize part symmetry.

7. Optimize parts handling.

8. Avoid separate fasteners where possible.

9. Provide parts with integral "self-locking" features.

10. Drive toward modular design.

Cost Reduction in New Product Design

Total Value Engineering

The distinction between traditional value engineering (VE), which concentrates on cost reduction while not deteriorating quality, and my version of total value engineering (TVE), which concentrates on maximizing customer "wow," loyalty, and retention, is covered in Chapter 10 and highlighted in Table 10-2. Both VE and TVE are among the most powerful cost reduction tools available to design engineers. For example:

■ An average reduction of 25 percent can be achieved, with a minimum of a 10 percent reduction. A 75 percent reduction is not uncommon.

■ A minimum return of 10:1 in investment is possible, with 100:1 returns frequently registered. Furthermore, the amount of investment required in design is modest.

Total value engineering's gains are even more spectacular because it concentrates on customer loyalty. A 5 percent increase in customer retention achieves a 35–120 percent increase in profit.

In addition to TVE, three other cost reduction techniques apply to new product design. Each of the following is covered in detail in Chapter 10:

■ SBU, Product, Model, and Part Number Reduction

■ Group Technology (GT) as a Discipline

■ Early Supplier Involvement (ESI)

Cycle Time Reduction in New Product Design

Customer-Marketing-Engineering Interface

In design, cycle time reduction starts with the customer. Keeping a finger on the customer's pulse should long precede product development, well ahead of its concept stage. The task starts even before the end of the launch of the previous design. The changing needs, requirements, and future expectations of the customer must be carefully monitored through quality function deployment, focus groups, clinics, panels, and—above all—in one-on-one mass customization sessions. Preparing the groundwork reduces the numerous delays that can be caused by customers changing their minds in the middle or at the end of a current design cycle. Furthermore, this should be a team effort where marketing, sales, and engineering work together in what is called the strategic business process.

Chapter 11 is entirely devoted to cycle time reduction, including techniques applicable in the design process.

Creativity and Innovation in New Product Design

In a larger sense, creativity and innovation are common to all human activity. They are certainly generic to all functions within a company—customers, leadership, organization, employees, suppliers, manufacturing, and services. However, because creativity and innovation are traditionally associated with the design function, it is convenient to include the principles and practice of creativity in this section. (It is beyond the scope of this book to treat the subject in depth. There are excellent references for that purpose; some of them are cited in the reference notes in the next few sections.)

Creativity Defined[1]

Creativity is a mental act that frees a person or an organization from self-imposed boundaries of common knowledge. It may also be defined as:

- Breaking out of traditional modes of thinking and seeing the world in new ways

- An expression of talents, hearts, and essence, individually and in groups

- Deferred judgment

Blocks to Creativity[2]

There are three sets of blocks to creativity—perceptual, cultural, and emotional.

Perceptual Blocks (obscure the view of the real problem)

- Difficulty in narrowing the problem, or the opposite—narrowing it too much.

■ Inability to define the problem owing to language difficulties.

■ Failure to use all of the senses in observation. (Physiologists identify not just the five primary senses but as many as fifteen or twenty different senses that account for hunches and premonitions.)

■ Difficulty in seeing remote relationships.

■ Difficulty in not investigating the obvious.

■ Failure to distinguish between cause and effect.

Cultural Blocks (caused by home, school, and societal pressures)

■ Desire to conform to an accepted pattern

■ Premature judgment for practical and economic reasons

■ Reluctance to investigate and tendency to doubt everything

■ Overemphasis on competition or cooperation

■ Too much faith in statistics, reason, and logic

■ Overgeneralization

■ Sticking to one's own viewpoint

■ Too much or too little knowledge in a particular field

■ Belief that indulging in fantasy is worthless

Emotional Blocks (irrational fears and anxieties)

■ Fear of making a mistake and being ridiculed or censored

■ Grabbing the first idea that comes along

■ Rigid thinking

■ Overmotivation to succeed quickly

■ Pathological desire for security

■ Fear of supervisors; distrust of colleagues and subordinates

■ Lack of drive to carry through to completion and verification

Methodology for Creativity:[3] A Seven-Step Approach
The methodology outlined here is similar to value engineering:

1. *Orientation.* Determine the true nature of the problem, eliminate misconceptions, and determine related problems.

2. *Preparation.* Gather storehouse of facts, general information, and past experiences.

3. *Analysis.* Consider the following questions:

■ Why does the problem exist?

■ What are the consequences of the problem?

■ Are the items causing the trouble really necessary? If not, consider doing without them.

■ Would a substitute item be better than replacement or redesign?

■ Is there any relationship between the subproblems?

■ Has elapsed time changed the conditions?

■ Is the problem really worth solving?

4. *Hypothesis.* Discard preconceptions; emphasize imagination unlimited. No critical evaluation is allowed in this step and no negative thinking.

5. *Incubation.* Allow time to invite subconscious thinking.

6. *Synthesis.* Put all the pieces back together after the analysis step.

7. *Verification.* Test and follow-up to determine the effectiveness of the final solution.

Training and Testing Results
Not all people are born with leadership; nor are they all born with creativity. Leadership can be learned. So can creativity, which is normally distributed in the general population. While there will always be a gap between the highs and lows of that creativity distribution, the whole spectrum of human creativity can be moved higher for all. But it requires training.

There are several training programs and tests for creativity. Two well-known tests are:

1. The AC Test for Creative Ability, from the AC Spark Plug Division of General Motors

2. The Purdue Creativity Test developed by Purdue University

In one such test, after a twenty-two-hour training program a group of thirty-nine engineers increased the average number of ideas from eight-two before training to 116 after the training. The group was then split into those who had contributed a relatively high number of ideas before the training (an average of 106 ideas) and those with a lower score (an average of 60 ideas). After training, the high group's contribution went up 25 percent to 133 ideas, while the low group went up 67 percent to 100 ideas. Similar gains have been registered in other areas such as suggestion programs. The moral of these stories is that 1) creativity can be learned and improved by all people, and 2) the lower the initial level, the higher is the gain in creativity.

A Blueprint to Raise Human Intelligence, Creativity, and Innovation for All

Training, important though it is, isn't enough. There must be leadership—not just at the CEO levels, but at all levels where people lead and influence others—and a nurturing, nourishing organization structure to maximize the potential for creativity and innovation. The elements of such an environment are:

■ *Trust.* Bob Galvin, the retired chairman of Motorola, states: "One's creativity depends on interaction with others—others one trusts—others who feel trusted. For one to be unfettered in risking interaction with another, the other must know the trust of openness, objectivity, and a complementary creative spirit. . . . [I]n order to trust, one must be trustable. Trust is a power. The power to trust and be trusted is an essential prerequisite quality to the optimum development and employment of a creative culture."[4]

■ *Help and Guidance.* In Japan, the CEO looks upon the care and feeding of the young as his primary responsibility. The help that enables people to grow is not a rigid master-to-apprentice regimen. It is guidance with a loose rein. Mentoring programs, which companies such as Ford Motor have institutionalized, are a good example of smoothing the road to creativity.

■ *Freedom to Explore and to Make Mistakes.* The true leader, recognizing that he is not God and does not have all the answers, gives his people the freedom to explore their own pathways, create their own solutions, and even make their own mistakes.

Freedom, however, is not a substitute for anarchy. The leader has to lead, set the direction, establish goals, and monitor results. Then, having done that, the leader gets out of the way. The mark of an outstanding leader, according to Jack Welch, retired chairman of GE, is the three Ds—direct, delegate, and disappear!

■ *Leader-Follower as an Iterative Role.* For a person to lead implies that others follow. But is the leader a breed apart or is he a better follower? A leader has many roles,[5] including that of:

- ■ Observer of the work his associates perform

- ■ Sensor of attitudes, feelings, and trends

- ■ Listener to ideas, suggestions, and complaints

- ■ Student of advisers, inside and outside of the institution

A leader is also the product of experience, both his own and other's,[6] and may mimic other leaders who have earned his respect.

■ *Team Synergy.* Today, the basic building block of an organization is not the department but the team. Not only are teams more productive; they have more fun. The team culture transforms the organization from separate islands of rugged John Wayne independence into a state of symbiotic interdependence. An *esprit de corps* develops, as in the world of sports.

■ *Problem Solving.* One of the most powerful tools in the creativity arsenal is problem solving "by talking to the parts." Chapter 9 details the various Shainin/Bhote Design of Experiments techniques that can coax answers from parts and processes much better than engineering guesses, hunches, theories, and opinions. And the joy of success in the eyes of team members is awesome to behold.

■ *Support, Encouragement, Celebration.* The psyche of employees can be fragile. Bossy attitudes, body language that demeans, and a tin ear to ideas can ruin motivation, creativity, and growth. So can harsh layoff policies and gross unfairness in income distributions for tangible gains by employees. By contrast, if the leader displays warmth and humility, has listening skills, is more of a coach and teacher, supports the efforts of workers, encourages and cheers them on, and celebrates their "wins," the potential for an advance in creativity and innovation in every employee is unbounded.

CASE STUDY

A BENCHMARK COMPANY IN THE AREA OF DESIGN— JAPAN'S AUTOMOTIVE INDUSTRY

Instead of choosing a particular company as a benchmark, I have selected a country and an industry within the country as a model for new product development. The country is Japan and the industry is its famed automotive industry (although one company—Toyota—dominates the field of car companies in Japan and worldwide and is unquestionably the benchmark *par excellence*).

Two comparisons are made:

■ *New Product Introduction.* Table 12-3 outlines the features associated with new product introduction in Japan vs. the West and explains the radical differences in their approaches.

■ *Performance Results.* Table 12-4 compares differences in performance results between Japan, the United States, and Europe. It is true that general financial and economic fluctuations on the world scene may have changed some of these figures in absolute terms, but the relative differentials remain. They should be a wake-up call to the West!

Table 12-3. Case study: a comparison of new product introduction (NPI) in Japan vs. the West (automobiles).

Feature	Japan	West
Project Manager	Leader, total authority, *shusa*: great power, most coveted position.	Coordinator must beg for resources and team members' time.
Team	Stays on project full-time; team members evaluated by *shusa*.	Team members available part-time; functional managers demand priority and do evaluations.
Engineer Rotation	Three months on assembly line, three months in marketing, one year in various engineering departments, then routine work on NPI, then more	Little or no rotation; start on the bench; one or two disciplines in a lifetime.

	fundamental work, then more training, then more advanced work, then other disciplines.	
Communication	Conflicts resolved early— *ringi* and *neemawashi*.*	Conflicts persist.
Development Method	Parallel development; die production and body design start at same time.	Series (i.e., sequential) development. Die making delayed until designers complete detailed part specs.
Range of Models	Wider range, short life, frequent replacement. Result: Innovations three or four product generations ahead of the West.	Narrower range, longer life for each model.
Outsourcing	Only core competencies retained in-house.	Vertical integration still favored in design.

Source: James P. Womack, Daniel T. Jones, Daniel Roos, *The Machine That Changed the World* (New York: HarperCollins Publisher,1991).

* *Ringi* is deferring a decision until group agreement is achieved; *neemawashi* is winning over opposition with a variety of advocates for the cause.

Table 12-4. Case study: automotive performance results— Japan vs. West.

Parameter	Japan	U.S.	Europe
Average engineering hours/new car (millions)	1.7	3.1	2.9
Average development time/new car (months)	46.2	60.4	57.3
Number of employees in project team	485	903	904
Number of body type/new car	2.3	1.7	2.7
Average ratio of shared parts	18%	38%	28%
Supplier share of engineering	51%	14%	37%
Ratio of delayed products	1 in 6	1 in 2	1 in 3
Die development time (months)	13.8	25.0	28.0
Time from production start to first sale (months)	1	4	2

(continues)

Table 12-4. (Continued.)

Parameter	Japan	U.S.	Europe
Return to normal productivity after new model (months)	4	5	12
Return to normal quality after new model (months)	1-4	11	12
Reliability (complaints/100 cars)	66	140	128
Quality: (Delivered defects/100 cars)	30	61	61
Productivity cars/employee/year	47.3	31.0	24
Cost: Japanese landed cost (into U.S.) advantage			
Small Cars	$2,600	—	?
Intermediate Cars	$3,000	—	?
Large Cars	$4,200	—	?

Source: James P. Womack, Daniel T. Jones, Daniel Roos, *The Machine That Changed the World* (New York: HarperCollins Publisher, 1991).

Self-Assessment/Audit on Design Practices: Implementing Disciplines by Company Type and Months to Complete

1. *Audit.* Table 12-5 is a self-assessment/audit by which a company can measure its design health. It has seven key characteristics and sixteen essential disciplines, with 5 points each for practical implementation. The total score is 80 points.

2. *Implementation Disciplines.* Only the most practical and results-oriented disciplines have been chosen.

3. *Timetable by Company Type.* The timetable to complete each discipline varies by company type. Specifically:

Type A companies, with a strong desire to be in the forefront of design, will embrace and implement these disciplines within twelve months.

Type B companies, with less background in benchmark design practices, are likely to have a longer incubation period.

Type C companies, which have traditionally had long design cycles alongside poor launch quality and high design costs, are doomed to implement some of these disciplines slowly or not at all.

Table 12-5. Design: audit and scores, key characteristics, essential disciplines, and timetable to complete—by company type (80 points).

Key Characteristics	Essential Disciplines	Rating 1-5*	Months to Complete, By Company Type		
			A	B	C
1-1 Organization for New Product Development	1. Concurrent engineering—a cross-functional team drawn from engineering, manufacturing, quality, sales/marketing, sourcing, service, and finance—is the full-time organizational building block for NPI.		6	12	36
1-2 Management Guidelines	1. A firm rule of no more than 25% of redesign of an existing product is permitted.		3	6	24
	2. A stream of new products with small changes (less than 25% new parts) is frequently and rapidly introduced to keep competition off balance.		12	18	—
	3. A "lessons learned" file to prevent mistakes in the next generation of design, and reverse engineering to evaluate strengths/weaknesses of competition, are essential requirements in the design function.		6	9	12
1-3 "Voice of the Customer"	1. All elements of customer "wow" have been considered in the concept phase of design, with				

(continues)

Table 12-5. (Continued.)

Key Characteristics	Essential Disciplines	Rating 1-5*	Months to Complete, By Company Type		
			A	B	C
	special attention to those features, unexpected by the customer, which would cause customer delight.		12	24	—
	2. All key parameters have been correlated between customer importance and engineering specifications to determine realistic, cost-effective specifications.		18	36	—
1-4 Design Quality/ Reliability	1. Quality/reliability tools, especially Design of Experiments (DOE) and Multiple Environment Over Stress Tests (MEOST) have been institutionalized in the design process.		15	30	—
	2. Product liability analysis (PLA) has been conducted to protect the company against product recalls and lawsuits.		9	15	36
	3. Design for manufacturability (DFM) rules are adhered to, in order to facilitate ease of production.		6	12	24
1-5 Design Cost Reduction	1. Cost reduction tools, especially total value engineering (TVE) and cost targeting, have been				

	institutionalized in the design process.			12	24	36
	2. The company has pursued a policy of retaining only those products where it has core competencies for its design efforts and outsources the rest.			12	24	–
	3. Incentives, including royalty incentives, have been designed to encourage partnership suppliers to generate cost reduction ideas in design.			12	24	—
1-6 Design Cycle Time Reduction	1. The customer-marketing-engineering team is in place to reduce delays and changes in customer requirements during the design cycle.			9	15	24
	2. Cycle time reduction tools, such as early supplier involvement, parallel development, group technology, have been institu-tionalized in the design process.					
1-7 Creativity and Innovation	1. Training and testing for creativity have been given to all design personnel and "skunk works" have been instituted to encourage freedom of design with results.			12	18	36
	2. A nurturing infrastructure to maximize creativity and innovation has been firmly established.			9	15	36

* The auditor or assessor grades each discipline on a rating scale of 1–5, with 1 being the least effective and 5 being the most effective.

CHAPTER 13

Manufacturing: From Sunset Obsolescence to Sunrise Enlightenment

A growing number of companies in electronics, toys, and consumer goods are coming home from abroad. . . . Companies
that sought cost reductions and manufacturing efficiencies
through foreign operations have learned the hard way that it
is easier to control your destiny through better management
techniques, local manufacturing effectiveness, just-in-time
[manufacturing], subcontracting, and training. The higher
quality product may again be your U.S. competitor that uses
these techniques. . . .

—DAVID M. RICHARDSON, *THE WALL STREET JOURNAL*

Why Has Manufacturing Been Sidelined?

For the last twenty years and more, manufacturing has been looked upon as a "sun-
set" discipline. It has lost the aura it used to have in the 1950s and 1960s. It has lost
the respect of top management; and its salaries are well below those of finance, marketing, and design. There are a number of reasons for this disenchantment:

■ *The Surge of the Service Industry.* The service industry accounts for 70 percent
of jobs as compared to manufacturing, which has declined to 25 percent. (There is a
parallel to the decline of agriculture, which once accounted for 90 percent of jobs in
the early-nineteenth century but has fallen to 10 percent half a century ago to three
percent today.)

■ *The Digital Age*. The third economic revolution—the digital age (after the agricultural revolution around 9000 BC and the industrial revolution a century and a half ago). E-commerce and the ubiquitous Internet now account for more than 75 percent of engineering jobs, while hardware is reduced to 25 percent.

■ *The Flight Offshore*. Manufacturers have moved operations to low-wage countries, with China leading the parade. The illogical rationale is lower cost, not recognizing the hidden costs of offshore procurement (see Table 8-3).

■ *The Influence of the Business Schools*. They churn out MBAs, who have no clue about what it takes to design or manufacture a product, but who aspire to be CEOs in five years after graduation.

■ *Single-Discipline Top Management*. Top management, with primarily a single background—finance or law (to quote William Shakespeare: "First, let's kill all the lawyers!")—has a hazy concept of manufacturing, at best. What insights can these two fields provide for manufacturing or running a successful business for that matter?

The Key Role of Manufacturing

Yet manufacturing need not be a stepchild, an appendage of other disciplines that have shunted it aside. Scores of progressive companies[1] have brought forth the renaissance of manufacturing in the last twenty years. These companies have run circles around their best offshore competitors, at a much lower unit cost; higher productivity; better quality; faster delivery; higher inventory turns; and higher profitability, despite higher pay to their line workers.

Why can manufacturing contribute so much to a company's welfare?

■ It makes a direct contribution to the customer. It is the "final answer"—to use the popular phrase from *Who Wants to Be a Millionaire*—to what the customer wants.

■ It integrates the functions of sales, marketing, engineering, and other disciplines. It is the only place where they come together.

■ It can be turned into a marketing weapon, according to Tom Peters, in his book *Thriving on Chaos*. Of manufacturing he says, "It is from hands-on interaction—among foremen, line operators, customers, suppliers, researchers, and distributors—that day-to-day advances in innovation and responsiveness flow."[2]

■ It is a breeding ground for small but continuous improvements, as opposed to the large but rare breakthroughs generated in design. An analogy is that the engineering function is the Babe Ruth who would hit a home run, but had many strikeouts in his career, whereas manufacturing is the Wee Willie, who could be counted on for a hit almost every time at bat.

Restoring Manufacturing to a Place of Honor:
Part I—What Not to Do

Before examining several key initiatives that can truly restore manufacturing to its rightful importance in a company, it is useful to list practices that should be given a wide berth.

1. *Mass Production.* Except in the rare instances where the market can sell millions of units of a standard product, mass production is as dead as the dodo bird. Today, more and more, we must consider a customer of one, who wants what he wants, how he wants it, where he wants it, when he wants it, and at what price he wants! Ours is the age of mass customization (see Chapter 9).

2. *Automation.* In the era of the 1970s and 1980s, the plaintive cry of the entrepreneur was "emigrate, automate, or evaporate." Emigrating industry to offshore locations is proving to be less and less of a bargain each year. Nonetheless, there is still an unseemly fascination with automation.

Example

An automated firm[3] processes molding, cutting, and painting parts for its product. Robots stack the parts from each automated fabrication step on pallets taken by automated guided vehicles to an automated storage. From there, the parts are taken automatically to an automated final assembly line, which can adjust its fixtures to hold any one of 100 models of the product and assemble it with pick-and-place robots. The direct labor head count: zero. The manufacturing support count: 3,600! Is the factory in the United States? No—it is in Japan, the land of Kanban! Automation can become a narcotic.

Automation is good if it reduces human slavery—fatigue, boredom, and drudgery. And it should only be used if it meets this inviolate rule: The cost of indirect technical support and high-tech tools added together should be less than the savings in direct labor.

Ross Perot bemoaned General Motors' expenditure of $40 billion for robotics-equipped plants and capital management. GM still lost market share and went from being the low-cost producer to the high-cost producer among the Big Three.

Even Toyota, which had religiously followed the precepts and practice of its great founder of just-in-time (JIT) manufacturing—Taiichi Ohno—was tempted to go the route of automation in its Tahara plant near Toyota City. It was a disaster. Toyota has never repeated the mistake again.

3. *MRP and MRPII: Systems Whose Time Has Long Gone.* MRP (materials requirements planning), a computerized system used to determine the quantity and timing requirements for materials, and MRPII (manufacturing resource planning), used for capacity planning and master schedules, were staple tools of the 1970s and 1980s. They are still used in those industries that have not switched to JIT. MRPII's main weakness is that it uses the old "push" system, where each workstation is gated by a preordained master schedule. As a result, inventories can pile up at each station if the next station doesn't require them.

Restoring Manufacturing to a Place of Honor: Part II—What Must Be Done

An Infrastructure of Support for Manufacturing Excellence

In a larger sense, the previous chapters of this book have prepared the groundwork for manufacturing excellence. Let's recap the highlights of their contributions to manufacturing:

1. *Leadership Contributions to Manufacturing*

- Releasing the genie currently locked up in the direct labor worker

- Trusting the line worker

- Giving workers freedom—even to make mistakes

- Training every worker

- Improving the quality of work life—creating joy in the workplace

2. *Organization Contributions to Manufacturing*

- Eliminating mind-numbing bureaucracy

- Converting from a department structure to a team-based process structure

- Changing the ways workers are hired, trained, evaluated, compensated, and promoted

- Designing meaningful and egalitarian gain sharing for all workers

3. Employee Contributions to Manufacturing

- Redesigning the dull, boring jobs of the line worker

- Creating power and joy in team competitions

- Adopting one of three approaches, or their composite, to industrial democracy: open book management, self-directed work teams, or the minicompany

- Moving up in the ten stages of empowerment

4. Supply Chain Management Contributions to Manufacturing

- Sending perfect parts directly from the supplier to the line

- Making drastic reductions in supplier lead time, yet ensuring no line stoppages or stockouts

5. Tools for the Twenty-first Century: Quality, Cost, and Cycle Time in Manufacturing

Of the eight powerful tools of Ultimate Six Sigma (covered in Chapters 9, 10, and 11), seven apply directly to manufacturing and should be used as a way-of-life. These are:

- Cost of Poor Quality (COPQ)—one of the most prolific ways to improve profitability

- Design of Experiments (DOE)—for chronic problem solving

- Multiple Environment Over Stress Tests (MEOST)—to prevent production processes and workmanship from degrading design intent

- Total Productive Maintenance (TPM)—to optimize machine/process effectiveness

- Benchmarking—to simulate and improve best-in-class company practices

- Poka-Yoke—to prevent operator-controllable errors

- Total Value Engineering—to reduce manufacturing costs

- Lean Manufacturing—to reduce inventory and cycle times

6. Design Contributions to Manufacturing

- Designing for minimum variability: $c_{pk} \geq 2.0$

- Adhering to the rules of design for manufacturability (DFM)

- Minimizing model numbers and part numbers

- Postponing mass customization to almost the end of a production line.

The Twin Engines of Quality and Cycle Time in Manufacturing

For manufacturing excellence, two disciplines are vital—quality and cycle time. Motorola calls them the twin engines that give a company its powerful thrust for world-class achievement. Motorola's 10:1, 100:1, and 1000:1 quality improvement drive has already been covered in Chapter 2. The company has a similar drive for 10:1 and 100:1 improvement in cycle time reduction. Each of these engines of change has been detailed in Chapters 9 (on quality) and 11 (on cycle time). At this point, though, a few additional techniques as they apply to manufacturing need elaboration.

Quality: Engine #1

Among the powerful quality improvement techniques applicable to manufacturing are:

- Design of Experiments

- Multiple Environment Over Stress Tests (miniversion)

- Poka-Yoke

- Cost of Poor Quality

In addition, there are a number of quality improvement techniques that are specifically in the realm of manufacturing.

1. *Product Robustness.* In production and in the field, there are a number of uncontrollable factors, sometimes called noise factors, that can adversely affect the quality of the product. Ambient temperature; humidity; static electricity; line voltage fluctuations and transients; lack of preventive maintenance; and some degree of customer misuse can degrade product quality and reliability. Product robustness means making it impervious to these noise factors. This cannot always be done, but robustness should be attempted in production before the product is launched into the field.

The necessary discipline is again DOE. Using a second round of a Variables Search experiment (see Chapter 9), the uncontrollable (noise) factors are deliberately introduced to determine their individual or collective impact upon the response (or Green Y). If the noise factors prove to be unimportant, they can be ignored. If they are important, some of the other product parameters must be modified so that we can live with the noise factors present. The objective is to increase the signal-to-noise ratio.

Example

An appliance manufacturer was experiencing an unacceptably high failure rate of its drier in consumer homes. Two of the principal reasons were 1) poor venting, with outlets clogged up, and 2) line voltage fluctuations. Both were beyond the manufacturer's control. The consumer could not be expected to worry about the venting, nor did he have control over line voltage fluctuations caused by the power utilities. A Variables Search experiment was run in production. It indicated that airflow was a parameter that could be increased with minimal cost increases, making the drier impervious to venting constrictions and line voltage fluctuations. The company now has a "robust" drier with a field failure rate reduction of over 10:1.

2. *Process Characterization and Optimization.* One of the frequent reasons for poor quality in manufacturing is that while much attention is paid to the design of the product, the process that makes the product is often treated as a stepchild. It may be selected as an afterthought to the product, with little compatibility between the two. Development engineers do not feel responsible for the process. They relegate that to the process engineer—who leans on the supplier of the process equipment. The result: arbitrary specifications, antiquated procedures, and arbitrary process parameters.

World-class quality companies start their process research two years ahead of product development, exactly the opposite of practices in the average company. When the product and process come together, a team consisting of the process engineer, the development engineer, and the equipment supplier conducts a DOE study—typically a Variables Search experiment—to define and characterize the process. The purpose is to separate the important process variables from the unimportant ones; open up the tolerances of the latter to reduce costs; and optimize the levels of the former to achieve c_{pk} of 2.0 or more, with a subsequent Scatter Plot technique (see Chapter 9).

3. *Positrol: Freezing Process Quality Improvements.* The purpose of Positrol, following optimization of the process, is to make sure that process gains and improvements are "frozen." Each important parameter (the what) is monitored by a "who, how, where, and when." It is described in somewhat greater detail in Chapter 9 and in my book *World Class Quality, Second Edition,* Chapter 18 (New York: AMACOM, 2002).

4. *Process Certification: Improving the Signal-to-Noise Ratio.* The purpose of this technique is to identify as many quality weaknesses of a peripheral nature and nip them in the bud. It makes the process robust by removing these noise factors and thus improv-

ing the signal-to-noise ratio. It is described in somewhat greater detail in Chapter 9 and in my book *World Class Quality, Second Edition* Chapter 19 (New York: AMACOM, 2002).

5. *Control Charts: A Technique Whose Time Has Gone.* Control charts, under the banner of statistical process control (SPC), have been widely used in Western industry ever since a 1980 NBC television documentary, "If Japan Can, Why Can't We," purported to show that Japan was way ahead in quality because of its use of control charts. Yet, for more than twenty-five years, Japan has abandoned control charts as being of marginal use (though occasionally they would roll out the old control charts to impress visiting Western firemen).

As a result, control charts, which had gone into limbo after World War II, were recalled from exile and given a coronation in the West. It has been a tyrannical reign, with several original equipment manufacturers (OEMs)—especially some of the automotive companies—demanding the use of control charts as a passport to doing business with them. They force control charts down the throats of unwilling suppliers; and they bludgeon into submission those knowledgeable suppliers who dare to point out that the control chart emperor wears no clothes. As often happens the royal court is filled with hangers-on and charlatans who exploit the desperation of companies to gain a foothold on the control chart bandwagon by offering courses, tutorials, and ubiquitous computer software programs on their methodology. It is a sad fact that control charts—along with their equally bumbling cousins, ISO-9000 and QS-9000—have done very little for the quality revolution. For a detailed treatment of control charts and their limitations, please see Chapter 20 of my book *World Class Quality, Second Edition* (New York: AMACOM, 2002).

6. *Precontrol: A Technique Whose Time Has Come.* Precontrol is much simpler, more cost-effective, and more statistical powerful than control charts. Another huge advantage is that it can be taught (the mechanics, not the theory) to line operators in five minutes. In fact, direct labor people and suppliers never, ever want to go back to control charts once they have sampled the east of Precontrol.

The rules of Precontrol are simple and shown in Figure 13-1. It can be charted in the same manner as control charts but is much easier for the operator to perform and for its interpretation of quality progress. For a detailed treatment of Precontrol, please see Chapter 21 of my book *World Class Quality, Second Edition* (New York: AMACOM, 2002).

7. *Poka-Yoke.* Discussed in detail in Chapter 9, Poka-Yoke is used instead of Precontrol when defect level requirements below 50 parts per million (ppm) make the Precontrol impractical from a sampling viewpoint. (It should be observed that control charts are ineffective when defect levels below 1,000 ppm are required.)

8. *Mini-MEOST.* The use of Multiple Environment Over Stress Tests for reducing and virtually eliminating field failures has been covered in Chapter 9. MEOST is

Figure 13-1. Precontrol: a technique whose time has come.

Simple Precontrol Rules:

1. Draw 2 Precontrol (P-C) lines in the middle half of the Specification Width.

2. To determine Process Capability, 5 units in a row must be within P-C lines (Green Zone).

3. In production, sample 2 units consecutively and periodically.

4. Frequency of sampling. Divide the time interval between 2 stoppages by 6.

Condition	Action
1. 2 units in Green Zone	Continue
2. 1 unit in Green and 1 unit in Yellow Zone	Continue
3. 2 units in Yellow Zone	Stop
4. 1 unit in Red Zone	Stop

*To resume production, 5 units in a row must be within the Green Zone.

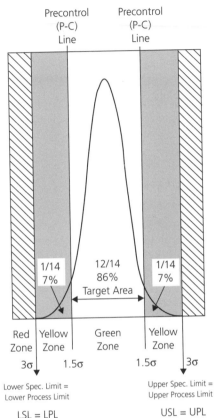

primarily used at the design stage to replicate and correct potential field failures before the product goes into production. But it is also a necessary discipline in manufacturing to ensure that workmanship, production processes, and supplier materials have not degraded design reliability.

However, a full-blown MEOST is not necessary here. Mini-MEOST is a truncated version of the technique with 1) fewer stresses and 2) somewhat lower levels of stresses. Again, the sample size for mini-MEOST testing remains unbelievably small: a maximum of ten units if the product is repairable or a maximum of thirty units if it is not repairable.

9. *The Elimination of Burn-in as a Reliability Tool.* Many companies subject their electronic products to a 100 percent high temperature test, often with power cycling to ensure that early-life failures are removed. The rationale is that high temperature can weed out the weaker components and improve reliability.

Table 13-1. Awareness and implementation of quality disciplines in manufacturing.

| | Leading Cos. | | Average Cos. | |
Discipline	% Aware	% Implementation	% Aware	% Implementation
1. Design of Experiments	10%	1%	—	—
2. Multiple Environment Over Stress Test	1%	0.05%	—	—
3. Product Robustness	5%	0.1%	—	—
4. Process Characterization/ Optimization	2%	0.05%	—	—
5. Positrol	5%	0.1%	0.1%	—
6. Process Certification	2%	0.1%	0.1%	—
7. Precontrol	40%	15%	10%	2%
8. Poka-Yoke	15%	1%	2%	—

If a company does not know what to do for reliability, it may use burn-in as a stopgap, brute-force measure. However, it has proven to be an ineffective technique.

10. *Field Escape Control.* Companies do not recognize that their earliest and largest service station is not in the field but in their own factories. During production testing, tabs should be kept on defects of a reliability nature (i.e., catastrophic failures). The discipline is called field escape control, which I introduced at Motorola nineteen years ago. During the course of a day or two, a single failure can be ignored. But if there are two or more failures, with the same failure mode and the same failure mechanism, the panic button should be pushed. The failures should immediately be analyzed and corrections instituted. If action is not taken on these factory failures, the probability of the same failures appearing in the field, in the hands of the customer, is unacceptably high.

11. *Analyzing Effectiveness.* Analyzing product fallout in the factory by human analyzers is not always 100 percent effective. Lack of time, knowledge, and accurate instrumentation, as well as intermittent failures, are the main causes. To some extent, computer testing of the product can overcome some of these weaknesses. However, a spot-check should be conducted on the products the analyzers troubleshoot to deter-

mine their effectiveness. A practice of "seeded defects," where a known defect is deliberately created to see if it would be detected by the analyzer, is encouraged. This practice can also be used to detect the effectiveness of mini-MEOST checks.

12. *Metrology*. Several product quality problems can be solved by making sure that the measuring instruments are accurate. There are four parameters in metrology that must be defined: precision, bias, accuracy, and discrimination.

1. *Precision* is the spread or range of a parameter; it can be measured as range of ^{c}p.

2. *Bias* is the deviation of the average of a parameter from the target value. It is the noncentering $\overline{X} = D$, where $\overline{X}$ is the average and D is the design center.

3. *Accuracy* combines precision and bias. It can be called $^{c}p_K$ if tied to a specification width.

4. *Discrimination* is the ratio of product spread to measurement spread, with a minimum ration of 5:1.

Reducing Instrument Variation. Reducing instrument variation should precede reducing product variation if the discrimination ratio is less than 5:1. The total instrument variation or tolerance T_T, is made up of three subvariations—within instrument tolerance (T_{WI}); instrument-to-instrument tolerance (T_{I-I}), and operator-to-operator tolerance (T_{O-O}). The total instrument tolerance is based on the root-mean-squared law, as follows:

$$T_T = \sqrt{T_{WI}^2 + T_{I-I}^2 + T_{O-O}^2}$$

The 5:1 rule means that the specification tolerance, T_P (where P stands for product) should be at least five times T_T.

■ *Routine Quality Disciplines in Manufacturing*. There are several other routine quality disciplines that are part of any good quality system. They are listed here, but without further explanation, in the interest of brevity:

- Plant Safety Guidelines

- Electrostatic Discharge (ESD) Protection

- Underwriters Laboratory (UL) or Equivalent Approval

- Quality Walk-through of Software

- Storage, Transport, Packing, and Shipping Control

- Effective Engineering Change Control System

- Traceability and Barcoding Control

- Effective Failure Analysis Down to Root Cause and Comprehensive Failure Analysis Lab

- Destructive Physical Analysis (DPA)/Teardown Audits

- Manufacturing Flowchart with Maximum Defect Targets at Each Workstation

Cycle Time Reductions: Engine #2—The War on Waste

The Importance of Inventory Reduction

Inventory was widely recognized twenty years ago as a liability, not an asset, and that's how nineteenth-century accountants living in the twenty-first century still label it. Furthermore, their faulty accounting practice artificially makes the balance sheet appear more profitable for a company than it should be! Yet inventory plays an important role in substantially increasing a company's return on assets (ROA). For instance:

Return on Assets $\geq$ Sales / Total Assets $\geq$ Sales / (Inventory + Fixed Assets + Receivables)

Of the total asset base, inventory often accounts for 40 percent. Therefore, reducing inventory to one-third could increase return on assets by 30 percent. Reducing it to one-tenth could increase ROA by almost 60 percent—a figure that world-class companies have far exceeded.

Cycle Time, the Integrator

Yet inventory, like profit, is a lagging indicator. Like profit, you cannot work on inventory. It is a result, not a cause; an output, not an input. But you can work on cycle time. In fact, cycle time is the great integrator of our times. Among the techniques specifically applicable to manufacturing cycle time reduction are:

- Focused Factories

- Unified Teams

- Product vs. Process Flow

- Multiskilled Workers

- Continuous Flow (Product Quality)

- Total Productive Maintenance

- Pull vs. Push Systems

- Small Lot Sizes

- Setup Time/Changeover Time Reduction

- Linear Output

- Material Control

- Dependable Supply and Demand

Chapter 11 was devoted to the dramatic reduction of cycle time in all operations, and Figure 11-5 captured these interrelated cycle time disciplines schematically.

Tracking Progress

Cycle time management in manufacturing requires only two macroscopic measurements to track progress: yield and cycle time. Figure 13-2 shows how a product line in a computer company's focused factory was tracked for yield and cycle time improvements. It also indicates the major techniques used to achieve these improvements both in quality and in cycle time.

Cycle Time Management: From Theory to Action

The most frequently asked question about cycle time management is: "Where do we begin implementation?" As with other processes (as opposed to "programs") of importance, the starting point should be top management exposure, education, and commitment. From that point forward, the following is a suggested sequence. It is not necessary, however, that these steps be taken in order. Parallel and iterative steps can be accommodated.

1. *Establish performance measurement parameters.* The focus must shift from profit to return on investment (ROI) for each strategic business unit (SBU); from

Figure 13-2. Manufacturing yield/cycle time.

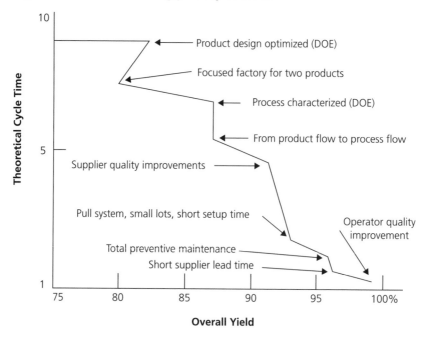

direct labor to manufacturing cycle time; from single workstation defect analysis to overall yield improvement; from manufacturing requirements planning (MRP) to just in time (JIT); from the vagaries of forecasting to "build and ship to order" with lightning speed.

2. *Create a pilot focused factory.* Rather than immediately breaking up a large plant into several focused factories, a single focused factory should be formed to act as a pilot to manufacture a product family based on similar processing requirements and using similar parts.

3. *Form a focused factory management team.* Forming a focused factory management team may be the hardest step of all from the point of view of human relations because it disrupts traditional functional organizations and breaks up empires. A first step is to assign a task force role to a selected focused factory management team. As the task force begins to pull together and succeed, it can become a permanent focused factory organization, with an autonomous team consisting of a product manager and members from every function within manufacturing, followed soon after by all supporting functions, such as sales, engineering, supply management, and quality assurance.

4. *Unleash people power.* A focused factory, with its small size, natural work units, client relationships, quick feedback on performance, and sense of ownership, has a far greater chance than a traditional factory of welding its people into a family and unleashing full people power. The Hawthorne effect—named after Western Electric's famous Hawthorne plant in Chicago where the noted Elton Mayo found, in the 1920s, that workers respond to the attention and support from management to achieve productivity gains—may also come into play as its success becomes more widely recognized. Training of the workforce in cycle time principles, multiple skills, and problem solving should begin with the creation of the focused factory.

5. *Attack poor quality—the first rock to blast.* In the "rocks in the river" analogy, there is no rock more formidable than poor quality. Tackling all quality problems must be the highest priority in the focused factory—from product yields to total productive maintenance, from incoming inspection to supplier process control.

6. *Adopt a pull system.* To convert from a push to a pull system, lot sizes must be reduced gradually but systematically, with some inventory banks between stations at the start leading to an eventual elimination of such banks. Setup time reduction should be pursued and an attempt made at stabilizing the total model mix at a nearly constant rate.

7. *Establish dependable supply and demand.* The last steps involve influencing suppliers and customers. A demonstration of achievement in one's own plant is worth a thousand exhortations to suppliers and pleas to customers. Such achievement can then become the best sales tool for requesting blanket contracts and smaller, more frequent deliveries from suppliers and to customers.

A Blueprint for Manufacturing Excellence

Dr. Richard J. Schonberger, in his landmark book *World Class Manufacturing: The Next Decade*,[4] lists sixteen principles with nonfinancial metrics required for manufacturing excellence.

1. Add customer/client representatives to each focus factory team.

2. Extend benchmarking to customers and competition on all key processes/functions continuously.

3. Sustain yearly improvements of 50 percent or more in quality (Q), speed (S), flexibility (F), and value (V).

4. Have frontline teams develop strategies and numeric goals, and self-monitor them.

5. Reduce parts, service operations, and suppliers by 90 percent.

6. Reduce setup time, cycle time, and product travel and space requirements by 90 percent.

7. Synchronize flow rate throughout production to the customer rate of usage.

8. Convert 80 percent of workers to certified, multiskilled operators.

9. Expand recognition of workers with gain sharing and stock options.

10. Achieve c_{p_k}s of 2.0 defects to <10 ppm; reduce rework and lateness by 99 percent.

11. Achieve a suggestions rate of more than twenty-five per employee per year, along with self-implementation.

12. Cut internal transactions (e.g., part number entires, work orders, move tickets) by 99 percent.

13. Concentrate on customer-oriented metrics—quality, speed, value—not on financial metrics.

14. Optimize current equipment (less downtime) instead of buying needless new equipment.

15. Use simple, flexible, low-cost equipment rather than "behemoth giants."

16. Selectively choose and limit your customers, not the other way around.

Although Schonberger has defined these excellent principles, the various chapters in this book—*The Power of Ultimate Six Sigma*—translate them into implementation and results with how to's, tools, and techniques.

CASE STUDY

A BENCHMARK COMPANY IN THE AREA OF MANUFACTURING—HEWLETT-PACKARD

While Taiichi Ohno started his famous Kanban system at Toyota and launched modern JIT,* several companies have successfully emulated the Toyota production system. Intel, Motorola, Dell Computer, Omark Industries, Lincoln Electric, and scores of others have rejuvenated their manufacturing operations. One company in particular is Hewlett-Packard—a model of quality, JIT, and manufacturing excellence. Table 13-2 documents the typical changes HP has wrought on a number of criteria.

Table 13-2. Breakthrough improvements in manufacturing at Hewlett-Packard.

Criteria	Before	After
Solder Quality	5,000 ppm	1 ppm
Repair/Scrap (% of direct labor)	35%	2%
Overall Equipment Effectiveness (OEE)	40%	99%
Number of Suggestions/Employee/Year	0.15	6.5
Plant Space (typical)	30,000 sq. ft.	7,500 sq. ft.
WIP Inventory	30–40 days	3 days
Number of Part Numbers	20,000	450
Number of Suppliers	2,000	200
Average Lot Size	500	5
Number of Skills/Operator	1	5
Ratio of Actual Time to Direct Labor Time	3,000–14,000:1	2:1
Process Speed: Sales Rate	100–1000:1	3:1

*Just-in-time (JIT) manufacturing did not start in Japan. Its originator was Henry Ford I in the 1910s. The total lapsed clock time for assembling an early automobile—from the time iron ore landed on the docks at Dearborn and was processed into engine blocks and machined, to the time the engine assembly was completed and the car readied for shipment to dealers—was forty-eight hours! Ford Motor today has not been able to capture old Henry's JIT recipe.

Self-Assessment/Audit for Manufacturing: Implementing Disciplines by Company Type and Months to Complete

1. *Audit.* Table 13–3 is a self-assessment/audit by which a company can measure its manufacturing health. It has four key characteristics and sixteen essential

disciplines, with 5 points each, for practical implementation. The total score is 80 points.

2. *Implementation Disciplines.* Only those disciplines that are the most practical and conducive to quick results have been chosen.

3. *Timetable to Complete by Company Type.* As explained in Chapter 3, the timetable to complete each discipline varies by company type:

Type A companies have a head start in introducing some of these disciplines in manufacturing, so the timetable for implementation is generally no more than one year.

Type B companies have had less exposure to the twin engines of quality and cycle time in manufacturing; the timetable for some of the disciplines can extend to eighteen months.

Type C companies, wedded to traditional and the *status quo,* may find it difficult to understand, much less accept, the power of the twin engines of quality and cycle time that drive manufacturing. Implementation, therefore, may be delayed for three years—and for a few disciplines, never.

Table 13-3. Manufacturing: audit and scores, key characteristics, essential disciplines, and timetable to complete—by company type (80 points).

Key Characteristics	Essential Disciplines	Rating 1-5*	Months to Complete, By Company Type		
			A	B	C
1-1 Manufacturing Resurgence	1. The company has an enlightened policy to manufacture in the region where it sells and to buy materials in the country or region where it manufactures.		9	15	—
	2. The company has discarded complex automation and MRPII as being counterproductive and				

	adopted pull systems and *Kanban* for maximum inventory reduction.	9	15	36
1-2 Quality Improvement in Manufacturing	1. The product is made robust by examining and compensating for uncontrollable (noise) factors present in production and in the field.	9	12	—
	2. Important processes have been characterized and optimized with Variables Search and Scatter Plots.	9	12	—
	3. Important process parameters are monitored with Positrol and potential, peripheral quality weaknesses are prevented through Process Certification.	6	9	18
	4. Precontrol is used to ensure defect levels of no more than 100 ppm on important parameters.	6	9	12
	5. Poka-Yoke is used to prevent operator-controllable errors and defect levels above 10 ppm.	9	12	18
	6. Mini-MEOST and field escape control are used to ensure that design reliability has not been degraded in production and in supplier materials.	12	18	36
	7. Design of Experiments are used by line workers to solve chronic quality problems by "talking to the parts."	12	15	30

(continues)

Table 13-3. *(Continued.)*

Key Characteristics	Essential Disciplines	Rating 1-5*	Months to Complete, By Company Type		
			A	B	C
	8. Metrology is used to ensure instrument precision, nonbias, accuracy, and discrimination.		6	9	15
1-3 Cycle Time Reduction in Manufacturing	1. Structured flow paths are employed to create: • Focused factories of dedicated product, with dedicated equipment and dedicated people. • Product flow—nor process flow—to minimize transport time. • Multiskilled operators to main group technology cells.		12	18	36
	2. Total productive maintenance (TPM) is used to achieve overall equipment effectiveness (OEE) >85%.		9	12	24
	3. Drastic reductions in lot sizes and setup/changeover time and space have been achieved.		9	12	30
1-4 General	1. Parts, service operations, and suppliers have been reduced by 90%.		12	18	30
	2. Employee suggestions are supported and sustained to achieve a level of 25 suggestions				

per employee per year, along with self-implementation.		9	15	30
3. Internal transactions, such as part number entries, work orders, move tickets, and general paper flow, have been reduced by >95%.		12	18	36

*This is a rating, established by the auditor, on the effectiveness of each discipline, with 1 being the least effective and 5 the most effective.

Services: From a Black Hole of Little Accountability to a Productivity Contributor

The Fisher [Body] man says: "Wait a minute. I did my job . . . fabricate a steel door and ship it to General Motors Assembly Division (GMAD). It's GMAD's fault." So you go to GMAD and say: "Listen. One more lousy door and you're fired." He says: "Wait a minute. I took the Fisher door and the car division's specs. And I put them together. So, it's not my fault." So you go to the Chevrolet guy and say: "One more lousy door . . ." He says: "Wait a minute. All I got was what GMAD made." So, pretty soon you're back to the Fisher guy and all you're doing is running around in great big circles.

—*FORBES* MAGAZINE INTERVIEW
WITH GENERAL MOTORS' FORMER CEO ROGER SMITH

Storm Clouds in the Service Industry

The service industry now accounts for over two-thirds of the gross domestic product of most industrial nations and for almost three-fourths of the workforce. Its value-added contribution is nearly ten times that of direct labor in manufacturing.

Yet, as Richard Quinn and Christopher Gagnon stated in a landmark article in the *Harvard Business Review*: "Daily we encounter the same inattention to quality, emphasis on scale economics, and short-term orientation in the service sector that earlier injured manufacturing." They add ominously: "If service industries are misunderstood, disdained, or mismanaged, the same forces that led to the decline of manufacturing stand ready to cut them to pieces."[1] The storm clouds are gathering:

■ There are far fewer winners of the Malcolm Baldrige National Quality Award in the service sector than in manufacturing.

■ A study by the Illinois Institute of Technology indicated that while blue-collar productivity in manufacturing has been consistently over 80 percent and rising, business (white-collar) productivity in office environments has been below 40 percent and falling.

■ In quality, manufacturing has made steady progress. But, among the services that support manufacturing—from marketing to engineering, from accounting to personnel—quality is off their radar screen. Service quality is not only twenty to twenty-five years behind manufacturing quality, it is an oxymoron!

■ In manufacturing, cycle time has become a household word, with synonyms such as JIT, zero inventories, stockless production, and lean manufacturing. But cycle time in service industries is a foreign word, relegated to another planet.

Objectives and Benefits of Next Operation as Customer (NOAC)

The objectives of this chapter are 1) to elevate the importance of the internal customer (i.e., the next operation as customer) in order to measure and greatly improve quality, cost, and cycle time in the service industry and in the business operations of a manufacturing industry, and 2) to apply the principles of NOAC to all service operations—from marketing/sales to the field, from services in manufacturing industries to the entire service sector.

Primary Benefits

■ *Achievement of Customer (and Employee) Loyalty.* It is an article of faith that a company can only achieve customer loyalty if it succeeds in achieving employee loyalty. By moving the goal posts of the external customer into a close coupling with the internal customer, we achieve a synergy between the external customer, the internal customers, and the internal suppliers—namely, the employees.

■ *Joy in the Workplace.* Chapter 7 indicated several ways to let the genie of employee empowerment, locked up in the bottle of bureaucracy, out of that bottle and give employees the freedom and job excitement they so richly deserve. These included open book management, self-directed work teams, and the minicompany. NOAC adds yet another dimension to that transformation—converting the boredom and frustration of white-collar employees to the joy of achievement in the workplace.

Secondary Benefits

- ■ *Improved Internal Customer-Supplied Communication*. There is a better knowledge of internal customers and their needs and of internal suppliers and their constraints.

- ■ *Teamwork*. Departmental walls and functional silos are broken down. There is a refreshing change from win-lose contests to win-win teamwork, from fire fighting to fire prevention.

- ■ *Better Evaluations*. The company puts a much greater emphasis on internal customer evaluation than the obsolete concept of performance appraisal by a single supervisor.

The Discovering of NOAC by Serendipity

In the early 1980s, I visited Japan several times as a member of various study missions. We kept bumping into a phrase "the next operation as customer," an idea initiated by Dr. Kaoru Ishikawa, the father of the quality movement in Japan. But when I sought to explore how Japan's leading companies implemented this simple but elegant concept, I found that they had not made the transition from concept to practice.

Upon my return, I started developing the principles and practices of NOAC in the business areas of my automotive and industrial electronics group at Motorola. NOAC had a successful launch. One reason for this was the inclusion of NOAC practices within the framework of Motorola's well-known participative management program (PMP)—an employee-involvement initiative tied in with financial gain sharing. This financial incentive helped every PMP team in putting NOAC into effect.

Motorola University then took our NOAC development and packaged it to extend Motorola's famous Six Sigma process from a manufacturing and product focus to all white-collar operations. More than 50,000 Motorolans were trained in NOAC techniques. It is to be hoped that just as Design of Experiments (DOE) is becoming the centerpiece of quality, Multiple Environment Over Stress Tests (MEOST) the centerpiece of reliability, and cycle time the centerpiece of manufacturing, so also will NOAC become the centerpiece of all service operations, many of which are mired in antediluvian practices.

Basic Principles of Next Operation as Customer[2]

Before developing a NOAC roadmap, its simple but powerful principles need to be enunciated.

1. *The Internal Customer as Prince.* It is universally recognized that the external customer is king. But the internal customer is given short shrift. In a logical customer-supplier flow, manufacturing is engineering's internal customer. In practice, however, engineering looks upon manufacturing as a second-class citizen. In NOAC, this attitude undergoes a metamorphosis. Manufacturing is now engineering's internal customer. If not a king, it is at least a prince. Manufacturing now measures and grades engineering performance on the basis of mutually agreed-on quality, cost, and cycle time targets. The same applies to all administrative areas, each of which has a major internal customer.

2. *Process, Customer, and Supplier.* All work—at a business, department, team, or worker level—is a process. The process user receives inputs from an internal supplier—the previous operation—adds value to that input, and converts it into an output for the internal customer—the next operation. Figure 14-1 shows this relationship between the internal supplier, process user, and the internal customer.

3. *Internal Customer's Requirements, Measurement, and Feedback.* The internal customer's requirements (or specifications) must be assessed by the supplier and a mutual agreement reached as to their validity and feasibility, consistent with the internal supplier's constraints and resources. (Lack of agreement can be kicked up to a higher "court"—the NOAC steering committee.) The method of measurement against the internal customers, the frequency of measurement and the feedback mechanics from customer to supplier must be mutually determined.

4. *Consequences.* There should be a careful assessment of the consequences of meeting or failing to meet the internal customer's requirements, both to the process user and to the organization. This entails appropriate incentives and penalties. Incentives could include recognition, pay raises, and even promotion. Penalties could include poor performance appraisals, done by the internal customer (in addition to or in place of the boss); no pay raises; and the internal customer having the right to go elsewhere within the company for the service or, in extreme cases, even going outside the company for such service.

5. *Continuous, Never-ending Breakthrough Improvement.* Measurements represent only a starting point—a baseline. The thrust of NOAC, however, is improvement in quality, cost, cycle time, and effectiveness. There is no finish line to improvement. It is continuous and never-ending. However, a distinct feature of

Figure 14-1. Next Operation as Customer (NOAC): a schematic representation.

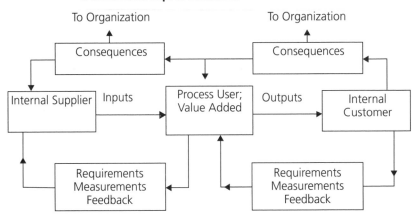

NOAC is out-of-the-box breakthrough creativity, where traditional and incremental approaches are cast aside and a revolutionary approach is put in place to achieve spectacular results.

Typical White-Collar (Business) Services in Manufacturing Industries

It is easy to visualize relationships between external customers, internal customers, and internal suppliers in traditional service industries, such as banking, insurance, airlines, hotels, car rentals, and a whole host of similar companies where no physical product is generated.

There are similar nonproduct services generated in manufacturing industries that are designated white-collar or business services; they are the focus of this chapter. Examples are:

Top Management	Human Resources	Finance/Accounting
Marketing	Public Relations	Information Technology (IT)
Sales	Security	Field (After-Sales Service)
Purchasing	Training	Product Control
Inventory Control	Logistics	Maintenace

Internal Customer–Supplier Relationship Charts

Figure 14-1 was a schematic representation of NOAC, where the requirements and measurements of the internal customer are fed back to the internal supplier, along with the consequences to the latter and to the organization. In actual practice, the relations between the internal customer and the internal supplier are more complex. For instance:

- There can be more than one customer, even among major customers.

- Often, there can be a role reversal, with the supplier becoming the customer and vice versa.

Figure 14-2 shows a typical internal-supplier relationship chart for the purchasing function. It has several customer-supplier links, some of them more important than others. Each link is represented by an arrow, with the shorter arrows being more important than the longer ones. The black arrowheads indicate purchasing's customers, while the white arrowheads indicate purchasing as customer.

An Organizational Framework for NOAC

NOAC is a process, not a program with limited goals or limited life. It needs organizational nourishment to sustain it through the vicissitudes of management changes, "program of the month" whims, and conflicting priorities. The process participants include:

1. *NOAC Steering Committee: The Lifeline Function.* Although NOAC can succeed without a top-level steering committee, initiatives taken solely at lower levels or by individuals often fizzle out without the organizational lifeline of a steering committee. The steering committee should have the president of the company as chairman and key members of his staff as members. A senior executive is selected as secretary. (At the division or plant levels, similar steering committees should be created and linked to the corporate committee.) The committee's tasks include:

- Defining critical business issues related to service operations

- Establishing quantifiable goals for quality, cost, and especially cycle time improvements, along with a timetable for their achievement

- Assigning a process owner to each key process (covered in the next section)

- Prioritizing and selecting a macroscopic cross-functional team for each key process

Figure 14-2. Internal customer-supplier relationship chart for purchasing.

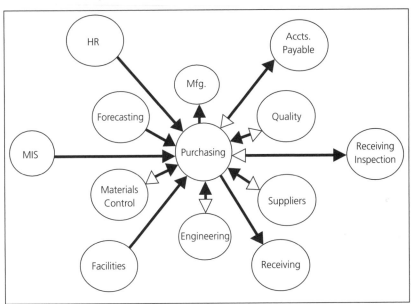

■ Acting as a "supreme court" to settle issues where there's a lack of agreement or other controversies between internal customers and internal suppliers

2. *The Process Owner: Wiring the Organization Together.* To prevent problems and real external customer issues from falling through the organization cracks of vertical management, progressive companies have appointed a process owner for each cross-functional (or macroscopic) process.

3. *The Improvement Team: The Basic Building Block of NOAC.* Team responsibilities, under the guidance of the process owners, include:

■ Determining major internal customers of a business process, their requirements, and measurements to gauge progress

■ Flowcharting the current or "is" process, then moving to a value-added "should" process with a shorter cycle time, using improvement tools

■ Using out-of-the box thinking for breakthrough improvements in quality, cost, cycle time, and effectiveness

An NOAC Roadmap—The Improvement Cycle

With the organizational infrastructure in place, a ten-step roadmap for implementing NOAC in any business process is ready to be initiated. The ten steps are summarized in Table 14-1 and further elaborated on in the next sections.

Step 1: Select the Business Process/Service

The selection of a relevant business process or service is based on 1) the priorities of attaining maximum external customer loyalty and 2) the business priorities of the company.

The NOAC team should also formulate a mission statement as if it were an outside contractor wanting to renew its contract with its major customer within the company. Objectives, goals, strategies, tactics, and plans should follow.

Step 2: Identify the Major Internal Customers of the Business Process/Service

As shown in Figure 14-2, there can be several internal customers for a service department or team, but only a few are the major customers on whom it must concentrate. Often, services pay scant attention to their real customers. As an example, I was consulting with a major university in the Midwest on introducing Six Sigma to its operations, but the faculty could not accept the fact that their students were their customers, rather than being looked upon as "chattel."

Step 3: Determine the Requirements of Major Internal Customers

There are several considerations associated with customer requirements. They should be:

- Consistent and in harmony with the needs and expectations of the external customer

- Consistent with the corporation's objectives and goals

- Clear, firm, meaningful, and mutually acceptable to the internal customer and the internal supplier

- Comprehensive yet realistic and measurable

Figure 4-4 in Chapter 4 depicts a network of elements of internal customer requirements in service operations that lead to customer "wow."

Table 14-1. The ten-step NOAC roadmap for business processes.

Step 1	Select the business process/service with a compelling need for improvement and establish internal targets.
Step 2	Identify the major internal customers of the business process/service.
Step 3	Determine the requirements of the major customers. Reconcile the requirements of the major customers with the requirements and specifications of the external customer.
Step 4	Reach agreement with the major customers on goals, method of measurement to charge progress, feedback intervals, evaluation, and consequences.
Step 5	Flowchart the entire "macro" process (i.e., an "is" chart).
Step 6	Determine the typical cycle time for each step in the flowchart and the total cycle time.
Step 7	Separate the value-added steps from the non-value-added ones.
Step 8	Estimate the number of steps and the cycle time saved by eliminating the non-value-added steps.
Step 9	Eliminate or reduce each non-value-added step using NOAC improvement tools, and redraw the flowchart from "is" to "should."
Step 10	Formulate and implement a totally different and radical approach to providing the service, including even the elimination of such service, using "out of the box" thinking and creativity tools.

Step 4: Reach Agreement with Major Customers on Goals, Methods to Chart Progress, Feedback/Evaluation, and Consequences

It is possible that some internal customer requirements cannot be met by the internal supplier because of resources, capital equipment, and time constraints. Usually, such "disconnects" can be mutually resolved by the customer and supplier. Sometimes, the steering committee is called in, acting as a supreme court.

Measurement of Internal Supplier Performance

There are several measures by which an internal customer can assess the internal supplier's performance. These include:

■ *External Customer Complaints.* At best, this is a post-mortem.

■ *Suggestions for Improvement from Support Service Personnel.* Companies measure the suggestion climate by counting the number of suggestions per employee per year. In manufacturing, the U.S. rate is a skimpy 0.1; in Japan it is more than ten, as an average, with leading companies registering over fifty suggestions per employee yearly. The rate of implementation of these suggestions is less than 20 percent in the United States, but over 75 percent in Japan. Similar statistics are not even recorded in white-collar operations, both in the United States and in Japan.

■ *General Statistics.* Several service operations use a variety of statistical measures to gauge NOAC progress, among them:

1. Ratio of number of employees in a given process to sales dollars generated by the process

2. Ratio of number of employees in the process to total number of company employees

3. Comparison of number of employees in the process to the number of employees in a similar process in a benchmark company

4. Impact of NOAC on business parameters (e.g., American Express, in sustaining process improvements in its customer service operations, increased its revenues by $17 million)

5. Industry reports such as those published by J. D. Powers and Consumers Union, as well as government regulatory agency reports to the media

Feedback from the Customer

In the final analysis, the most important measure of NOAC progress is not what management thinks, but what the customer says it is. Here are a few suggested feedback techniques:

1. *Customer Effectiveness Index (CEI).* As explained in Chapter 4, this metric, evaluated by a core customer, assesses a company's effectiveness in serving the customer. It quantifies several key attributes important to a customer and integrates them into a traditional scoring system of 1 to 100. The same CEI index can be used in service operations, where the internal customer can measure the effectiveness of the internal supplier. Table 14-2 shows an example of how a team in charge of preparing training manuals was valued by its "customer"—the development project manager.

Table 14-2. Internal supplier effectiveness index (ISEI): case study of a training manual team rated by the development project manager.

Requirement	Customer Importance (I) Scale: 1–10	Customer Rating (R) Scale: 1–5	Customer Score (S) S = (I) x (R)
1. Quality			
• Comprehensiveness	7	4	28
• Accuracy	9	1	9
• Clarity	8	3	24
• Meaningfulness	10	2	20
2. Timeliness			
• On-time Delivery	8	1	8
• Cycle Time	5	1	5
3. Cost (to Customer)	6	3	18
4. Dependability			
• Promises Kept	4	2	8
• Credibility	6	3	18
• Trustworthiness	7	2	14
5. Cooperativeness			
• Responsiveness	5	4	20
• Flexibility	4	3	12
• Approachability	7	5	30
• Courtesy	4	5	20
6. Communication			
• Listening	4	4	16
• Feed-Forward Information	5	2	10
Total Score	*Total (Y) = 99*		*Total (T) = 260*

Company (Internal Supplier) Effectiveness Index = $\dfrac{T}{5Y}$ x 100 = $\dfrac{260}{490}$ x 100 = 53%

where:

T = sum of the S (Score) column

Y = sum of the I (Customer Importance) column

Table 14-3. Image survey scorecard.

Internal Customer: Parts and Service

Internal Supplier	Customer Requirements	Supplier Performance: Actual				Image	Score*
		1st Qtr	2nd Qtr	3rd qtr	4th Qtr		
1. Purchasing	Parts available (within 1 hour)	2 days	1.4 days	1.1 days	7 hrs	Rate of progress too slow	1
2. Engineering	Fix for repetitive problems (1 month)	2 mos	2 mos	1.3 mo	1.25 mo	Rate of progress fair, but not sufficient since engineering delays other Parts & Service suppliers	2
3. Publications	Field bulletins each month	1.5 mo	1.75 mo	1.25 mo	1 mo	Service stations pleased with progress	3

*Index for Score:

1 = Well below expectations; progress too slow

2 = Below requirements; progress fair

3 = Meets requirements; progress good

4 = Above requirements; progress superior

5 = Well above requirements; progress excellent

    2. *Image Survey.* Another measurement instrument is the image survey, where the internal customer lists its major suppliers in priority order, along with the requirements for service from these internal suppliers in quantified terms. Table 14-3 is an example of a parts and service operation scoring its three internal suppliers—purchasing, engineering, and publications.

3. *Feedback from Several Customers.* Table 14-3 is an example of one internal customer (parts and service) with a few major suppliers. Table 14-4 is an example of a single internal supplier involved with providing several services or functions to several customer constituencies. The supplier is a team responsible for developing a participative management process (PMP) as part of the company's gain sharing initiative. Its functions include providing information assistance, feedback surveys, and training to all PMP participants and to the PMP council task force. The requirements of these customer constituencies are timeliness, accuracy/completeness, cooperation, responsiveness, guidelines/options alternative, and overall effectiveness. The internal customers use a rating sale of 1 to 3. The score card shows the strengths and weaknesses of the PMP administration the latter involving training in general and participative problem-solving in particular.

Feedback Frequency

The frequency of feedback from customer to supplier varies with the complexity of the process, the urgency of the improvement, the difficulty of measurement, and the interpersonal relations between customer and supplier. The usual period is once a month. In the early stages of NOAC, some companies even have customer-supplier meetings each day for ten to fifteen minutes until they develop a more practical *modus vivendi*. In NOAC, as in most business dealings, integrity, mutual help, and trust form the solid foundations upon which the superstructure of partnership can be built.

Step 5: Flowchart the Entire "Macro" Process (the "Is" Chart)[3]

Flowcharting is a key tool in NOAC. After this step, workers who have been involved with an administrative/business process for years are often amazed at how much they did not know. To undertake this step, first let's review some definitions for the flowchart:

Macro Process	A process that cuts across departmental, business, or divisional boundaries.
Micro Process	A process confined to within a department or group's jurisdiction.
Block Diagram	A diagram that traces the various paths by which materials, paperwork, and information flow between suppliers and customers.
Flowchart	A pictorial representation of the detailed steps by which a process works. It can uncover potential sources of trouble (sometimes called "disconnects" or "white spaces").
Mapping	Another term for a block diagram or flowchart. There are three types of maps or charts:

Table 14-4. Measurement of the administration of participative management.

Service Provided by Priority Order by the Department Administering the Participative Management Program OV(PMP)	Timeliness	Accuracy/ Completeness	Cooperation	Responsiveness	Guidelines Options Alternatives	Overall Effectiveness
Information/Assistance						
• Group Staff Support	2.0	2.0	3.0	2.75	2.3	2.3
• Steering Committee Assistance	3.0	2.5	2.9	2.9	2.9	2.9
• Goal Committee Assistance	2.9	2.5	2.7	2.0	1.5	2.5
• Improvement Team Assistance	2.6	2.6	2.9	2.8	2.6	2.8
• Assistance During PMP Implementation	2.5	2.5	2.5	2.5	2.3	2.5
• Assistance in Culture Progression						
Feedback Survey						
• Survey Results Preparation	2.9	2.6	2.8	2.9	2.4	2.7
• Survey Analysis	2.8	2.7	2.9	2.8	2.4	2.8
• Manager Briefing	2.8	2.6	2.8	2.8	2.7	2.9
• Results Management Support	2.6	2.76	2.9	2.9	2.6	2.7
Training						
• Training Classes	2.2	2.2	2.6	2.6	2.2	2.7
• Training Schedule	2.0	2.0	2.1	2.1	2.0	2.0
• Training Status Report	1.6	1.9	2.0	2.1	2.0	2.0
• Participative Problem: Solving Training	N/A	N/A	N/A	N/A	N/A	N/A
Council Task Force Representation						
• Representation	2.6	2.0	2.5	3.0	2.5	2.8
• Knowledge of Subject	N/A	3.0	N/A	2.0	3.0	3.0
• Level of Participation	3.0	N/A	2.5	2.0	3.0	2.5
• Pilot Program Support Follow-up	3.0	2.5	3.0	3.0	2.5	3.0

Overall effectiveness of PMP department _____

Comments _____

1. "Is" chart (the current process flow)

2. "Should" chart (improved process flow, implemented by the NOAC team but without the necessity for additional resources)

3. "Could" chart (improved process flow requiring additional manpower or capital resources)

It is important to verify the flowchart by actually walking through the process. The NOAC team can then determine whether:

■ The flowchart can be changed from "is" to "should."

■ The flowchart is acceptable, but its execution is poor.

■ The process is poorly managed.

Step 6: Determine the Typical Cycle Time for Each Step in the Flowchart and the Total Cycle Time

In Chapter 11, cycle time was described as the great integrator because it can be used as a single metric to measure quality, cost, delivery, and overall effectiveness. Because of this integrating power, cycle time is used by several companies, starting with Motorola, as the only metric needed for any business process/white-collar operation.

The number of steps in a flowchart may vary from less than ten to several hundred. It is necessary to determine the typical cycle time for each step. (Some teams use three estimates—pessimistic time, optimistic time, and realistic time.) The total cycle time is the sum of the typical or realistic time of each step.

Step 7: Separate Value-Added Steps from Non-Value-Added Ones

It is surprising how many white-collar people are unaware of non-value-added factors in any business process. They include:

■ Waiting (queue) time

■ Setup/changeover time

■ Transport time

■ Downtime (equipment)

■ Inspection time

■ Priority shuffling

- Shortages (material/manpower)

- Rejection/rework time

- Approval time

- Poor job redesign

- Overproduction

Chapter 11 explains the removal of non-value-added operations as a general approach to cycle time reduction. Many non-value-added steps depicted in Figure 11-3 are also applicable in service operations.

Step 8: Estimate the Number of Steps and the Cycle Time Saved by Eliminating Non-Value-Added Steps

As a rule of thumb, at least 60–75 percent of the total number of steps in a flowchart are non-value-added. Furthermore, they account for at least 50 percent of the total cycle time. These steps, therefore, can either be eliminated or substantially reduced. Many companies make the mistake of spending an inordinate amount of effort in mapping. However, as will be pointed out in step 10, a totally revolutionary approach to the business process may obsolete mapping altogether. Hence, use mapping, but only as a fast preliminary exercise.

Step 9: Redraw the Flowchart from "Is" to "Should" Using NOAC Improvement Tools

NOAC principles, organizational structure, and teams are important. Measurement is important. But as seen in Chapters 9, 10, and 11, unless there are tools—powerful tools—to give to our good people, process improvement is likely to be modest and temporary.

Traditional NOAC Tools

- *Pareto Charts and Cause-and-Effect Diagrams. Pareto charts* separate the vital few causes (20 percent or less by numbers, but 80 percent or more by effect) of a problem and are useful in service work to prioritize actions. *Cause-and-effect diagrams* are useful in developing a laundry list of the causes of a problem, but if there are too many such causes, the team may be bewildered about where to start an investigation.

- *Brainstorming, Nominal Group Technique, Multi-Voting.* Brainstorming is an old technique to tap the creative thinking of the NOAC team to generate and then distill a large list of ideas and solutions. It is a useful starting point for improving a business process. One variant is a nominal group technique, where the team establishes a priority or rank order for each idea. Another variant of brainstorming is getting each team member to vote on each idea. The ones with the most votes are selected. The process generally yields two to five ideas. Grade: B.

■ *Benchmarking.* The virtues of benchmarking as a problem-solving tool in manufacturing and in product design are well known.[4] But benchmarking is equally useful in service operations. There is always out there, somewhere, a best-in-class company whose proficiency and success factors in business processes can be studied and emulated by a company. Benchmarking can offer quick results *vis-à-vis* the slower longitudinal progress an organization can make on its own steam. Grade: B plus.

■ *Technology: Going Beyond Silicon and Software.* There is probably a more general understanding of improvement in support services through technology breakthroughs than of the other tools discussed in this section. Computers and the Internet have revolutionized white-collar operations even more than they have in manufacturing. Yet heavy investments in information technology have not resulted in the hoped-for bonanzas. Computerizing a business process to make it efficient, when it can be redesigned or eliminated altogether, is worse than useless. Instead of embedding business processes in silicon and software, we should dismantle them, using creative approaches (discussed later in the next sections) to achieve the needed breakthroughs in quality, cost, and cycle time. Grade: B.

Step 10: Use Out of-the-Box Thinking and Creativity Tools to Formulate and Implement a Radical Approach to Providing Service (Including Even the Elimination of Such Service)

Most service improvement efforts confine themselves to mapping and cycle time reduction. That approach can and does result in, say, a 50 percent reduction in cycle time. But it still represents thinking "within the box," where the NOAC practitioner draws a self-imposed boundary of conventional measures of improvement.

What's needed is the free flow of creativity, of radical ideas to achieve breakthrough improvements. Step 10, therefore, concentrates on these highly creative tools—as distinguished from those in step 9. These truly creative tools and their grades are as follows:

Tool	Grade
Total Value Engineering (TVE)	A+
Design of Experiments (DOE)	A+
Process Redesign	A+

Total Value Engineering (TVE)

Chapter 10 discussed total value engineering as an alternative to traditional value engineering (VE) in product work. The latter concentrates on cost reduction only, without lowering quality. TVE, by contrast, concentrates on maximizing customer loyalty, even if it means incrementally added costs. Total value engineering has equal merit in services as a powerful creative tool. Its algorithm is as follows:

- What is the service?

- What does it do and what does it cost?

- Who is the customer?

- What does the customer really want?

- What else would do the job that would "delight" the customer?

- What will that cost?

Total value engineering has—as one of its tools—the five "whys." It is disarmingly simple, but when applied to any business process or service, it packs a powerful punch. Its cardinal rule is to challenge everything; question every rule, every procedure, every system, every assumption. It asks the first question—Why is the process or step necessary?—then questions the response with another "why," going five "whys" deep—probing, digging, challenging. The creativity of TVE can raise questions such as:

- Can the process/procedure/system be eliminated altogether? (This is a zero-based approach.)

- Can it be substituted with a totally different and radical approach?

- Can the final customer's requirement be exchanged for a "wow"—an unexpected "delight" feature?

- If the process/procedure/system cannot be eliminated, can it be simplified, minified, or combined with another?

- Can it be executed in parallel with a previous process—instead of in series—to save time and costs and prevent hand-off discontinuities?

- Can it be performed better (with greater customer enthusiasm) by another department or team, or even another company?

Design of Experiments in Service Work

The application of this powerful quality tool in production and in design has been amply detailed in Chapter 9. My research in the last ten years has been extended to the application of the Shainin/Bhote DOE to business processes, services, farms, schools, hospitals, and government. There are five DOE techniques applicable to white-collar work: Multi-

Vari, Components Search, Paired Comparisons, B vs. C, and Scatter Plots. For examples of such applications, please refer to my book *World Class Quality, Second Edition.*

Process Redesign: Exploding Taylorism—Twice

1. *Dismantling the Assembly Line.* Chapter 6 was an eloquent testimonial to the evil of Taylorism on the production assembly line. What is not generally recognized, however, is that the "assembly line" syndrome is alive and well even in businesses processes. Each clerk and each white-collar operator moves a limited task forward to the next operator, with only a tunnel view of the overall task and of the client or customer. This hand-off practice promotes errors, delays, discontinuities, and white spaces within the same department and between departments. In addition, the process gets cast in concrete with rules and regulations imposed by a stifling bureaucracy.

Instead of each person performing a few steps in the process chain, assembly-line fashion, one person can perform all the steps in the entire process. In fact, the same implementing concepts described in job redesign for manufacturing in Chapter 7 (see Figure 7-3)—namely, combining tasks, forming natural work units, client relationships, vertical job enrichment, and opening feedback channels—can, with equal validity, be applied to business processes.

Example

A large life insurance company required thirty steps—involving nineteen people and five separate departments (such as credit checking, quoting, and underwriting, etc.) to approve customer applications. The total cycle time ranged from five to twenty-five days. (The theoretical cycle time—that is, the actual working time—was only seventeen minutes!) The company completely revamped its approval process. It created case managers who could perform all the tasks for an insurance application. They were supported by powerful PC-based workstations, along with an expert system that acted as a coach. The results: Cycle time was reduced to two to five days. The company eliminated 100 field positions, despite a doubling of the applications volume.

---

2. *Reducing Support Services.* It is well known that there are seven support service personnel for every production line worker. That is bureaucracy raised to the power of seven. Intelligent NOAC reverses this trend by:

■ Giving inspection and test back to line workers, instead of an overhead quality function

■ Giving cost accounting back to manufacturing, where computers and expert systems can be deployed, instead of setting up a separate cost accounting department

■ Disbanding production control and planning, with their cumbersome MRPII systems, and converting a cumbersome "push" system into an automatic "pull" system with *Kanban*

■ Eliminating or drastically reducing the need for forecasts by sales department by reducing cycles times from weeks and days into hours and minutes

■ Disbanding the need for a separate MRO section within purchasing by giving departments authority to order inexpensive items directly with a simple credit card system

■ Pulverizing accounts payable operations by having checks cut directly to partnership suppliers, based on quantities shipped by manufacturing

In short, support operations such as quality assurance, accounting, purchasing, human resources, and others should become one- or two-person operations—with highly qualified people who can command respect as coaches and helpers—not bloated control cops, information carriers, and paper shufflers.

CASE STUDY

THE DEPARTMENTAL ANNUAL BUDGETING PROCESS

This is a time-worn ritual each year in thousands of companies. Each department is asked to prepare a budget for the next year. The submitted budget then travels in circles from each level in the hierarchy to the next higher level and back until—well into the middle of the following year—the budget is finally approved thousands of dollars and many months later! On a national scale, this antediluvian practice wastes billions of dollars.

The conventional solution would be to flowchart (map) this budgeting process and eliminate or shorten non-value-added steps, such as the ritualistic approval/disapproval cycles in the management chain. Automating the process using parallel steps and the concept of zero-based budgeting could also shorten the cycle time. At best, these measures could cut the total cycle time from six months to, say, three months.

NOAC "out of the box" thinking challenged the need for the whole kit-and-caboodle process. With a few of my clients, I introduced the following plan:

- The president or general manager determines the overall budget, based on sales forecast for the next year, tempered by a 10 percent factor of safety to allow for forecast inaccuracies.

- Each department, then, is given a percentage increase/decrease over the previous year, again with a further factor of safety.

- Only a few exceptional departments, with unavoidable increases or decreases, are reviewed.

- There is no need to budget for subaccounts. The department manager is given total authority/responsibility to live within the total budget.

The results: The budgeting process was reduced to one week! If forecasts change in the succeeding months, the percentages are automatically changed accordingly.

CASE STUDY

TRAINING EFFECTIVENESS—ASSESSING NEEDS DELIVERY AND RESULTS

Here is a side-by-side comparison of conventional and NOAC approaches for a training function in a large multinational company.

Conventional Approach

Assessing Needs: Verify the scope, priority, and sequence of training topics with general managers and line managers.

Delivery: Training is done in the classroom.

Assessing Results:

- For classroom training, evaluate the subject relevance, instructor competence, participant involvement, the adequacy of training materials, and the length of course with students at the end of the training session.

- Conduct pre-tests and post-tests of student absorption of curriculum.

(continues)

NOAC Approach: "Out of the Box" Thinking

Assessing Needs:

■ Benchmark training topics at "best in class" companies.

■ Conduct surveys of general managers, line managers, customers, suppliers, and employees on training topics—their scope, priority, and sequence.

■ Tie-in training needs with business plans, especially areas of weakness.

Delivery: The NOAC solution moves beyond classroom training alone and involves:

■ Gauging the effectiveness of teaching and learning methods through teacher-student iterations and interactions.

■ Cascade teaching, which starts with the general manager acting as teacher to his staff, followed by staff workshop projects. This dual approach then cascades through the organization chain.

■ Consultants (internal or external), who serve as hands-on coaches.

Assessing Results: Classroom training is assessed using methods similar to those used in the conventional solution, but in addition the NOAC solution uses:

■ Three-month and six-month follow-up surveys of line managers' perceptions and participants' perception of training implementation

■ Evaluations of results, as a percentage of improvement in quality, costs, cycle time, and innovation

---

CASE STUDY

A BENCHMARK COMPANY IN THE AREA OF SERVICE OPERATIONS—SOLECTRON CORP.

Solectron, a contract manufacturer for several Fortune 500 companies, is headquartered in San Jose, California. It has the unique distinction as the only company that has won the Malcolm Baldrige National Quality Award twice in the twelve-year history of the prize. (In the last two years, Solectron has been hit hard in the stock market, as have many technology companies. Nevertheless, it remains a model worthy of emulation in the area of service operations.) Its business performance has been stellar.

■ Its stock rose 525 percent in three years.

■ It has a compound annual growth rate of over 50 percent.

■ Its return on equity doubled—from 11.1 percent to 22.2 percent in five years.

■ Its sales/employee increased 2.5:1 in four years

■ Its profit/employee rose from $2,700 to $8,000 in four years.

■ Its sales/square foot went up from $180 to $390 in two years.

■ Its profits/square foot increased from $10 to $24 in two years.

Solectron's devotion to the customer—both external and internal—is legendary. Every week it holds a meeting, presided over by its CEO, for about a hundred of its senior management, where each team/department presents the score it receives from its external and internal customers, on alternate days. The meeting lasts only an hour, with each team allowed five minutes on the average to flash both customer scores—called the customer satisfaction index (CSI). Quality and delivery performance are objective measurements; communication and service are subjective. Grading is on a severe scale. The only acceptable response is A (100) for maximum satisfaction. A grade of A minus (90) is lower than the corporate goal of 97. Grades of C and D are worth zero and −100, respectively. Only the poor scores are grilled by management at these meetings.

Solectron has a ten-step NOAC process for improvement of each of its business processes, called quality improvement process (QIP), where several business parameters are tracked. Table 14-5 gives examples from sales, human resources, finance, MIS, and safety/telecommunications.

The conclusion: The stock market may go up. The stock market may go down. But the odds are that you will always win with Solectron!

Table 14-5. Tracking business improvement parameters at Solectron.

Sales	Human Resources	Finance	MIS	Safety/ Telecommunications
• Internal Customer Satisfaction Index (CSI)	• Internal CSI	• Internal CSI	• Internal CSI	• Accidents
• Sales actual vs. projection	• Compensation competitiveness	• Receivables (days outstanding)	• Training hours	• Lost time
• Quotes won/lost	• Benefits competitiveness	• Payables (days outstanding)	• Errors per line of code	• Safety audits
• Quotation cycle time	• Benefit costs	• Number of reworked journal vouchers		• Safety training
	• Employee opinion survey	• Month-end close cycle time		• Environmental compliance
	• On-time filling of positions	• Forecast accuracy		• Telephone response time
	• First pass yield on interviews	• Order entry verification		
	• Employee turnover			
	• Late reviews of performance appraisals			

Self-Assessment/Audit on Service Operations: Implementing Disciplines by Company Type and Months to Complete

1. *Audit.* Table 14-6 is a self-assessment/audit by which a company can measure its service health. It has four key characteristics and sixteen essential disciplines, with 5 points each, for practical implementation. The total score is 80 points.

2. *Implementation Disciplines.* Only those disciplines that are the most practical and results-oriented have been chosen.

3. *Timetable to Complete by Company Type.* As explained in Chapter 3, the timetable to complete each discipline varies by company type. Generally, over 90 percent of companies are unfamiliar with Next Operation as Customer (NOAC) practices. Hence a period of nine months is considered to be a gestation period for all companies. Once a NOAC baseline is established, the supporting structure and implementation can follow within a few months of additional effort.

Type A companies clearly see the need to improve white-collar operations for a quick return on a modest investment in NOAC.

Type B companies are more manufacturing-oriented, so it takes more time and more convincing for them to use NOAC as a tool for service improvement.

Type C companies are stuck with guerrilla-type obstructionism from their service constituencies and may lack the will and momentum to run with NOAC.

Table 14-6. Service operations: audit and scores, key characteristics, essential disciplines, and timetable to complete—by company type (80 points).

Key Characteristics	Essential Disciplines	Rating 1-5 *	Months to Complete, By Company Type		
			A	B	C
1-1 NOAC Principles/ Practices	1. The Next Operation As Customer (NOAC) is used as a primary technique in all business processes in all service operations throughout the company.		9	15	30

(continues)

Table 14-6. (Continued.)

Key Characteristics	Essential Disciplines	Rating 1-5 *	Months to Complete, By Company Type		
			A	B	C
	2. The internal customer specifies his requirements (which must be in accord with those of the final external customer) and reaches an agreement with the internal supplier to meet such requirements.		9	15	30
	3. The internal customer is the main evaluator and performance appraiser of the internal supplier.		9	15	30
	4. Consequences, including incentives and penalties, are clearly identified for internal suppliers meeting or failing to meet internal customer requirements.		9	15	30
1-2 NOAC Structure	1. There is an active steering committee of senior executives to lead, guide, and measure the effectiveness of all service operations.		12	18	36
	2. A process owner and cross-functional NOAC teams have been established to improve major business processes.		12	18	36
	3. Internal customer-supplier relationship charts have been				

	carefully constructed by each team (Figure 14-2).	12	18	36
	4. Top management reviews the progress of major NOAC teams a minimum of once a month, based on internal and external customer evaluations.	12	24	42
1-3 NOAC Implementation	1. The ten-step roadmap (Table 14-1) has been established and followed as a guide for all business process improvement.	12	18	36
	2. Measurements to determine supplier performance against customer requirements are tracked, using the company effectiveness index (CEI)— Table 4-1.	12	18	36
	3. Flowcharting is employed to determine the total cycle time and craft the "is" chart, and to reduce/eliminate non-value-added steps to craft the "should" chart.	12	18	36
1-4 NOAC Improvements: "Out of the Box Thinking"	1. Brainstorming, force field analysis, and other creativity techniques have been used to achieve improvements.	12	18	36
	2. Benchmarking is extensively employed to short-cut improvements in functions/ practices associated with business processes.	12	18	36

(continues)

Table 14-6. (Continued.)

Key Characteristics	Essential Disciplines	Rating 1-5 *	Months to Complete, By Company Type		
			A	B	C
	3. Total value engineering is extensively practiced to achieve breakthrough improvements in customer enthusiasm at lowest cost.		12	18	36
	4. The assembly-line method used in business processes is dismantled to improve productivity.		12	18	36
	5. The overhead departments of quality, accounting, human relations, production control, etc. are drastically reduced in headcounts and greater authority transferred to line operations.		15	24	48

*The auditor uses a scale of 1–5 to rate each discipline, with 1 being given the lowest rating and 5 the highest.

Part Five

The Power of Ultimate Six Sigma
Results

CHAPTER 15

Results:
From Mediocrity
to World Class

Never mind your golf swing . . . let's see where your ball
lands . . .

—CARL LINDHOLM, MOTOROLA VICE PRESIDENT

A Seesaw Battle Between Process and Results

Many management gurus decry senior executives paying attention only to formulating goals and measuring results but ignoring the all-important in-between process by which their people translate goals into results. As a consequence, the pendulum seems to be swinging the other way. It has become almost fashionable to ignore results. ISO-9000 and QS-9000 standards are examples of such omission. Only the more recent Malcolm Baldrige National Quality Award and the European Quality Award list results as an important category in their guidelines.

Granted, results are effects, not causes; outputs, not inputs. Nevertheless, results do represent the final proof of achievement. They cannot be explained away. They draw a firm line in the sand. They constitute the bottom line.

The previous chapters concentrated on process initiatives. This last chapter focuses on results—in two parts. The first is on the primary factors, few in number but vital in measuring the success of a business enterprise. The second is on secondary factors that embellish and circumscribe the primary factors. (These few primary factors and the larger secondary factors are intended as guidelines. A company can select its own primary and secondary factors from these lists.)

The Primary and Secondary Factors That Assess the Success of a Business

In the final analysis, there are four primary constituencies on which a business must concentrate in terms of results—customers, leadership, employees, and financials. This is similar to the balanced scorecard concept that has gained currency in recent years—that is, a balance between financial and nonfinancial metrics.

Rationale for Choosing Success Factors in Assessing Primary Results

Customers

In terms of results, the customer takes top priority; for without customers, there can be no company, no results. Companies that worship only the god of profit wind up with neither profit nor customer loyalty. While there are several types of customers, as detailed in Chapter 4, only the external customer is highlighted in the primary parameters. Others are included in the secondary parameters.

Four primary factors are key to customer results:

1. *Core Customer Loyalty.* The customer retention rate as a percentage of the total customer base is crucial for the success of a company. Yet over 90 percent of companies are either totally ignorant of their customer retention rate or its direct contribution to profit and are incapable of measuring it.

2. *Value-Added to the Customer.* A company's primary objective is to add value to the customer—*as perceived by the customer*. If that value-added is insufficient, customers could (and should) change suppliers or take on the product/service themselves. Yet very few companies attempt to define their value to the customer; and very few customers quantify the value they have received.

3. *Customer Base Reduction.* Not all customers are worth keeping. In fact, the mark of a smart company would be to give poor customers—the bronze and tin customers—to its competition! The concentration decision, as Peter Drucker calls it, enables a company to serve its core customers—its platinum and gold customers—much more effectively and profitably.

4. *Public Perceptions of the Company.* When all is said and done, a company grows in stature or fades away based on the perceptions of the public at large about the com-

pany as a good employer and as a responsible citizen in terms of the environment, safety, freedom from lawsuits or unfavorable publicity, and social responsibility.

Leadership

Next only to customers, leadership is the most important criterion for results. In this first decade of the twenty-first century, more and more companies are earnestly trying to define the characteristics required for determining the leadership potential of their senior staff and for making the much-needed metamorphosis from management to leadership. A company without true leadership is rudderless. Four primary factors are vital to leadership results:

1. *Releasing the Full Potential of All Employees.* The true measure of successful leaders is their ability to release the creative genie of each employee, which is currently locked up in a bottle of bureaucracy, and give it full scope to flower and bloom for the betterment of the employee and of the company. This means breaking the chains of enervating Taylorism and instead encouraging, supporting, promoting, and celebrating the growth of each employee.

2. *Transforming Managers Into Leaders.* Most employees estimate that the ratio of leaders to managers in companies is 1:99. The measure of a successful, results-oriented company is the extent to which this dismal ratio has been reversed to favor enlightened leaders over autocratic managers. This is, indeed, a relatively unexplored frontier for the vast majority of companies.

3. *Adhering to Principles of Ethics, Trust, and Help—The Hallmarks of Leadership.* As stated in Chapter 5, the personal philosophies and values of true leadership are embedded in three keywords—*ethics, trust,* and *help.* Without ethics, the company is not likely to survive in the long run. Without trust, employees will always feel alienation. Without active, concrete help, they will not rise to the maximum of their God-given potential. Leadership involves uncompromising integrity in all business dealings, even at the expense of the bottom line. It involves trust in people so that they can earn that trust. It involves helping people technically, managerially, administratively, or emotionally, as coach and guide, rather than as an overbearing boss.

4. *Practicing Equitable Gain Sharing.* One of the distinctive differences between a truly successful company and a mediocre one is the differential in gain sharing between managers and those employees who have earned it by their tangible contributions to profitability. The average company, if it considers gain sharing at all, would grant its employees, who have made a direct contribution to the company's bottom line, a grudging 10 percent of base pay. By contrast, successful companies, those that smile all the way to the bank, generously allow gain sharing to their deserving

employees in the range of 25–80 percent of base pay. Their leaders recognize that if it is fair to give senior executives incentive pay, it is equally fair to give line workers, who have earned it, a comparable incentive pay.

Employees

Behind customers and leadership, employees are next in the rank order. How often have we heard the slogan: "Employees are our greatest asset." Yet how often those words ring hollow and false in actual implementation. In this age, when the customer is elevated to prime importance, it is becoming axiomatic that you cannot have customer loyalty without a corresponding employee loyalty. Four primary factors are essential in generating employee loyalty:

1. *Joy in the Workplace.* Most visitors to a company can sense the mood of the workers with a brief walk-through. If employees have a hangdog, unsmiling expression with eyes glazed over, visitors know that the prevailing climate is one of boredom, even alienation. On the other hand, if they observe cheerful, enthusiastic faces, visitors can sense a happy, productive atmosphere. I use a rule-of-thumb to gauge a company's productivity and employee morale when I first visit its plant. I observe the first ten people I encounter. If they appear busy, happy, and "hustling," I gauge good productivity. If they are furtive, cowed, bored, or sullen, I sense a poor work climate and poor productivity. On the Bhote "meter," progressive companies have productivity of over 70 percent. W. Edwards Deming has said that a company "must create joy in the workplace." I go further. When a company's workers can go from TGIF (thank God, it's Friday) relief to TGIM (thank God it's Monday) excitement, heaven has been ushered in! The extent of the change can be measured in employee attitude surveys.

2. *The Ten Stages of Empowerment.* Chapter 7 depicts the ten stages of empowerment of workers in a company—from stage 1 (passivity) to stage 10 (industrial democracy). Although several companies have advanced to stage 4 or 5 (problem solving) in the last fifteen years, very few have conceded the reins of operational management to their employee teams. With the introduction of open book management, self-directed work teams, and minicompanies, an organization can make a leap of faith to the full potential of empowerment stages 9 and 10.

3. *Ratio of CEO Salaries to Line Worker Salaries.* No rational worker would ever begrudge the higher salaries of top managers, who have the onerous responsibility of guiding companies in these turbulent times. But when the ratio of total CEO compensation to that of the lowly line worker far exceeds the Japanese figure of 10:1, or even the German figure of 30:1, and instead reaches astronomical levels of 100:1 and 500:1 in the United States, the gap is the harbinger of a potential revolt. What is worse, those figures are in the public domain for the whole world to see. It con-

tributes to worker dejection, frustration, and alienation. What loyalty can be squeezed out of these unfortunate workers? There is an even greater danger. While capitalism has been the engine of economic development for the last century, we are beginning to sprout the seeds of its decline in the public mind. CEO greed and collusion are the main reasons for the decline in the stock market and a burning public outcry to throw the culprits in jail. If free enterprise is to survive, this ratio must, by design, be reduced—voluntarily—by a company's reassertive board of directors, or if not, by a self-correcting impact on its stock prices.

4. *The Number of Organization Layers Between Top Management and the Worker.* One sure mark of a company's employee health is the number of organizational layers between the CEO and the lowly worker. For a large company (generally one with more than 3,000 employees), the typical number is fourteen to eighteen management layers. This many levels lead to bureaucracy, micromanagement, and middle managers acting mostly as carriers of information back and forth from top management to the line worker. Modern organizational development recommends no more than five layers, even for the largest of companies. When managers have to shepherd fifty to a hundred employees each instead of six to ten, they can no longer micromanage them. They must have faith in their employees, give them the freedom to attain corporate goals, and get out of their way. This transforms autocratic managers into coaches and teachers.

Financials

Most companies, financial analysts, and the stock market concentrate on a company's financials as the only tangible measure of its performance. Although financials are important, they are only lagging indicators, not leading ones. That is why they are listed last among the four primary categories in our group.

Three primary factors give a well-rounded perspective on financials:

1. *Return on Investment (ROI).* The most common yardstick of financial performance is profit on sales. However, since profit is not tied to money invested, it is a poor measure as compared to other parameters of financial performance such as:

Return on Investment (ROI)	Income after interest and taxes, divided by assets minus current liabilities
Return on Assets (ROA)	Income divided by assets (inventory and receivables plus fixed assets)
Return on Net Assets (RONA)	Income before interest and taxes, divided by assets minus current liabilities

Return on Equity (ROE)   Income after interest and taxes, divided by stock-
                                            holders' equity

Of these, return on investment and return on net assets are the most meaningful of yardsticks because of the multiplier effect of asset turns on profits:

ROI = Profit on Sales x Asset Turns

where:

$$\text{Asset Turns} = \frac{\text{Sales}}{\text{Assets (Inventory + Receivables + Fixed Assets)}}$$

A mediocre profit on sales of one percent can be turned into an outstanding ROI
of 25 percent with asset turns of twenty-five.

2. *Market Position*. Several companies consider market share to be particularly
attractive and strive mightily to increase it. Yet market share is, at best, a cloudy
crystal ball. A company may be lulled into a false sense of well-being as its market
share increases while customer defections may slowly be pumping air out of its
balloon. By contrast, market position *vis-à-vis* other companies in the same business gives a clearer signal of performance. General Electric's Jack Welch jettisoned
any business if it did not achieve the number-one or number-two position and
maintain that position in the marketplace. A company that is fifth or sixth in market rank clearly has a tougher road to travel than its competitor whose market rank
is number one or two.

3. *Value-Added per Employee*. Frequently, companies use the metric of sales per
employee, per year as a measure of their financial/productivity performance. In the
last two or three decades, that number has steadily climbed from below $50,000 to
over $800,000. However, this metric is only good to measure a company's longitudi-
nal (i.e., year by year) progress against time. It cannot easily compare the productivity
of different companies because their material dollar content, associated with outsourcing, varies widely from company to company and skews the numbers dispro-
portionately.

A truer productivity measure is value-added per employee (i.e., sales dollars
minus material dollars). Then comparisons across companies become meaningful.

Table 15-1. Company rating of results: by business health and by equivalent sigma levels.

Company Rating	Equivalent Business Health	Equivalent Sigma Level
1	Terminally ill	2 Sigma
2	Major surgery needed	3 Sigma
3	Poor health; continual monitoring by doctor essential	4 Sigma
4	Good health; but periodic checkups (audits) urged	5 Sigma
5	Robust health	6 Sigma

Rating of Results

The criteria, developed in Table 3-4, for gauging a company's business health are repeated in Table 15-1. Ratings 1 through 5 are given correspondingly equivalent business health attributes. Also, in a bow to sigma metrics, ratings of 1 to 5 are given—nonmathematically—equivalent 2-Sigma to 6-Sigma levels, respectively.

Self-Assessment/Audit

Table 15-2 is a company's self-assessment/audit of its primary results. It has four key characteristics and fifteen success factors, each worth 5 points for a maximum score of 75 points.

Considerations in Choosing Secondary Parameters for Company Results

Although secondary parameters are not as vital as the primary parameters listed in Table 15-2 for assessing a company's results, they lend support to the primary factors and put results in a total perspective. They have been included as a comprehensive guide to companies that may wish to consult them in assembling a results list of their own. As with the primary list, Table 15-1 can again be used to convert the ratings of 1 to 5 to equivalent business health levels or to equivalent sigma levels of 2-Sigma to 6-Sigma, respectively.

Table 15-2. Primary results: key characteristics and success factors (75 points).

Key Characteristic	Success Factors	Rating*				
		1	2	3	4	5
1-1 Customer	1. Core customers retained per year as a % of total	?	60%	75%	90%	99%
	2. Value-added to customers (as perceived by them)**	1	2	3	4	5
	3. Customer base reduction, as % of total	0%	5%	10%	30%	60%
	4. Public perceptions of company—as employer and responsible citizen (i.e., on ethics, environment, social responsibility)	1	2	3	4	5
1-2 Leadership	1. Ability to abandon bureaucracy: % of full creativity of employees released	0%	5%	10%	25%	50%
	2. Transformation: % of managers transformed into leaders	0%	2%	5%	20%	50%
	3. Leadership: Ethics, trust, help (as perceived by employees)**	1	2	3	4	5
	4. Gain sharing: % of base pay for average worker	0	5%	10%	25%	>50%
1-3 Employees	1. Joy in the workplace (as perceived by employees)	1	2	3	4	5
	2. Stage of empowerment (refer to Table 7-5)	1	5	7	8	9,10
	3. Ratio of CEO to lowest line worker total compensation (salary = bonuses, stock options)	500:1	200:1	100:1	75:1	50:1
	4. Number of layers between CEO and line worker (large companies)	>15	12	9	7	5
1-4 Financials	1. Return on investment (ROI)	<2%	5%	15%	30%	>50%
	2. Market position (vis-à-vis competitors)	>6th	5th	4th	3rd	1st,2nd
	3. Value-added per employee/year: ($ x 000)	30	70	150	300	>600
	4. Inventory turns	10	20	30	40	>50

*The sigma levels associated with ratings of 1, 2, 3, 4, and 5 are 2, 3, 4, 5, and 6 Sigma, respectively.
**Whenever ratings are nonquantitative, a subjective scale of 1–5 is used, with 1 being the least effective and 5 the most effective, as perceived by those surveyed.

This secondary list of results is divided into two groups (see Table 15-3):

- *By Area* (Table 15-4). Each area—leadership; organization; employees; supply chain management; design; manufacturing; and services—corresponds to an appropriate chapter in this book.

- *By Discipline* (Table 15-5). The disciplines are quality, cost/productivity, cycle time, and innovation.

In choosing the specific milestones for the ratings of each parameter, the following guidelines have been chosen:

1. They are based on personal experiences with more than 450 companies with which I have consulted.

2. They are stretch (i.e., reach-out) goals, especially for ratings of 4 and 5 (i.e., for sigma levels 5 and 6). There is no need for groveling in mediocrity.

3. The ratings apply more to larger companies with over 10,000 employees. They can be modified and toned down for smaller companies.

Table 15-3. Secondary list of results.

By Area	Number of Secondary Parameters
A. Customers	10
B. Leadership	20
C. Organization	10
D. Employees	10
E. Supply Chain Management	10
F. Design	15
G. Manufacturing	10
H. Services	10
By Discipline	
A. Quality	10
B. Cost/Productivity/Financials	14
C. Cycle Time	5
D. Innovation	10

4. Most parameters are measured in percentages/year or in ratios.

5. For some of the parameters, the evaluator (scorekeeper) is the customer. The usual scale is 1–5, with 1 being the least effective and 5 being the most effective.

6. Where the customer, as evaluator, can compare a parameter associated with a company's performance *vis-à-vis* its best competitor, a scale of –5 (very unfavorable) to +5 (very favorable) is used.

7. For other parameters, employees (at appropriate levels) are the evaluators. This is generally done in employee attitude surveys, where training, in terms of background and meaningfulness and impact, is given by human resources departments prior to such surveys. Honesty, transparency, and freedom from spying or recriminations are emphasized at such training sessions.

8. Milestones in some sections of Table 15-4 and Table 15-5 are repeated in other sections for a better perspective. Sometimes, the milestones so repeated are not exactly the same because of differences in the requirements of different departments.

In summary, from Tables 15-4 and 15-5, a company can choose the most appropriate secondary parameters to fit its purpose and culture.

CASE STUDY

OF A BENCHMARK COMPANY IN THE AREA OF RESULTS—GENERAL ELECTRIC

General Electric, as a whole, and Jack Welch, its retired chairman in particular, have been held up as model phenomena of the corporate world. Every management textbook pays due homage to their achievements. It is true that GE's success has sometimes been on the backs of people who've been used and discarded. In January 2001, GE announced the layoffs of 75,000 employees— one of the largest layoffs in corporate history. Jack Welch has been derisively labeled "Neutron Jack" for saving buildings while destroying people. It is also true that many of GE's businesses were jettisoned for not climbing to number one or number two in market position.

Furthermore, in the light of the Enron/Andersen scandals, GE is increasingly besmirched as an unethical company for gouging the Defense Department with many overcharges and for engaging in shady accounting practices and auditing irregularities.

Nevertheless, GE's results have been spectacular. The prestigious magazine,

The Economist, calls "General Electric more country than company and its boss, Jack Welch a legend. . . . If there is a corporate equivalent to the American presidency it is the post of chairman and chief executive of General Electric."[1]

GE's results are nothing short of the unbelievable. In the last year, according to the company's annual report:[2]

■ Revenues rose to more than $125 billion, up 4 percent in a disastrous year for industry as a whole.

■ Earnings increased to almost $14 billion, up 11 percent, while average earnings for the S&P 500 declined by more than 20 percent.

■ Earnings per share grew to $1.41, up 18 percent.

■ Operating margin rose to more than 19.6 percent, up almost one full point.

■ GE share owners experienced a total return on a share of GE stock of 27 percent.

■ GE has averaged a 24 percent per year total return to share owners for the last eighteen years.

■ The generation of $9 billion in free cash flow allowed an investment of $21 billion for 108 acquisitions.

■ The record cash flow allowed the company to raise dividends by 16 percent.

What a stellar record! But is it worth achieving at the altar of repeated overpricing to the government of the United States and accounting sleight of hand?

Table 15-4. Parameters for secondary results: By area.

Recommended Parameters	Rating*				
	1	2	3	4	5
A. Customers					
A.1 Loyalty of Core Customers					
• Longevity: in years	—	One-time	1	3	>5
• Repeat purchases: number of times	—	2	3	4	>5
• Referrals by customers: number	—	1	5	8	>15
• Company effectiveness index (Table 14-3): score %	—	40%	60%	80%	>95%
• Customer ideas for improvement: number	—	1	5	10	>20
• Frequency of senior management visits to customers: number per year	1	5	15	50	>100
• Amount of senior management time spent with customer: days per year	1	5	30	100	>200
A.2 Customer Satisfaction					
• Differential rating *vis-à-vis* competition (–5 to +5)	–5	–1	+1	+3	+5
• Customer complaints/claims: % of units sold	20%	5%	1%	0.1%	0.01%
• Lawsuits upheld against company: number in five years	>10	6	4	2	0
B. Leadership					
B.1 Leadership Effectiveness Index (Table 5-3)	—	25%	50%	75%	>90%
C. Organization					
C.1 Dismantling Taylorism: % dismantled	—	25%	50%	75%	>95%
C.2 Conversion of Departments Into Cross-Functional Teams: % conversion	—	20%	40%	65%	>90%

C.3 Decentralization: % reduction in corporate staff	0%	20%	40%	60%	>80%
C.4 Employee Hiring (based on team player potential, customer sensitivity, entrepreneurship, growth potential): % departure from previous practices	0%	10%	20%	40%	>60%
C.5 Training: benefit-to-cost ratio	—	2:1	5:1	10:1	>30:1
C.6 Performance Appraisal: % change from boss evaluation to internal customer evaluation	—	10%	25%	50%	>75%
C.7 Compensation: % change from pro forma, minor merit increases to no merit increases, but generous incentives based on performance	—	5%	10%	25%	>50%
C.8 Promotion: % change from performance criteria to growth and leadership potential	—	5%	10%	25%	>50%
C.9 Safety/Environment: number of accidents/injuries/EPA violations a year	>20	10	5	2	0
C.10 Time Allocation: % of managers' time spent in meetings	>50%	30%	15%	10%	<5%

D. Employees

D.1 Number of Layoffs: % of employee population/year	>25%	10%	3%	1%	0%
D.2 Voluntary Employee Turnover: % of employee population/year	>30%	15%	7%	3%	<1%
D.3 Employee Readiness for Empowerment (Table 7-3 Score)	<9	9–18	19–27	28–30	>30
D.4 Number of Jobs Redesigned for Vertical Job Enrichment: % of total jobs	0%	10%	20%	50%	>80%
D.5 Management by Walking Around (MBWA) for Each Senior Manager: average number of hours/week	0	1	2	3	>4

(continues)

Table 15-4. (Continued.)

Recommended Parameters	Rating*				
	1	2	3	4	5
D.6 Training: hours per employee per year	<5	10	20	50	>100
D.7 Teaching Employees Financials: % of total number of employees	0%	5%	20%	50%	100%
D.8 Self-Directed Work Teams: % of total number of employees	0%	10%	20%	30%	>60%
D.9 Formation of Minicompanies Within Company: number	0	2	5	10	>20
D.10 Gain Sharing for Employees with Tangible Savings: as a % of employee pay	0	5%	10%	25%	>50%
E. Supply Chain Management					
E.1 Management Practices					
• Supplier/distributor evaluation of company (Table 8-6)	1	2	3	4	5
• Levels of subsuppliers influenced/helped	0	1	2	3	4
E.2 Active/Concrete Help to Suppliers: Effectiveness					
• Man months of help per commodity team/year	–	4	10	25	>50
E.3 Quality/Reliability Effectiveness					
• Supplier defect levels (ppm)	>10K	5K	1K	100	10
• Supplier reliability levels (failure rate/in ppm year)	>100K	30K	5K	500	<100
E.4 Cost-Effectiveness					
• Material cost decreases/year: %	0	5%	10%	15%	>25%
• Material inventory turns/year	<3	10	40	80	>150
• Profit % increases for partnership suppliers	–	2%	5%	10%	15%
• Financial incentives/penalties: % of total number of key parts	–	<1%	5%	20%	>50%

	—	100:0	90:10	70:30	50:50
• Savings sharing on VE, ESI ideas: company-to-supplier ratio	—				50:50
E.5 Cycle Time Effectiveness					
• Lead time on important parts: in days	100	40	15	3	<0.5
• Lead time from subsuppliers to partnership suppliers: in days	100	40	15	3	<0.5
F. Design					
F.1 Management Guidelines Effectiveness					
• Maximum % of parts allowed in new design	100%	80%	67.5%	50%	25%
• Number of new products each year as % of total products	5%	10%	20%	35%	>50%
F.2 Design Quality/Reliability Effectiveness					
• First-time overall yield at launch: %	<40%	60%	80%	90%	>95%
• Months of engineering changes after job 1	>18	12	6	3	1
• Parts derating ratio	—	1.1:1	1.2:1	1.5:1	>2:1
• "Wow" features vs. competition: customer perception (−5 to+5)	−5	−0	+1	+3	+5
• Product liability costs: % of sales	>500%	60%	20%	2%	0%
• Number of design flaws prevented per product through MEOST	—	0	2	4	>6
F.3 Design Cost-Effectiveness					
• Product cost vs. competition: customer perception (−5 to +5)	−5	0	+1	+3	+5
• Early supplier involvement (ESI) savings: % of product costs	—	3%	6%	12%	>20%
• Value engineering (VE) savings: % of product cost	—	0	5%	10%	>20%
• Part number reduction: % of total parts	—	20%	40%	60%	>80%
• Number of parts cost targeted: % of total parts	—	5%	10%	25%	>50%

(continues)

Table 15-4. (Continued.)

Recommended Parameters	Rating*				
	1	2	3	4	5
F.4 Design Cycle Time Effectiveness					
• Time to market (from concept to launch): in months	>25	18	12	9	<6
• Time to recover (cost/time profile) costs of human inventory: in months	>15	12	10	8	6
G. Manufacturing					
G.1 General					
• Ratio of Kanban to MRPII	0:100	1:20	1:1	20:1	100:0
G.2 Quality Effectiveness					
• Cost of poor quality (COPQ): % of sales $	>25%	15%	7%	3%	<1%
• Total defects per unit (TDPU)	>8	1.5	0.5	0.1	<0.1
• Outgoing quality (PPM)	>10%	3000	500	100	<10
G.3 Cost-Effectiveness					
• TPM: overall equipment effectiveness (OEE)	–	<50%	65%	85%	>95%
• Inventory turns/year	3	10	25	60	>100
• Number of suggestions/employee/year	0.1	0.5	5	50	>100
G.4 Cycle Time Effectiveness					
• Work in process (WIP) cycle time: in days	>30	10	3	1	0.1
• Average setup times: in minutes	>180	60	15	4	<2
• Number of multiple skills/employee	1	3	6	9	>12
• Space reduction through cycle time reduction: %	0%	20%	40%	60%	80%

H. Services

H.1 Structure

• Customer-supplier relationship charts in effect: % of total teams	—	5%	20%	50%	>95%
• Processes redesigned: % of total processes	—	5%	20%	50%	>90%

H.2 Implementation/Progress

a) Quality

• Internal Supplier Effectiveness Index (Table 14-2)	—	25%	50%	75%	>90%
• Image survey (Table 14-3)	1	2	3	4	5
• Major internal customer feedback (Table 14-5)	—	1	1.5	2.5	3
• Industry reports: J. D. Powers, Consumer Union, etc. vs. competition (−5 to +5)	−5	−1	+1	+3	+5

b) Cost

• Service team generated sales increases: % of total sales $	—	2%	5%	8%	>15%
• Savings generated by service teams: % of total sales $	—	3%	7%	10%	>20%

c) Cycle Time

• Number of process steps reduced: % of total steps	—	5%	25%	50%	>80%
• Cycle time reduced: % of total cycle time	—	20%	50%	75%	>90%

Table 15-5. Parameters for secondary results: by discipline.

Recommended Parameters	Rating*				
	1	2	3	4	5
A. Quality (company as a whole)					
• Cost of poor quality (COPQ): % of sales $	>25%	15%	7%	3%	<1%
• Field reliability: ppm/year	>15%	5000	1000	100	<10
• Outgoing quality: ppm	>10K	3000	500	100	<10
• Total defects/unit (TDPU)	>8	1.5	0.5	0.1	<0.1
• First-time overall yields: %	<40%	70%	90%	95%	>99%
• C_{pk}S on critical/important parameters	–	<1.0	1.33	2.0	>3.0
• Product liability costs: % of sales	>500%	60%	20%	2%	0%
• Ergonomics vs. competition: customer perceptions (–5 to +5)	–5	–1	+1	+3	+5
• "Wow" features vs. competition: customer perceptions (–5 to +5)	–5	–1	+1	+3	+5
• Safety features vs. competition: customer perceptions (–5 to +5)	–5	–1	+1	+3	+5
B. Cost/Productivity/Financials					
• Profit: % of sales after tax	–	2%	6%	12%	>20%
• Asset turns	<1	2	4	8	>15
• Sales/employee/year: ($ x 000)	50	100	300	700	>1000
• Satisfaction of all stakeholders: rated 1 to 5	1	2	3	4	5
• TPM: overall equipment effectiveness (OEE)	–	<50%	75%	85%	>95%
• Inventory turns per year	3	10	25	60	>100

• Supplier cost reductions/year: %	0	5%	10%	15%	>25%
• Value engineering (VE) savings: % of product costs	–	1%	5%	10%	25%
• Early supplier involvement (ESI) savings: % of product cost	–	2%	5%	10%	>20%
• Sales wins to sales losses: ratio	50:50	60:40	70:30	80:20	>90:10
C. Cycle Time					
• Manufacturing cycle time (raw materials, WIP, finished goods): in days	>60	20	6	3	1
• Business process cycle time reduced: % of historic	–	20%	50%	75%	>90%
• Design cycle time reductions: % of historic	–	20%	50%	75%	90%
• Lead time from partnership suppliers (A items): in days	100	40	15	3	<0.5
• Lead times from subsuppliers to partnership suppliers (A items): in days	100	40	15	3	<0.5
D. Innovation					
• Sales/year of new products: % of total sales	0%	5%	10%	25%	50%
• Frequency of stream of new products (with 25% change from previous models) per year	–	1	2	3	4
• Number of "skunk works" projects launched per year	–	1	4	8	>15
• Number of ideas lifted from competition through reverse engineering per year	–	5	10	20	>50
• Number of patents generated per year: % of technical population	–	1%	3%	5%	>10%
• Number of patents commercialized per year: % of technical population	–		1%	2%	>3%

(continues)

Table 15-5. (Continued.)

Recommended Parameters

		Rating*			
	1	2	3	4	5
• Number of benchmark projects/year	—	2	5	10	>20
• Number of suggestions/employee/year	—	0.1	1	15	>50
• Number of customer "wow" features added per major product	—	—	1	2	>3
• Number of incentive payments to partnership suppliers/year for ideas accepted	—	2	10	20	>50

Conclusion

New Hope, New Horizons for Corporations

From Profit as a Desert Mirage to Profit as an Oasis

Why are so many large and, hitherto, respected corporations wallowing around in deep red ink, while a few are riding the crest of solid black ink? The answer in the first case is their lack of knowledge or their lack of implementation (or both) of the techniques and disciplines described in *The Power of Ultimate Six Sigma*. These fifteen chapters have detailed 200 disciplines that can sow the seeds of a bumper harvest of profitability. To highlight but a few, Table C-1 is a list of the more promising of these disciplines and the range of profit improvement each can generate. Table C-1 also indicates the small percentage of companies that are even familiar with each discipline and the even smaller percentage of companies that have implemented it.

2:1, 3:1, and 4:1 Profit Improvements

Granted, there is some degree of overlap among the ten disciplines. However, a simple addition reveals that a 2:1 improvement in profit would be a no-brainer. Furthermore, if a company truly embarked on pursuing many of the 200 disciplines detailed in this book, profit increases of 3:1, 4:1, and even higher would be within its reach.

From Questionable Ethics to "True North"

Once a company can get over its obsession to slash costs indiscriminately, with layoffs and a slavish catering to the tyranny of unscrupulous financial analysts, it can bask in the freedom of sustained profits. No longer will it be shackled by questionable ethics, payoffs, lobbying for favors in the halls of Congress, and other shoddy practices that have prevented it from reaching "true north."

Table C-1. Disciplines to dramatically increase corporate profit.

Technique/Discipline	Range of Profit Improvement	% of Companies Aware of the Discipline	% of Companies Implementing the Discipline
1. 5% increase in customer retention (Chapter 4)	35% to 120%	<10%	<1%
2. 20% reduction in customer base (Chapter 4)	20% to 30%	<5%	<0.2%
3. 50% reduction in cost of poor quality (Chapter 9)	50% to 150%	<20%	<5%
4. 50% improvement in overall equipment effectiveness (Chapter 10)	10% to 75%	<15%	<1.5%
5. 5% reduction in bill of materials (Chapter 8)	30% to 70%	<50%	<5%
6. Increase in inventory turns: from 10 to 30 (Chapter 11)	30% to 50% (ROI)	<40%	<10%
7. 2:1 reduction in design cycle time (Chapter 12)	1 to 2 years of improvement in cash flow	<10%	<2%
8. 2:1 reduction in white-collar cycle time (Chapter 14)	20% to 60%	<15%	<1%
9. Empowerment from stage 4 to stage 8 (Chapter 7)	10% to 100%	<25%	<5%
10. Total Customer Satisfaction team competition: 50% completion (Chapter 7)	20 % to 60%	<10%	<1%

From a Customer Focus to Social Responsibility

Once it finds "true north," a company can begin to enlarge its horizons to tackle the several avenues of social responsibility within the community it serves locally, regionally, nationally, or globally.

From Social Responsibility to Solving the Ills of Society

Once a company gets a taste of success in serving the public, it can then band together with other companies—in a grand alliance business Marshall Plan—to pursue the visions that only corporations can achieve, namely, solving the problems of the less fortunate of the world, with profit at the end of the rainbow. That will be fulfilling God's mission for humanity on earth!

KEKI R. BHOTE

Reference Notes

Chapter 1

1. Women's American ORT Annual Report: "WAO 2000" (New York: WAO, 2000).

2. Hugh Dellios, "Poverty Fighters Tout 'Micro-Loan' Promise," *Chicago Tribune* (April 2, 2002).

3. Dinshaw Tamboli, World Zoroastrian Organization Annual Report (Mumbai, India: WZO, 2001).

4. Ahmed Rashid, *Jihad* (New Haven: Yale University Press, 2002).

5. William Neikirk, "Lieberman Issues Call for a New Corporate Social Contract," *Chicago Tribune* (April 2, 2002).

6. "An Expense by Any Other Name—The Wrong Way to Treat Stock Options," *The Economist* (April 6, 2002).

7. Special Committee on Financial Reporting, "Improving Business Reporting—A Customer Focus, Meeting the Information Needs of Users" (New York: AICPA, 1994).

8. Michael Hammer, "Process Management and the Future of Six Sigma," *MIT Sloan Management Review* (Winter 2002).

Chapter 2

1. Keki R. Bhote, "Plan for Maximum Profit: The 12 Critical Success Factors That Guarantee Increased Profits from Total Quality," in Volume 5, *The Total Quality Portfolio* (Zurich, Switzerland: Strategic Direction Publishers, 1996).

2. Keki R. Bhote, "The Quality Project Alert: The Early Warning Signals for Any Quality Initiative in Danger of Costing More Than It Earns," in Volume 6, *The Total Quality Portfolio* (Zurich, Switzerland: Strategic Direction Publishers, 1996).

Chapter 4

1. Keki R. Bhote, *The Ultimate Six Sigma—Beyond Quality Excellence to Total Business Excellence,* First Edition (New York: AMACOM, 2002).

2. Keki R. Bhote, *Beyond Customer Satisfaction to Customer Loyalty—The Key to Greater Profitability* (New York: AMACOM, 1996).

3. A. T. Kearney, *The Customer Satisfaction Audit* (Zurich, Switzerland: Strategic Direction Publishers, 1994).

4. REL Consultancy Group, "Study on Customer Retentions," *Quality Digest* (June 1995).

Chapter 5

1. Bennett Davis, *TWA Ambassador* (December 1995).

2. Robert W. Galvin, *Idea of Ideas* (Schaumburg, IL: Motorola University Press, 1991).

3. Harry Mark Petrakis, *The Founder's Touch: The Life of Paul Galvin of Motorola* (New York: McGraw Hill, 1965).

4. "The Secret Skill of Leaders," *U.S. News and World Report* (January 14, 2002).

5. Christopher A. Bartlett and Sumantra Ghoshal, "Changing the Role of Top Management Beyond Systems to People," *Harvard Business Review* (May-June, 1995).

6. Peter F. Drucker, "Change Leaders," *Inc.* (June 1999).

7. Michael Arndt, "3M: A Lab for Growth?" *Business Week* (February 4, 2002).

8. Yankelovich Poll: Christopher, 1998.

9. James O'Toole, *Leading Change* (Boston: Harvard Business School Press, 1996).

10. Bill Ginnodo, "Leading Change: An Interview with Motorola's Bob Galvin," *Commitment Plus*, Pride Publications (May-June 1996).

Chapter 6

1. *The Washington Monthly* (July 1986).

2. Michael Hammer and James Champy, *Reengineering the Corporation* (New York: Harper Business, 1993).

3. Hammer and Champy, *Reengineering the Corporation*.

4. A. T. Kearney, "Seeking and Destroying the Wealth Dissipators" (1985).

5. Gary D. Zeune, "Outside the Box Performance—How to Beat Your Competitor's Brains Out" (1996).

6. Mary Walton, *The Deming Management Method* (New York: Putnam Publishing, 1986).

7. Motorola Benchmarking Team, Internal Report.

8. Tom Peters, *Thriving on Chaos* (New York: Alfred A. Knopf, Inc., 1987).

9. Walton, *The Deming Management Method*.

10. Peters, *Thriving on Chaos*.

Chapter 7

1. M. Scott Myers, *Every Employee a Manager* (New York: McGraw Hill, 1970).

2. Roy Walters, Internal Publication (New York: Roy Walters and Associates).

3. Anne Stevens, "Mentoring—Expanded Program Creates a Win-Win Situation for Ford Associates," *Profiles in Diversity Journal* (January/February 2002).

4. Jack Stack, *The Great Game of Business* (New York: Currency Doubleday, 1992).

5. John Case, *Open Book Management: The Coming Business Revolution* (New York: Harper Business, 1995).

6. Chris Lee, "Open Book Management," *Training Magazine* (March 1995).

7. Stratford P. Sherman, "The Mind of Jack Welch," *Fortune* (March 27, 1987).

8. Jack Osborne, *et al.*, *Self-Directed Work Teams* (Homewood, IL: Business One Irwin, 1990).

9. Kiyoshi Suzaki, *The New Shop Floor Management* (New York: Free Press, 1993).

10. Ricardo Semler, *Maverick: The Success Story Behind the World's Most Unusual Workplace* (New York: Warner Books, 1993).

11. Stack, *The Great Game of Business*.

Chapter 8

1. Peter Hines, "Toyota Supply System in Japan and the U.K.," Lean Enterprise Research Center, White Paper (U.K.: Cardiff Academic Press, 1994).

2. James P. Womack and David T. Jones, *Lean Thinking* (New York: Simon and Schuster, 1996).

Chapter 9

1. Keki R. Bhote, *World Class Quality—Using Design of Experiments to Make It Happen* (New York: AMACOM, 1991); and Keki R. Bhote, *World Class Quality—Using Design of Experiments to Make It Happen*, Second Edition (New York: AMACOM, 2000).

2. Bhote, *World Class Quality*, Second Edition.

3. *Ibid*, Chapter 8.

4. *Ibid*, Chapter 10.

5. *Ibid*, Chapter 11.

6. *Ibid*, Chapter 12.

7. *Ibid*, Chapter 13.

8. *Ibid*, Chapter 15.

9. *Ibid*, Chapter 16 and Chapter 17.

10. *Ibid*, Chapter 18.

11. *Ibid.*

12. *Ibid*, Chapter 22.

13. Shigeo Shingo, *Zero Quality Control, Source Inspection, and Poka-Yoke* (Cambridge, MA: Productivity Press, 1986), and Nikkan Kogyo Shimban, *Poka-Yoke* (Cambridge, MA: Productivity Press, 1988).

14. Bhote, *World Class Quality*, Second Edition, Chapter 19.

15. *Ibid*, Chapter 22.

Chapter 10

1. Lawrence D. Miles, *Techniques of Value Analysis and Engineering*, Second Edition (New York: McGraw Hill, 1972).

2. Keki R. Bhote, *Total Value Engineering* (Singapore: Singapore National Productivity Board Conference, September 1990).

3. Nancy L. Hyer and Urban Wemmerlov, "Group Technology and Productivity," *Harvard Business Review* (July-August 1984).

4. Raymond J. Levulis, "Group Technology," Internal Publication (K. W. Tunnell Consulting Co., 1998).

5. Hyer and Wemmerlov, "Group Technology and Productivity."

Chapter 11

1. Seichi Nakajima, *TPM Development Program* (Cambridge, MA: Productivity Press, 1989) and Nachi Fuji Koshi, *Training for TPM* (Cambridge, MA: Poductivity Press, 1990).

2. Shigeo Shingo, *A Revolution in Manufacturing: The SMED System* (Cambridge, MA: Productivity Press, 1985).

Chapter 12

1. These definitions of creativity emerged from sessions held at an Illinois Institute of Technology Faculty Retreat, September 12, 1992.

2. A. L. Simburg, *Creativity at Work* (Boston, MA: Industrial Education Institute, 1964).

3. Alex E. Osborne, *Applied Imagination* (New York: Charles Scribner's Sons, 1963).

4. Robert W. Galvin, *The Idea of Ideas* (Schaumburg, IL: Motorola University Press, 1991).

5. *Ibid.*

6. Illinois Institute of Technology, Faculty Retreat, September 12, 1992.

Chapter 13

1. Richard J. Schonberger, *World Class Manufacturing Case Book* (New York: Free Press, 1987.

2. Tom Peters, *Thriving on Chaos* (New York, Alfred A. Knopf, Inc., 1987).

3. James P. Womack and David T. Jones, "*Lean Thinking* (New York: Simon & Schuster, 1996).

4. Richard J. Schonberger, *World Class Manufacturing: The Next Decade* (New York: Free Press, 1996).

Chapter 14

1. Richard Quinn and Christopher Gagnon, "Will Services Follow Manufacturing Into Decline?" *Harvard Business Review* (November-December 1986).

2. Keki R. Bhote, *Next Operation as Customer: How to Improve Quality, Cost, and Cycle Time in Service Operations* (New York: AMACOM Books, 1991).

3. Geary Rummler and Alan Brache, *Improving Performance: How to Manage the White Spaces on the Organization Chart* (San Francisco: Jossey-Bass, 1990).

4. Michael J. Spendolini, *The Benchmarking Book* (New York, AMACOM, 1992).

Chapter 15

1. *The Economist* (1999).

2. General Electric Annual Report, 2001.

Index

About the Author

Keki R. Bhote is the president of Keki R. Bhote Associates, a company specializing in quality and productivity improvement. He has consulted with more than 420 companies all over the world, ranging from manufacturing and service industries to universities and governments. As one of the quality gurus of America, Mr. Bhote's primary focus is on:

■ Design of Experiments to improve quality over 100:1

■ Multiple Environment Over Stress Tests to improve reliability over 10:1, even 100:1

■ The Ultimate Six Sigma to go beyond quality excellence to total business excellence

Before he retired from Motorola, he was senior corporate consultant for quality and productivity improvement. He played a key role in Motorola's winning the prestigious Malcolm Baldrige National Quality Award—the first company to win this honor as a total corporation—and in launching its renowned Six Sigma process for continuous improvement. At Motorola, he was responsible for twenty-three quality innovations in his forty-two-year career there.

Mr. Bhote received a B.S. in Telecommunications Engineering from the University of Madras and his M.S. in Applied Physics and Engineering Sciences from Harvard University. He joined Motorola as a development engineer and rose through the ranks to become group director of Quality and Value Assurance for Motorola's Automotive and Industrial Electronics Group before his promotion to senior consultant for the entire corporation worldwide.

He is a seminar leader for the American Management Association, the Management Center of Europe, and the Management Center for the Middle East. He is an adviser to the Celerant Consulting Company of Europe and America, specializing in chronic problem solving and Six Sigma. He has been an associate professor at the Illinois Institute of Technology and a visiting professor at the University of San Diego and Northwestern University. He is on the editorial board of the *National Productivity Review* and *Strategic Insights into Quality*, a British Business Strategy publication. He has published more than 200 papers, addressed numerous professional societies, and has lectured and consulted in thirty-three countries of the world.

Books by Keki R. Bhote

World Class Quality: Using Design of Experiments to Make It Happen (also translated into German, French, Italian, and Portuguese)

Supply Management: How to Make U.S. Suppliers Competitive

Strategic Supply Management: A Blueprint for Revitalizing the Manufacturer-Supplier Partnership

Next Operation as Customer: How to Improve Quality, Cost, and Cycle Time in Service Operations

Critical Success Factors in Effective Benchmarking

The Customer Loyalty Audit: A Self-Assessment

Plan for Maximum Profit: The 12 Critical Success Factors That Guarantee Increased Profits from Total Quality

The Quality Project Alert: The Early Warning Signals for Any Quality Initiative in Danger of Costing More Than It Earns

Beyond Customer Satisfaction to Customer Loyalty: The Key to Greater Profitability (also translated into Japanese and Portuguese)

World Class Quality: Using Design of Experiments to Make It Happen, Second Edition

The Ultimate Six Sigma: Beyond Quality Excellence to Total Business Excellence

Books Coauthored by Keki R. Bhote

Value Analysis Methods

AMA Management Handbook

Forthcoming Books by Keki R. Bhote

Supply Chain Management: Optimizing Profits for the Entire Supply Chain

Powerful Tools for the 21st Century

The Four Stages on the Road to Excellence: Meeting a Company's Health in Quality, Supply Management, Customers, Design, Manufacturing and Service

Business Excellence: A Self-Assessment in 12 Areas

Releasing the Human Spirit: On the Road to Industrial Democracy

World Class Reliability: Breakthrough with Multiple Environment Overstress Tests

Awards and Honors for Keki R. Bhote

Cecil B. Craig Award, American Society for Quality

Distinguished Service to the United Nations—United Nations Association of the United States of America

One of the New Quality Gurus of America—*Quality Digest Magazine*

Outstanding Zoroastrians of the World—World Zoroastrian Organization, London, U.K.

Outstanding Young Men—Junior Chamber of Commerce, Chicago

Outstanding Naturalized Citizens of Chicago—The Immigrant Service League

Who's Who in the Midwest

Who's Who in Finance and Industry

Who's Who in Global Business Leaders

Who's Who in National Registry

Zero Defects Award, U.S. Department of Defense

Mr. Bhote lives with his wife Mehroo, in Glencoe, Illinois, where their four children—Safeena, Shenaya, Adi, and Xerxes—grew up. He has been active in civic affairs locally, regionally, nationally, and in the world.